D1188185

RECRUITING
FOR UNCLE SAM

Modern War Studies

Raymond A. Callahan
J. Garry Clifford
Jacob W. Kipp
Jay Luvaas
Theodore A. Wilson
Series Editors

RECRUITING FOR UNCLE SAM
Citizenship and Military Manpower Policy

David R. Segal

University Press of Kansas

© 1989 by the University Press of Kansas
All rights reserved

Published by the University Press of Kansas (Lawrence, Kansas 66045), which
was organized by the Kansas Board of Regents and is operated and funded by
Emporia State University, Fort Hays State University, Kansas State University, Pittsburg State University, the University of Kansas, and Wichita State
University

Library of Congress Cataloging-in-Publication Data

Segal, David R.
    Recruiting for Uncle Sam : citizenship and military manpower
policy / David R. Segal.
    p. cm. — (Modern war studies)
    Bibliography: p.
    Includes index.
    ISBN 0-7006-0391-3
    1. United States—Armed Forces—Recruiting, enlistment, etc.—
History. 2. Draft—United States—History. 3. Sociology,
Military—United States—History. I. Title. II. Series.
UB323.S44 1989
355.2'23'0973—dc19   88-34461
                                                            CIP

British Library Cataloguing in Publication Data is available.

Printed in the United States of America
10 9 8 7 6 5 4 3 2 1

The paper used in this publication meets the minimum requirements of the
American National Standard for Permanence of Paper for Printed Library
Materials Z39.48-1984.

To my mother, Daisy,
and to the memory of my father, Harry,
who enjoyed careers as civil servants when service was valued
and who taught me that value

Contents

Acknowledgments

The gestation and birth of this volume were influenced by a large number of people and organizations over a long period of time. With one exception these influences were all positive.

My interest in and understanding of military manpower—a term I use reluctantly, following convention, to include modern, gender-integrated military forces—and personnel issues have been guided by the work and the friendship of two scholars who preceded me on the faculty at the University of Michigan: Morris Janowitz (of whose death I learned as this book was going to press) and Charles C. Moskos (now at Northwestern University). They established the intellectual agenda for the study of the relationship between armed forces and society, and if there is value in this book, it is because I have sought to continue the work that they began.

The conceptualization of the book began in the early 1970s, when the United States Army, seeking to reestablish the sociological research capability it had during World War II, invited me to take a leave of absence from Michigan to participate in that enterprise. I am grateful to J. E. Uhlaner, then technical director of the Army Research Institute, to E. Ralph Dusek, then director of its Individual Training and Performance Research Laboratory, and to Colonels Richard Rooth and William Maus, who commanded the institute during my years there. They had the wisdom to see the potential applications of sociological knowledge at a time when the discipline of sociology itself was ambivalent about being applied, particularly to military problems.

In the mid 1970s I rejoined the academic world at the College Park campus of the University of Maryland, one of the few American universities that offered a course in military sociology and where now, under the auspices of the Center for International Security Studies at Maryland (CISSM), scholars who are concerned primarily with missiles and throw weights talk to scholars concerned with military personnel and organization. I think that Maryland is the only university where this happens on a regular basis. I am particularly indebted to Catherine Kelleher and to George Quester in this regard. I am also grateful for the ongoing stimulation, guidance, and collaboration of sociology colleagues at Maryland, past and present, who share my interests in peace, war, and the military: Mady Wechsler Segal, John D. Blair, Melanie Martindale, R. E. Canjar, Barbara Foley Meeker, and Joseph J. Lengermann. These collaborations extend beyond the College Park campus. Jere Cohen, at the university's Baltimore County campus, and Jay

Stanley and Sandra Carson, at Towson State University, have also been valuable colleagues.

I am grateful to the dozen or more graduate students who have done degree work in military sociology at Maryland and have allowed me to bombard them with, and reacted to, the ideas in this book as they developed. I owe a particular debt to Katharine Swift Gravino, who served as my research assistant on this project. I am also indebted to the several hundred undergraduate students in my military-sociology classes over the past decade who have had these ideas tried out on them.

I have learned over the years that it is difficult to write a book while sitting in one's own office: people know that you are there, and they know your telephone number. From 1981 to 1984, pieces of the manuscript took shape in the library at the Brookings Institution, which generously appointed me as a special guest scholar during this period. More importantly, this venue allowed me to chat frequently with Martin Binkin, a most insightful analyst of military manpower. I do not always agree with him, but I always learn from him.

One has no business writing about soldiers unless one goes where soldiers go. Since 1982 I have been given the opportunity to do that as a guest scholar in the Department of Military Psychiatry, Walter Reed Army Institute of Research. I am grateful to David H. Marlowe, chief of the department, and to Jesse J. Harris, Joseph M. Rothberg, and Theodore P. Furukawa, my primary collaborators at WRAIR, who have contributed significantly to my understanding of American soldiers. I am also indebted to the hundreds of military personnel who filled out my questionnaires, allowed me to interview them interminably, shared their rations with me, and taught me how to build bunkers in the field.

The early stages of this research were supported by a foundation located in New York. That this book was not published under its auspices reflects our having had several differences of opinion. However, I would like to acknowledge the continuing support of two of the three program officers who were responsible for overseeing my work there: James Smith and Robert Fancher.

The book received its fine tuning during my year as visiting professor of sociology at the United States Military Academy. I am grateful to Colonel Howard T. Prince II, head of the Department of Behavioral Sciences and Leadership, and Colonel John M. Wattendorf, director of the sociology program, for having encouraged me to help build military sociology at USMA. Members of the United States Corps of Cadets had not only to listen to these ideas but to read and criticize them as well.

My wife, Mady, and our daughter, Eden, lived with the joys and frustrations of my writing longer than any of the above and frequently had to remind me when I was angry at my muse not to take it out on them. I am grateful for their patience.

1
Social Trends
and the Citizen-Soldier

A debate has raged among Americans for the last half century about how the manpower component of their national-security needs can be provided most effectively and still be consonant with their basic national values. Shall we maintain a system of selective military conscription—a draft? If so, what shall the criteria for selection be? Alternately, might we be best served by a system of universal military service or training or by some system that embeds military service in a broader matrix of national service with non-military alternatives? If we adopt a system of universal service, to what degree should it be coercive? Or should we, as we currently do, depend on the dynamics of the labor market to provide our military manpower and continue to maintain an all-volunteer force?

All of these alternatives, as well as several variations of them, have been discussed during the last five decades. This debate, in turn, has been an extension of a public discourse that began with the birth of our Republic. During the early years it focused on the rights of the federal government vis-à-vis the rights of the several states. More recently it has focused on the right of the federal government to call people for military service versus the right of individual citizens to decide for themselves whether or not to serve. Throughout our history, the debate has been waged on two levels. One is the issue of principle: Do we believe that military service is an obligation of citizenship? The other is our actual practice: To what degree has our military force been manned by citizen-soldiers?

From the outset, the principle that linked citizenship to military service prevailed, and the right of the states to maintain militias was not questioned. On the other hand, the degree to which citizens fulfilled their militia responsibilities and the conditions under which those state militias could be called to federal service were at issue. As historian Philip Gold, among others, has argued, and as we shall see in the next chapter, "the American people displayed a marked reluctance to serve, except for very short periods, usually close to home, and often at rather extortionate financial terms."[1] At best, the militia was suited to local defense but not to the international military responsibilities that were to come with the evolution of the United States as a world power.

As we shall see in chapter 2, the militia system that provided our base for mobilization proved untenable. Ultimately, the maintenance of a national armed force became a federal responsibility, and the principle that linked military service to citizenship became increasingly tenuous. The states did retain the right to maintain militias, which could be federalized in the event of national emergency. These militias, however, came to be based on selective principles of National Guard organization, rather than on principles of the universal obligation to serve in a common militia. Thus the base for mobilization was narrowed. Moreover, the right of the federal government to deploy National Guard units to foreign soil remains a sensitive political issue.

In recent decades, the dispute over military manpower has shifted from a concern with states' rights to the issue of individual rights versus collective responsibility. Does citizenship still assume an obligation to serve the nation? And if so, must this service be in a military capacity? The current debate embeds the principle of national service in the broader issue of national service as a civic responsibility.

The contemporary debate has been shaped largely by five social trends in America that reached important turning points in the middle part of the century and affected the relationship between the individual and the state, as well as the nature of American military organization.

The first of these trends was the movement away from a military manpower policy that was based on mobilization during wartime and demobilization after wars toward a policy of maintaining a relatively large force-in-being at all times, in response to changes in military technology and to polarized power relationships in the post–World War II world. That is, our basic manpower policy was shaped by the worst-case scenario—a full-scale war between the East and the West. However, the second trend was a more optimistic shift from a mission of fighting total wars toward one of peace keeping or fighting limited wars, in response to the same technological changes. The third was the advent of the welfare state and the pattern of benefits to which citizens and groups came to regard themselves as being entitled.

The fourth trend was the continuation of the ongoing citizenship revolution in the industrialized nations of the West, which was reflected both in the growth of industrial democracy and in the extension of citizenship rights to new sectors of the population. And the fifth was the passing of the post–World War II baby-boom generation through the age of prime eligibility for the military, and the arrival at that age of the subsequent "birth dearth" generation, which reflected lower birth rates during the late 1950s and thereafter. This generation will continue to be the primary age group for the eligible military population into the 1990s.

In the short run, the effect of the confluence of these trends in the mid-twentieth century was that the United States military became a laboratory for the development of social-welfare programs in the United States, primarily in the areas of family benefits and educational assistance. Since these benefits were granted in exchange for military service, they served to symbolize the complementarity of citizen obligations and citizen rights. In the longer run, however, as the range and magnitude of benefits or entitlements of citizenship grew and as threats to national security seemed less imminent relative to the size of the defense establishment, benefits became separated from the notion of service. Thus, citizenship came to be reflected more in rights than in responsibilities.

Moreover, since the entitlements that came to be regarded as citizen rights were manifested primarily by financial grants, the connection between the individual and the state came to be defined in terms of cash rather than participation. In the era of the all-volunteer force, the military entered the labor market as an employer of first-term enlisted personnel; the military competed with other employers primarily on a wage basis, thus further asserting that even in the realm of military service, the link between the citizen and the state is a fiscal one. The United States has managed to maintain its active-duty military forces on an all-volunteer basis throughout the 1980s by using labor-market principles. However, the waning of the principle of the citizen-soldier has deprived the nation of the mobilization base that it is likely to need in the event of a major war.

THE DECLINE OF THE MASS FORCE
AND THE MOBILIZATION MODEL

Recognizing both that the maintenance of large standing armies during peacetime was an inefficient use of resources and that the existence of such a force was a potential liability to the democratic political process, the industrial nations of the West, at least from the period of the American and French revolutions through the first part of the twentieth century, utilized a mobilization model of military manpower. During peacetime, these nations maintained relatively small nuclei of military organizations, and during times of conflict, they expanded the force by taking large numbers of people out of civilian pursuits and making soldiers of them. This was accomplished largely through conscription.

The American and French revolutions contributed to the expansion of the definition of the citizenry and defined participation in armed conflict as part of the normative definition of citizenship.[2] The mobilization of "mass armies" through the conscription of the citizenry was accompanied by economic mobilization, with the productive resources of society being expanded and converted from consumer-oriented production to the production of war materials. The mobilization model assumed that in the event of war, the involved states would have time to raise, train, and field their fighting forces and that the peacetime nucleus could fill organizational and training functions until the newly mobilized force was ready to take the field. Technological changes in the mid-twentieth century, however, have deprived nations of the luxuries of time and distance from the battlefield that the mobilization model had assumed.

The mass army reached the peak of its importance in the Western world during the first half of the twentieth century. The armies of that era were mass ones in terms of size, with the United States Army alone numbering almost 6 million during World War II and with double that number serving in all the U.S. forces. They were mass ones in terms of having low levels of organizational differentiation, with the infantry serving as the prototypical model of the soldier. And they were mass ones in terms of the mobilization of people and resources drawn from the civilian sector.[3] Indeed, the wartime industrial mobilization, which drew unprecedented numbers of women into the full-time industrial labor force to maintain defense production, provided impetus to the citizenship revolution—the fourth trend noted above.

Shortly before the middle of the twentieth century, the political scientist Harold D. Lasswell noted changes in military technology that he proposed would change the relationship between military forces and their host civilian societies.[4] In a world in which modern military technology (then conceived of as air power) would make civilians as vulnerable to attack as military personnel were, Lasswell projected that "specialists in violence"—that is, military elites—would add management to their repertoire of skills and would become a major force in ruling elites. Among their skills they would count the manipulation of symbols, in the interest of mobilizing the entire population for defense efforts. Income would be somewhat equalized, in order to reduce opposition to the regime on the part of the underprivileged. Herein was an anticipation of the welfare state, but it was closely linked to the development of a warfare state. Economic production would be regularized and geared primarily toward military rather than consumption goods.

Note that Lasswell did not intend to apply this "garrison state" model to the United States, and indeed, evaluating the model a quarter of a century after its formulation, he found it most applicable to the Warsaw Pact nations.[5] What is important about the garrison-state model is that even among those who have explicitly rejected it, it has shaped the conceptual agenda for the analysis of civil-military relations in America, and that it links welfare and warfare spending.[6] Other theorists have argued that we have been forced to make a choice between purchasing guns or butter and that we have frequently chosen guns. However, as we shall see in chapter 4, the United States has actually attempted to buy both.

At a minimum, Lasswell's formulation makes us face the facts that in the post–World War II world, military affairs are of concern not only during periods of overt hostility; they are an ever-present feature of the political landscape. Also, large military expenditures are an ever-present feature of federal budgets, which in a sense is a statement about civil-military relations in America. Military manpower policy, in turn, is a direct reflection of our conception of civil-military relations.

World War II added nuclear weapons to the air power that had concerned Lasswell. These two new technologies undermined the mobilization model's assumptions of time and distance from the battlefield and contributed to a postwar emphasis on air power, rather than land power, as the major component of America's armed forces. World War II ended with the major nations of the world divided into two ideologically opposed camps: one centered on the United States and its allies in Western Europe; the other, on the Soviet Union and Eastern Europe. Given the need to respond rapidly to external threats that were expected to emanate from the Soviet bloc, the United States began to maintain a larger and more expensive peacetime force in the post–World War II period than it had previously. Early in the century, our active-duty strength numbered in the hundreds of thousands. It increased to more than 4 million at the peak of World War I. Between the World Wars it returned to less than 0.5 million. It was more than 12 million at the height of the World War II mobilization, and never thereafter did it dip below the million mark. Indeed, having reached 3.7 million during the Korean War, it remained at about the 2 million mark after Korea.

The number of personnel under arms was not the only change, however. The new technologies dictated changes in the kinds and levels of skill required by military personnel. The advent of increasingly sophisticated air power, armored-weapon systems, and electronic warfare and the expanded use, more recently, of computer and laser technology have required personnel with higher levels of basic aptitudes, who receive lengthy and costly training and who must be retained in the force for considerable terms of service if the return on expenditures for recruiting and training is to be economically viable.

The complexity of military technology has forced the United States to move from a principle of equipping the man to a principle of manning the equipment, and such a change of emphasis is consequential for the kinds of people who are needed for the armed forces. The economist Harold Wool has reported an increase in the percentage of electronics specialists in the enlisted force from 5.8 to 14.2 between 1945 and 1963.[7] Martin Binkin has noted an increase in enlisted technical workers from 13 percent after World War II to 29 percent in 1985.[8] While it is difficult to chart precise trends because of ever-changing categories, it is clear that during the 1980s, more than a quarter of all enlisted personnel were in technical specialties. And all of the services predict increasing needs for technical specialists over the next decade.

While it is possible to draft and train personnel during wartime to serve for tours of duty as combat infantrymen, it is less plausible to expect to draft and train large numbers of technicians for long periods of service during peacetime. Thus, the tendency in the Western world has been for the trend from a mobilization force to a force-in-being either to be accompanied by a conversion from conscription to volunteer forces, as in the United States, Great Britain, and Canada, or, at a minimum, to experience debate on the continued viability of military conscription, combined with a greater dependence on a nonconscripted and more technological career force, as in the cases of France and West Germany. And while there is no inherent contradiction between volunteer military forces and citizen-soldiers—people can volunteer for short periods of military service—the accompanying trend has been toward a larger proportion of longer-term career-oriented personnel.

PEACE-KEEPING MISSIONS AND LOW-INTENSITY WARFARE

The same technologies and international alignments that contributed to the decay of the mobilization-based *levée en masse* and its replacement by the force-in-being also required modern nations to rethink the missions that they wanted their military forces to perform.[9] In pre-Napoleonic Europe, wars had been limited in size, scope, and objective and had ended when the political purposes of sovereign states had been served.[10] After the Napoleonic Wars and the French Revolution, however, with the adoption of the mobilization model, the European states raised larger armies and fought larger-scale wars to achieve military objectives. It was regarded as normal for nations to use the most powerful weapons at their disposal in pursuit of their objectives. The epitome of this model was the pattern of world war that developed in the first half of the twentieth century.

More than two decades ago, however, Morris Janowitz suggested that in response to pragmatic constraints in the international arena and particularly in recognition that a major war between superpowers or their surrogates would in all likelihood result at best in a Pyrrhic victory, the mission of armed forces was shifting from one of war-fighting operations to one of constabulary, or peace-keeping, operations.[11] Constabulary military organization is "committed to the minimum use of force, and seeks viable international relations, rather than victory."

A decade after Janowitz had suggested the concept, Larry L. Fabian reviewed the organizational and political experiences of peace-keeping forces that were operating as agents of the United Nations, with a view toward improving the preparedness posture of peace-keeping forces. One of his major recommendations was that the superpowers (the United States and the

Soviet Union) maintain "distance and detachment" from the peace-keeping system.[12] Shortly thereafter, Charles C. Moskos, Jr., reaffirmed this principle in more general terms when he hypothesized that "soldiers from neutral middle powers are more likely to subscribe to the constabulary ethic [absolute minimal force and impartiality] than soldiers from major powers."[13] However, as we shall see in chapter 6, although the American military doctrine that has been developed since World War II emphasizes major conflicts, high-intensity warfare, and capital intensive air power, recent military missions have involved an expanded peace-keeping role and other forms of lower-intensity warfare that involve primarily labor-intensive land power—soldiers.

Under the mobilization model, military expenditures had not been a major issue on the federal agenda. Not only was military technology relatively inexpensive, but also during peacetime the force was small and absolute expenditures were low. During wartime, of course, expenditures grew markedly. However, at such times, there was an external enemy, national security was threatened, and victory was more important than budgetary considerations. During the current era, by contrast, the external enemy is less apparent, the existence of the force and the technology for it are themselves expensive, and deployments for peace-keeping and other low-intensity operations raise the ante, in lives as well as in dollars.

THE ADVENT OF THE WELFARE STATE

The same era that witnessed the rise of military forces-in-being during peacetime and the deployment of American military personnel for purposes of keeping international peace rather than defending national sovereignty also witnessed the rise of social-welfare institutions and programs that, during the current period, we now find competing with the military for federal budget dollars. Like the advent of military forces-in-being, the emergence of welfare states has been a twentieth-century trend among the industrial nations of the West. In one sense, the United States has lagged behind other nations in this movement,[14] both because the movement seemed to conflict with the very high value placed on individualism in America and because the American doctrine of states' rights prevented the federal government from promulgating a set of social rights to which one was entitled as a consequence of being a citizen of the nation.

The idea of a welfare state developed gradually in the Western world. Germany was perhaps the first Western state to develop broad social-welfare reforms, under Bismark in the 1880s. Other European countries began similar programs of government-assured assistance and social reform, particularly in the areas of medical, disability, and old-age insurance between the 1880s and the 1920s. The welfare state in the United States, by contrast, has generally been traced to the Social Security Act of 1935. The term "welfare state" was in wide use by the 1940s.[15]

In another sense, however, the beginning of the welfare state in the United States might be traced to earlier programs based on military service: the Civil War pension system and the mortgage assistance programs that started after World War I.[16] By the first decade of the twentieth century, the former covered more than half of the white native-born males in the North, and the latter, while extremely modest, opened the possibility of property ownership to lower strata of the social structure, thus contributing to the redistribution of economic resources that Lasswell's garrison-state model was to propose.

The major turning point, however, was the Great Depression, which, during the 1930s, led the government to become sufficiently concerned with insurrection on the part of the unemployed and the destitute so that the government rethought the meaning of the value of individualism.[17] Whereas individuals previously had been seen as responsible for their own economic well-being and whereas poverty had been seen as the result of sin, sloth, and stupidity, poverty came now to be regarded as a social rather than a personal condition, and the state assumed the responsibility for providing the mechanisms by which the individual could succeed according to his own efforts.[18] This was formalized in the terms of the original Social Security Act of 1935, which was based on contributions by employers and employees but not by the federal treasury. This contributory funding made access to benefits a right for those who had been gainfully employed.[19]

Major growth in welfare programs and expenditures occurred during the post–World War II years with priority shifting from the income-maintenance concerns of the Social Security program back to mortgage assistance and to expenditures for higher education, both of which were strongly influenced by the Serviceman's Readjustment Act of 1944 (the original GI Bill of Rights). While cynics might argue, with some justification, that educational benefits were extended to returning servicemen in order to prevent them from becoming a massive army of discontented and unemployed after demobilization, the GI bill nonetheless established the principle that entitlement to benefits could be achieved through service to the nation, not merely through cash contributions. Veterans' benefits exceeded federal expenditures for health, education, and manpower and for community development and housing into the mid-1960s. Federal contributions to nonveteran welfare programs went predominantly into education until well into the 1960s; they exceeded expenditures for health and for community development and housing, although they still lagged behind veterans' benefits.

The decade of the 1960s was the period during which, through court decisions, "benefits" became "entitlements" of citizenship.[20] Through litigation, access to benefits became a citizenship right, to be administered universalistically. All welfare sectors grew markedly, and health benefits grew most rapidly and indeed outstripped veterans' benefits. Educational expenditures that were not tied to military service also grew, producing what some analysts have referred to as "the G.I. Bill without the G.I." The ensuing redistribution of resources clearly improved the quality of life of less-privileged strata of society, and it is difficult to argue that this was not a social good. One might indeed reasonably argue that rationalizing the relationship between the citizen and the nation, as the welfare state has done,[21] and minimizing the affect and particularism that had characterized the relationship in the past was a benefit. However, it is wise to recognize the concomitant costs as well. The rationalization of citizenship rights in the welfare state virtually stripped the conception of citizenship of any notion of obligations that accompanied the rights. Whereas Social Security in the 1930s had assumed cash contributions and whereas the GI Bill of Rights had assumed service, the interpretations of the 1960s assumed neither.

THE CITIZENSHIP REVOLUTION

The advent of the welfare state can itself be seen as a reflection of an ongoing transformation of Western societies, which "have steadily moved to a condition in which the rights of citizenship are universal."[22] In the nations of Western Europe, the most dramatic manifestation of this citizenship revolution has been the extension of citizenship to historically repressed lower economic classes. New middle-class and working-class groups also had to be progressively incorporated into the citizenry of the United States. However, the absence of a long history of repressive class politics in this country, as compared to Europe, made the extension of citizenship based upon characteristics other than class—such as race, gender, and age—more pronounced in this country.[23]

T. H. Marshall has noted the importance of military service as an obligation of citizenship.[24] Historically, the role of combatant in warfare has been restricted to the most politically relevant strata of society. Until the end of the eighteenth century, military leadership was the privilege of a hereditary warrior class. The mounted cavalry, which was restricted to the nobility, held the place of honor on the battlefield. Even after the advent of artillery and muskets, the chevalier strove to maintain his monopoly over the right to bear arms.[25] During the nineteenth century, however, the infantry developed the ability to break up the cavalry charges of the knights, thereby in a real sense democratizing the battlefield and Western society in general.

The association between the right to bear arms and the citizen role grew out of the American and French revolutions, as noted above. Both of these events emphasized the right of every citizen to bear arms and to belong to the officer corps. From these revolutions came the concept of the citizen-soldier, the modern mass military formation discussed earlier, and the growth of parliamentary institutions. Janowitz has noted: "The political democracies which these revolutionary movements sought to establish rested on their having armed their citizens, who in turn demonstrated their loyalty through military service. . . . Military service emerged as a hallmark of citizenship and citizenship as the hallmark of a political democracy."[26] Thus, Janowitz found himself in agreement with Friedrich Engels's assertion that compulsory military service surpasses the general franchise as a vehicle of democracy. This effect has been even more pronounced in recent years than it had been in the immediate postrevolutionary period. "From World War I onward, citizen military service has been seen as a device by which excluded segments of society could achieve political legitimacy and rights."[27]

Military service as a path to citizenship has been an American tradition since the Revolutionary War. Foreigners who fought with the colonial forces in that conflict were made citizens. During the Civil War, both the Union and the Confederacy made provision for the naturalization of alien soldiers. Naturalization was used as an inducement to aliens to serve in World War I, and in the World War II period, virtually all requirements for citizenship, including lawful admission to the United States, were waived for alien military personnel. Current naturalization laws still extend special benefits to aliens who serve honorably in the American armed forces.[28]

As we shall see in chapter 5, in twentieth-century America, the relationship between military service and citizenship has been most dramatic with regard to the racial integration of the armed forces. Through the World War II period, the incorporation of black Americans into the civilian citizenry was only minimally effective, and blacks in the military served in segregated units, under a quota, were for the most part limited to noncombat jobs, and had an infinitesimally small likelihood of being commissioned as an officer.

During World War II, except for a short period of integration under battle conditions in the Ardennes, blacks continued to serve in segregated units, performing primarily quartermaster, construction, and transportation functions. Even the black combat units that did exist were used largely as a source of unskilled labor. The demand for recognition of the "right to fight" became a major slogan of black organizations that wanted to demonstrate the willingness of the black community to fulfill citizenship obligations. However, an army board in 1945 recommended the continuation both of racial segregation and of the quota system, as well as the use of blacks exclusively in support rather than combat functions.

It was not until 1950, under the direction of President Harry S. Truman's

1948 executive order to desegregate the armed forces and, most importantly, the manpower requirements of the Korean War, that segregation, the quota, and exclusion from combat on the basis of race truly disappeared. The racial integration of the armed forces during the Korean War preceded the gains achieved by the civil-rights movement toward racial integration and equality in American civilian institutions during the 1960s. The integration of blacks into the armed forces and into civilian institutions preceded by about three decades parallel issues raised regarding the extension of full citizenship rights to women.[29]

The relationship between military service and political citizenship was more recently demonstrated in the case of young adults. One of the themes of the movement against the Vietnam War during the 1960s was that young men between the ages of eighteen and twenty-one, who were liable for military conscription, were not eligible to vote. They were, therefore, not able to participate in the political processes that selected the members of the executive and legislative branches of the federal government who determined United States military policy, including policies regarding the waging of war. The contribution that the antiwar movement made to the end of the Vietnam War and to the end of conscription was preceded by its contribution to the Twenty-Sixth Amendment to the United States Constitution, which lowered the age of political majority to eighteen, thus allowing those who were liable to military conscription to participate in the electoral process. The unfortunate lesson of the Korean and Vietnam wars with regard to the extension of citizenship rights to blacks and to young adults may be that the military serves as a vehicle for the citizenship revolution primarily during times of war.

The social strains that reflect the extension of equality to women, in both military and civilian institutions in America, can be seen as the current phase of the citizenship revolution. The major barrier to women's participation in the armed forces has been a cluster of cultural values about the appropriate roles for women in society. Such values have had two interrelated thrusts. First, women have been perceived as being psychologically different from men. The stereotypical feminine personality traits include warmth, nurturing, dependency, submissiveness, and lack of aggressiveness—characteristics that are not highly valued in the military or, indeed, in the world of work. Second, the belief that psychological differences exist between males and females has reinforced the cultural acceptance of a division of labor based on gender. The world of work has been viewed as a man's world, whereas a woman's world has revolved around the family.[30]

There is a clear parallel between the service role in which women are viewed today and the service role in which blacks have been seen in the past. Both cases assume low levels of citizenship participation. A quota, sometimes referred to as a goal, still limits female participation in the United

States armed forces to roughly 12 percent of the force, even though women constitute more than 50 percent of the age-eligible population. It is only within the last two decades that organizationally segregated women's branches, such as the Women's Army Corps, have been abolished and that women have been integrated into the force structure. Opportunities for advancement in the officer corps have been opened to women, but these are constrained by the fact that the military establishment rewards combat specialists and combat performance, whereas women are still excluded from combat assignments by regulation in the army, and by statute in the navy and in the air force.

A second facet of the citizenship revolution, beyond the extension of citizenship rights to new social groups, also has potential implications for the armed forces. Not only are citizenship rights being extended to larger segments of the population; they are also being extended to new social arenas. Whereas purely political definitions of citizenship focus on the rights and obligations of individuals vis-à-vis the state, a more sociological definition of citizenship focuses more broadly on the rights and obligations of individuals vis-à-vis society at large. In terms of the first perspective, military service, as opposed to civilian employment, can be seen as an obligation of citizenship.[31]

The second perspective supplements political citizenship with industrial citizenship and asserts the rights of workers both to decide where they will work (which is influenced, of course, by economic rationality) and to participate in the decision-making process within the work place.[32] To the extent that military service is seen as a form of employment—an assumption that is required by the labor-market model of the all-volunteer force—this perspective would expect the accession process of military manpower to be based upon the self-interest of those in the service, rather than upon a principle of citizen duty, and would anticipate that military personnel would be able to pursue improvements in the quality of their work life through such means as collective bargaining.[33] Indeed, in the mid-1970s, one of the major concerns of Congress and the Defense Department was the threat of unionization of the all-volunteer force.[34] That threat did not become a reality, but the degree to which the military can be expected to be influenced by principles of industrial democracy remains ambiguous, and the extension of these principles to military service can be expected to change the nature of military service and military organization in significant ways.

THE CHANGING DEMOGRAPHIC CONTEXT

The changes in military manpower policy and in the definition of military mission, as well as the expansion of welfare and citizenship rights, discussed above, have taken place in the context of fluctuating demographic patterns.

Prior to World War II, the birth rates in most industrial nations of the West reached their nadir during the depression of the 1930s: people could no longer afford large families. And birth rates remained low when a generation of young men went to fight World War II and young women went into the civilian labor force. With the return of the young male population and of economic prosperity, birth rates rose during the 1940s and 1950s; and indeed, while they declined again starting in the late 1950s, they remained above the depression level until the early 1970s. The average number of births per woman in the United States had fallen to about 2.2 during the depression. It reached a zenith of 3.3 in the late 1950s and subsequently has returned to the lower level.

The growth of the population during the 1940s and 1950s, which was influenced both by the fact that there were large numbers of young women in the population and by the fact that these women were, on the average, having more babies, is the period referred to as the "baby boom." The baby-boom generation is notable in three important regards. It was the first generation to profit from the advent of the welfare state from an early stage in the life cycle. This generation was in its youth during the 1960s when court decisions expanded welfare benefits, which at the time were largely family benefits.

Because the benefits were largely concerned with the welfare of children who had not reached the age of political majority and had no clear citizenship obligations, this was also the generation for which citizenship obligations and rights were unassociated from the outset.[35] For this generation, the pattern was continued with the expansion of federal aid to higher education based upon need rather than military service: the GI bill without the GI. And it was the generation that came of military age eligibility between the late 1950s and the late 1970s, during most of which time the United States had a system of military conscription, fought a war in Southeast Asia that was increasingly opposed by the American people, and saw, in 1973, the advent of the contemporary all-volunteer military force.

The decline in fertility since the late 1950s reflected the fact that people were postponing marriage longer than they had during the 1940s and the early 1950s. This trend has continued in the civilian population, thus reducing the pool of young men on whom the armed forces draw for personnel, although interestingly, armed-forces personnel have been getting married younger than their civilian counterparts, which perhaps is a reflection of the family benefits available to them.[36]

In addition, Americans have postponed having their first child longer and have spaced their children more widely. In part, this reflects the widespread adoption of new and more effective methods of contraception during the 1960s and 1970s, which has allowed parents to exert some choice in the size of their family. Preferences for smaller families, in turn, may reflect to some extent a general ecological concern with the consequences of population growth.[37]

Whatever the reason for declining fertility, it has implications for military personnel policy. The number of males between the ages of eighteen and twenty-one in the American population peaked in 1978. This was the last baby-boom cohort. There was a modest decline from 1978 to 1982: less than 1 percent per year. The major effect of the "birth dearth" of the 1960s occurred between 1983 and 1987, when the decline in cohort size increased to 2.5 percent per year. By 1990, the number of 18-to-21-year-old Americans will be 17 percent below the 1978 level, and the military-age-eligible population will continue to decline into the mid-1990s. This population decline has been one of the major reasons for the increasing intensity and frequency of debate on military-manpower policy.

Two important points must be noted to put the discussion into perspective. First, it is a short-term phenomenon. The military-age-eligible population will again begin to expand in the mid 1990s. To the extent that the declining size of the cohort will produce a manpower-based "window of vulnerability," that window will close before the turn of the century. Second, and more important, we should remember that at the lowest future point of military-manpower supply, in the mid 1990s, there will still be more young men in the American population than there have been during any previous wartime period. The population of young adult male Americans is, and will continue to be, larger than it was for the mobilizations produced by either world war, the Korean War, or the Vietnam War. However, the population of adult males in the Soviet Union is larger still.

THE DECADE PAST

At the beginning of the 1980s, in response to criticisms about the quality, quantity, and social unrepresentativeness of the all-volunteer military force and to the projected decline of manpower availability just discussed, the debate intensified about whether the United States should maintain a voluntary military manning system, return to conscription, or move to a more general system of national service.[38] The American military was given a great deal of media attention, and the prestige of organizations such as Stanford University's Hoover Institution, the American Assembly, and the Atlantic Council was thrown behind a series of conferences, symposia, and workshops, leading to analytic publications that were intended to inform the public debate.[39]

These forums focused primarily on whether the economic assumptions that served as the basis for the all-volunteer force could be expected to provide the military manpower needed for America's national security in the future.

They avoided addressing the implications of rejecting the principle that service to the nation in the interest of collective security is an obligation of citizenship and the question of the degree to which this principle had been important in meeting our needs for military manpower in the past.

By the early 1980s, discrepancies between civilian pay levels and military compensation, which had arisen during the early years of the all-volunteer force and favored civilian employment, had disappeared. A problem with the selection test for armed services' personnel, which had appeared in the mid 1970s and had led to the enlistment of large numbers of less-qualified people, had been resolved. And problems in the nation's economy had driven youth unemployment up. The manpower picture had improved markedly, with manpower goals being met early through the recruitment of highly qualified personnel. There was general agreement that whatever problems remained in the manpower and personnel equation, neither the quantity nor the quality of the force would be changed markedly by a reintroduction of conscription.[40] Moreover, since any military draft in a peacetime environment would conscript only a small proportion of the eligible population, a perception of inequity would taint the armed forces.

As noted above, a draft would not produce the large numbers of technical specialists required by the modern military force of the United States. And indeed, under the economic assumptions of the early 1980s, with military compensation comparable to civilian pay and with youth unemployment high, the all-volunteer force has been working. However, the debate should go beyond this point. The sole question is not, or should not be, whether we can recruit enough bodies to fill the boxes in the organization charts of a peace-time standing force through voluntary means. The question of whether a force so recruited can fulfill America's national-security needs by winning battles and wars if need be should also be addressed.[41] In other words, the basic question should not be whether the quantity and the quality of personnel in the all-volunteer force constitute a problem. These are important issues, but they are less basic than the implications of the concept of wholly voluntary military service, driven by self-interest rather than by citizenship obligation.

Also in need of deliberation is the relationship that the nation desires between the individual and the state. Recently a working group of the Atlantic Council confronted the question of whether members of the generation who were born in the industrial nations of the West after World War II are "adequately educated with respect to the heritage, values and basic principles of our common Western civilization to play a fully responsible part in strengthening our heritage and way of life."[42] In the United States, the generation being discussed was the generation that grew up under the welfare-state conditions described above. The working group's response to the question was a resounding no.

THE DECADE TO COME

The advent of the welfare state has redefined the relationship between the citizen and the state in terms of economic support. The military, if it is not merely a welfare-oriented employer of last resort, is, to many, primarily an employer nonetheless.[43] The Republican administration that steered America's course through most of the 1980s, while it attempted to reduce welfare programs, also rejected the collectivistic assumptions of compulsory military service and found that an all-volunteer military force shaped by labor market dynamics was more compatible with its ethic of individualism.

Only recently have there been a return to the inclusion of obligations in analyses of the concept of citizenship and a recognition that the concepts of citizenship and patriotism have consequences for military organization and military performance. Empirical support for the principle that the United States population will support the military establishment when there is a clear sense of national purpose and need comes from survey data that show growing support for registration and a military draft, a general willingness of a plurality of young American males to volunteer for service in the event of a necessary war,[44] and from the generally high level of compliance with the current requirements to register for Selective Service.[45] One of the emerging issues in the debate over military manpower, however, is how citizenship and military service are to be articulated in a welfare-state context in which citizenship itself is increasingly defined in economic rather than political terms.[46] And in more pragmatic national-security terms, it has become increasingly clear that the peacetime all-volunteer force lacks the mobilization base it would need in order to fight a major war.

While the Defense Department, which in the 1960s warned against the adoption of an all-volunteer force, now argues against all potential alternatives to the volunteer force, the viability of such alternatives is now frequently raised in the policy community. The alternative that is most frequently suggested—and most dramatically rejected by the defense establishment—is national service. Is this the direction in which the nation is headed? Should such service be voluntary or compulsory? Should it be limited to males, or should women serve as well? To what extent should it involve civilian as well as military service? Is a force based on national service suited to the role of the United States in the international system? These issues and the questions they subsume are among the concerns of this book.

2
Changes in United States Military Manpower Policy

The contemporary debate on United States military manpower policy has tended to be ahistorical; it has either romanticized or failed to attend to the lessons of the past. The issues facing us today are not new. They have recurred since the birth of the Republic. Military manpower policy for our first century and a quarter was based on the principle of a widespread obligation to serve—a principle that was more an expression of sociopolitical values than an effective military manpower policy.

The principle, as manifested in the organization of the militia, was ambiguous, in part because the sometimes-competing principle of states' rights limited the effective control of the armed forces. Indeed, the evolution of the United States military from decentralized colonial militias to a large standing federal force reflects the process of nation building in America, and the concomitant transformation of the locus of citizenship from the state to the nation-state. The early militias did not in fact accomplish the goals of the obligation principle, and the nation lacked an effective base for mobilization. However, despite frequent attacks, the militia model stood until the beginning of the twentieth century.[1]

As the new century began, the obligation principle was itself compromised in order to generate a more effective military organization. The Dick Act, by establishing greater federal control over the National Guard, substituted voluntarism for obligation as the basis for the military service of citizen-soldiers. Attempts were occasionally made to reassert the principle of obligation, and wartime drafts demonstrated that the principle could be applied in times of crisis. Attempts to establish the principle more generally, however, such as President Truman's support for universal military training, were unsuccessful.

The Gates Commission, which in the 1960s developed the blueprint for the all-volunteer force that the United States adopted in 1973 and maintains today, dealt a mortal wound to the principle of obligation by explicitly identifying financial inducements as the major incentive for voluntarism. In this context, reactions to the subsequent resurrection of selective-service registration by President Jimmy Carter and its continuation by an ambivalent President Ronald Reagan, coupled with persistent problems of raising and mobilizing a military reserve, have led to serious questions about whether the current military manpower policies of the United States will provide for national-security needs in the future. In order to avoid the liabilities associated with forgetting the past, a review of how the country got to where it is today is in order.

THE COLONIAL PERIOD

America's military traditions, which were inherited from the British, included both a favorable predisposition toward militia organization and a distrust of centralized standing peacetime forces. The militia, as a military organization composed of civilians enrolled and trained as a defensive force against invaders, developed from the Anglo-Saxon fyrd—a national levy based upon the duty of all free men to serve in the military when needed. King James II had maintained a standing peacetime army of some thirty thousand men in the seventeenth century and had used it to suppress the freedom of the English and to threaten religious and military despotism. England's Glorious Revolution in 1688–89 deposed James, brought William III and Mary II to the throne, and produced a bill of rights that redefined the relationship between monarch and subjects and forbade the crown to maintain a standing army in peacetime without parliamentary consent.

The North American colonists, as British subjects, inherited both the English militia system and a memory of the excesses of James's army. The colonists were in a defensive posture, being threatened both by Native Americans and by rival colonial powers, and were in need of military force. Their solution was the militia—a force of citizen-soldiers who manifested the notion of universal military obligation in their own colonies.

Military manpower systems receive their greatest support in the face of pressing military need. As the colonies became more secure and as the threats faded, the colonial militia system deteriorated in much the same way that military conscription deteriorated two centuries later: through a system of deferments and exemptions that moved away from the principle of universal obligation and made the burden of military service increasingly inequitable.

The "common militia" was in theory composed of all able-bodied free white men. It was to serve as the mobilization base of the colonies, with the "volunteer militia" providing the long-term military nucleus. However, a considerable proportion of the citizenry was exempted from militia service by more than two hundred militia laws.[2] The Massachusetts Militia Act of 1647, for example, exempted officers, fellows, and students of Harvard College; church elders and deacons; schoolmasters; physicians; surgeons; captains of ships of more than twenty tons; fishermen who were employed year round; people who had physical problems; members of the General Court; and people who were excused from service by the General Court or by the Court of Assistants. The burden of service was progressively lifted from the shoulders of the wealthy and placed upon the shoulders of the poor.[3]

When the volunteer militia failed to produce a sufficiently large force and when legislative calls for additional volunteers failed to expand the force sufficiently, men were drafted from the common militia. Such drafts increased the inequity of the distribution of the burden of service; the results were both desertions and draft riots.[4] Both forms of opposition to conscription were to become commonplace in America during periods of military draft.

During the Revolutionary War, the colonies temporarily had to centralize control over the militias and resort to conscription in order to raise the Continental Army. Since the Articles of Confederation constrained the Continental Congress from implementing an equitable draft, the process was left up to the states, which continued past inequities and led again to draft riots.[5] After the victory of the Continental Army over the British, George Washington urged Congress to accept the principle "that every Citizen who enjoys the protection of a free government, owes . . . his personal services to the defense of it."[6] On the basis of this principle of universal national military obligation, he recommended the establishment of a small peacetime army, backed by a national militia, which would consist of citizens from eighteen to fifty years of age, who would be equipped and trained at federal expense. Congress, recalling the experience of James II, ruled against General Washington, declared that standing armies in times of peace were inconsistent with the principle of republican government, and discharged the Continental Army, except for "twenty-five privates to guard the stores at Fort Pitt and fifty-five to guard the stores at West Point, with a proportionate number of officers," none of whom were to be above the rank of captain.[7]

FROM THE REVOLUTION
TO THE SPANISH-AMERICAN WAR

The victory of the Antifederalists in preventing the formation of a national military institution did not remove the need for an armed force. With hostilities against the British ended, there was still a western frontier to protect. On June 3, 1784, the day after it had dismissed the Continental Army, Congress requested that the states of Connecticut, New Jersey, New York, and Pennsylvania recruit a total of seven hundred militiamen for a year of service on the frontier. A year later, the term of frontier service was extended to three years, and the militiamen were replaced by regular soldiers.[8] The First Regiment of the United States, operating on the frontier under the dual authority of the states, which supplied its officers and enlisted men, and the Congress, which provided its authorization, was plagued by problems of morale, drunkenness, and desertion; it proved to be ineffective even in the protection of its own garrisons.[9]

This inability of Congress to provide for the security needs of the new nation was reflected as well in Shays' Rebellion in Massachusetts in 1786–87, which was led by debt-ridden former Continental soldiers, whom the militia tended to support, and which the army was not able to combat. It was in the context of such events that the Constitutional Convention, convened in Philadelphia, had to deal with the issue of whether the responsibility for the maintenance of an armed force resided with the states or with the central government.

The resolution was a compromise. The new government was given the power to "raise and support armies," with a two-year limit on appropriations; to "provide and maintain a navy"; and to "make rules for the regulation of the land and naval forces." The right of the states to control their militias was confirmed at the same time, and these state troops were to be the country's major land force in the event of a crisis. The navy, which was not subjected to the same two-year limit on appropriations as was the army, would be the major defense of the isolated nation against foreign powers. The small voluntary national army would protect the frontiers and would handle any encroachment by colonial powers or problems with native American tribes, and the militias would help maintain internal order, reinforce the regulars on the frontier when necessary, and provide a mobilization base for the national army in case of emergency.[10]

Although controlled by the states, the structure of the militia was dictated (more or less) by the Militia Act of 1792, which called for universal liability for service, with few exceptions, among able-bodied white male citizens between the ages of eighteen and forty-five. The act specified how the militia units were to be organized and how the militiamen were to equip themselves. The act did not specify how it was to be enforced or how the militia was to be mobilized.

The weaknesses of the militia system were demonstrated by the Whiskey Rebellion. During the summer of 1794, opposition to the central government evolved into insurrection in western Pennsylvania. Federal revenue agents were assaulted. The rebellion was supported by, if not organized within, the local militia.[11] President Washington lacked the legal authority to use regular troops to deal with domestic rebellion, and he did not want to use them for such purposes in any case; so he called up thirteen thousand militiamen from neighboring states to be prepared for national service in the event that he could not negotiate the peaceful reestablishment of national authority.

The state militias proved to be undermanned, because many citizens had elected to pay fines in lieu of service. The militias were poorly trained, and in many cases, their sympathies lay with the insurgents. Ultimately, all states that were called to assist met their quotas, but not through the normal mobilization of the common militia. Rather than representing a cross section of the citizenry, the militia that followed Washington into western Pennsylvania was composed for the most part of substitutes, who were paid to serve in the place of those who had been called, and of volunteers from the youngest and poorest strata of society.[12]

The Whiskey Rebellion was put down, but it was clear that the state militia system had not provided a broadly representative force of citizen-soldiers. Moreover, the performance of the militia troops in the rebellion, coupled with their failures in the Indian wars and their poor performance in those wars in comparison to that of regular soldiers, led the Federalists to press again for a national militia or a standing army—proposals that the Republicans opposed. In 1792, Congress had approved a request from President Washington for five additional regiments of regular soldiers to serve on the frontier. This was in addition to the infantry regiment and the artillery battalion that had been established in 1784 and a second regiment of infantry that had been added in 1791. However, the Republicans continued to oppose a standing army, and Congress did not act on what appeared to be the sole viable alternative—an effective national militia. Indeed, the Republicans' opposition to such a militia, which was based upon the principle of states' rights, seemed to be a driving force toward what was to them a more odious alternative—a standing army. Thus, by the end of the eighteenth century, while America was evolving as a confederation of states toward nationhood, it adopted a military manpower format that tenuously balanced local and national interests and that included an expanded national army, but with the mobilization base still belonging to the states.[13]

Events across the Atlantic also helped shape the evolution of United States military manpower policy. The success of the French Revolution and the establishment of the *levée en masse* by the Committee for Public Safety tied citizenship to military participation for all French men, women, and children, who were required to provide support for the army if they did not themselves serve. This was the extreme manifestation of the mass armed force that was to characterize the Western nations in a much more moderate form a century later. It demonstrated to the Americans, Federalist and Republican alike, the potential ugliness of a national militia. And it frightened the Americans by its military successes over professional European soldiers.

Relations between America and France deteriorated, and with skirmishing on the high seas and with a threat of an invasion by France, Congress expanded the navy, established the separate Navy Department, and passed the Provisional Army Act in 1798, which provided for the recruitment and training of a ten-thousand-man reserve force, and the New Army Act, which added twelve regiments and more than ten thousand volunteer soldiers to the Regular Army. Both acts were designed to remove responsibility for national security from the state militias and to give it to the central government. The Republicans anticipated that this all-volunteer force would be recruited from members of the lowest strata of society, who, motivated by pecuniary concerns, would be unlikely to fight for the principles of the Republic. The European threat also led to the development of an industrial support base for the military: iron mines, foundries, musket factories, and navy yards for the production of the materials of war. Indeed, Eli Whitney's assembly-line production of muskets established a pattern of industrial dependence on governmental contracts and of the failure to complete such contracts on time.[14] Thus we created a small nineteenth-century military-industrial complex.

At the beginning of the nineteenth century, with Napoleon's ascent to power in France having removed the threat from that quarter and with the election of Thomas Jefferson to the presidency, the Federalists' initiatives to establish a strong national army were reversed. While sending naval forces to the Mediterranean to deal with the Barbary pirates at Tripoli, Jefferson also restructured the navy by eschewing large ocean-going frigates in favor of small, shallow-draft gunboats, which carried small crews and only one cannon. These boats seemed ideal for the coastal defense of a nation that did not have international pretensions, although they had proven themselves effective in Tripoli as well. The gunboat fleet was actually a naval analogy to the militia, prepared for rapid mobilization; but it was a national, rather than a state, force.

In his Inaugural Address, Jefferson had emphasized his belief that the state militia should be the major defensive force of the nation; and in his first message to Congress, he had requested and received a reduction in the size of the Regular Army, to about thirty-three hundred soldiers. In 1802, in response to the president's request for a review of the militia, Congress reaffirmed the Militia Act of 1792. Interestingly, in that same year, recognizing the increasing complexity of war, Jefferson asked Congress to establish a military academy. In the following year, the president was given discretionary powers to call the militia into service, but the organization, arming, and equipping of the militia remained responsibilities of the states.

With a major war being waged between England and France, Jefferson maintained a position of neutrality, using his forces to prepare to defend the United States coastline and to explore, organize, and protect the western frontier, especially the new Louisiana Purchase, the crown jewel of which—New Orleans—was the gateway to the Mississippi.

The maintaining of neutrality became increasingly difficult. In 1807 the British warship *Leopard* attacked and defeated the United States frigate *Chesapeake* off the Virginia coast and impressed several members of the *Chesapeake*'s crew. Jefferson, while continuing to seek neutrality, called for an increase in the size of the army, and in 1808, Congress made the organization and arming of the militia a federal responsibility. James Madison, who was elected as the fourth president, inherited a nation committed to neutrality and to a militia-based military organization.

The impressment of United States seamen and the British interference with American shipping continued and, in combination with the opportunity to expand into British Canada and Spanish Florida, led to a declaration of war in June, 1812. The British had only a few thousand troops in Canada, and there was virtually no Spanish garrison in Florida, but the United States was not in a significantly better position to wage a land war. At the time that war was declared, there were fewer than seven thousand regular troops, scattered over scores of posts. The state-based militia was theoretically large, numbering in the hundreds of thousands, but it was poorly equipped and trained.

Congress sought to improve the United States posture through an expanded regular (albeit temporary) force, recruited through economic incentives and supplemented by militiamen. The new regiments—commanded by veterans of the Revolution and manned by a combination of regular soldiers from previously existing units, new regulars recruited for this war, volunteers, and militiamen—did not fare well against the British professional soldiers in Canada. It fell to the navy, at Lake Erie and Lake Champlain, to prevent the British from bringing the campaign south.

After the defeat of Napoleon in 1814, the British could make a larger investment in the war in North America. The British advance down the Champlain waterway proved the efficacy of the United States Navy, but it also once again demonstrated the weakness of the state-based militia system. When the British reached Plattsburgh, New York, the governor of Vermont sought to withdraw the Vermont militia from the battle, noting that the Vermont militia was constitutionally required to "repel invaders" but that an invasion of New York did not constitute an invasion of Vermont.[15]

After the British drive south had been halted and an attack on Baltimore had been repelled by forces at Fort McHenry, both sides sought peace, and a treaty was signed in December, 1814. News of the treaty did not travel rapidly enough, however, to prevent Gen. Edward Michael Pakenham from marching his ranks of professional British soldiers toward the entrenched citizen-soldiers, regular soldiers, and pirate-soldiers who were under the command of Andrew Jackson at New Orleans during the second week of January, 1815. The relative losses—the British, advancing in ranks, lost one-third of their force; and the Americans, firing from cover, lost seven soldiers— probably tell us more about maneuver formations than about the relative merits of professional, as against "citizen," armed forces; and the difficulties experienced by Jackson in controlling his militia after the battle added to the accumulating evidence of the weakness of the militia system.

If the War of 1812 indicated illness in the militia system, the Mexican War pointed to the terminal nature of the disease. The militia did not do well in the Indian Wars of the 1830s, because its members were poorly armed, poorly trained, and convinced that they were obligated to only three-month tours of service. During the 1840s, Joel R. Poinsett, President Martin Van Buren's secretary of war, attempted to reform the militia, but he met with no greater success than had his predecessors.

Texas had declared its independence from Mexico in 1836, and after the massacres at Goliad, Texas, and the Alamo, the likelihood of a war with Mexico had increased. In 1844, President John Tyler submitted to the Senate a treaty to annex Texas, and when James K. Polk was elected president that fall, the nation seemed to be committed to a war with Mexico.

The annexation of Texas was accomplished in the summer of 1845, and Zachary Taylor, with roughly fifteen hundred regular troops, was sent to Corpus Christi. Such reinforcements as the nation could afford were sent to him, but at the end of the year, he had less than four thousand troops. In April, 1845, the Mexican army crossed the Rio Grande and destroyed one of Taylor's outposts.

Having previously been authorized to mobilize the militia, Taylor called for five thousand militiamen from Louisiana and Texas. He in fact got ten thousand, but they arrived too late for the early battles of the war, and because they were committed to only three-month terms of federal service, they left too early to participate in the subsequent Mexican campaign. In any case, the militia was protected by law from being required to fight on foreign soil. Thus, the militia played a negligible role in the Mexican War.

The war was fought for the most part by volunteers who, while they were nominally federal troops, fought in units that were raised by the states and were commanded by officers appointed by the governors. By statute, the troops were to serve for one year or for the duration of the war, which President Polk interpreted as a term of service not to exceed one year. Thus, like militia units, these regular regiments faced the risk of disintegrating at key points in the campaign, as the soldiers' tours of duty expired.[16] The victory of the United States over Mexico cannot be credited to the militia system. Rather, just as the War of 1812 demonstrated the efficacy of the navy, the Mexican War demonstrated the importance of a professional officer corps. The senior commanders in Mexico had learned their trade in the War of 1812 and in the Indian Wars, while the company and junior field-grade officers were the graduates of the Military Academy, which Jefferson had created. However, as had also been the case in the War of 1812, the military victory convinced the nation, erroneously, that the state militia organization, based upon the principle of obligatory service, was sufficient for the nation's needs.

The Mexican War had caused the mobilization of some 104,000 American soldiers, primarily volunteers. In keeping with the mobilization model, after the war, the volunteers were sent home, and the regular army was reduced to about ten thousand soldiers. The militia model, based upon the rights of the states as against the central government, was to continue to serve as the basis for the land forces. Yet the issue of states' rights itself was to lead to the attempted dissolution of the Union and to our first national military draft.

Tensions between the Northern and Southern states, largely over the issue of slavery, had been building. The election of Abraham Lincoln as president catalyzed the crisis, and in December 1860 South Carolina declared itself a separate and independent state. Six other Deep South states followed South Carolina, and in February, 1861, formed the Confederacy. Lincoln was willing to concede much on the issue of slavery, but he was not willing to concede the right of secession. Although he attempted to find a peaceful resolution, the Confederacy fired on Fort Sumter in Charleston harbor on the morning of April 12.

Technological advances in communication, transportation, and weaponry increased both the rate and the scale of mobilization over what had been experienced in past conflicts. Congress sought to mobilize an army of 500,000 soldiers, while the Confederacy sought to amass a force of 400,000. In the course of the war, the two armies mobilized almost 2.5 million men: the Confederate army was 261,000 strong at its peak, while the Union army reached 622,000.[17]

The militia organization of the Union forces in 1861 and the fact that the president had to seek mobilization through the states, calling militiamen to serve three-month tours of federal service, forced the border states to choose sides, and the South benefited from this situation. The greater part of the Regular Army, having been recruited primarily in the North, remained loyal to the Union. In order to raise the manpower it needed, the Confederacy enacted conscription one year and four days after Fort Sumter was fired upon. Eleven months later, the Enrollment Act of 1863 in the North established the first federal conscription and lengthened the term of service for conscripts to three years. The military was responsible for most of the administration of the draft. Enrollment officers sought people out in their homes; however, individuals could provide substitutes or purchase their way out of military service.

Conscription was neither equitable nor popular in either the North or the South. Both systems favored the rich. In the North, draft liability could be commuted for a $300 fee, while in the South, owners of slaves were exempted. More importantly, although the Confederacy had adopted a more centralized manpower system than had the Union, the Southern states, having seceded on the basis of states' rights, were not willing to yield, even to Jefferson Davis, a principle they had refused to yield to Abraham Lincoln.

The governors of the Confederate States exempted tens of thousands of men from draft liability.[18]

In the North, opposition to conscription was more violent. The commutation provision led to complaints that poor mens' blood was going to be spilled in rich mens' interests. As we will see in chapter 5, opposition to the draft in the North had important racial undercurrents as well. When the first federal draft lottery got under way in New York City, an angry mob stormed the Provost Marshal's Office and burned it to the ground. About fifty thousand people continued to riot for four days in one of the largest acts of collective violence ever experienced in the United States. A great deal of property was destroyed, and roughly a thousand people were killed. It took six regiments of Union troops, returning from the Battle of Gettysburg, to restore order. Additional riots took place in Massachusetts, Ohio, New Hampshire, and Vermont.[19]

Interestingly, while the draft was a major issue, it was not directly a major source of military manpower in the Civil War, which, like previous United States military engagements, was fought primarily by volunteers. Only about 2 percent of the soldiers who served in the Union army were federal draftees. The draft did, however, provide an incentive to enlist, beyond the bounties and bonuses that were offered to volunteers, and yielded America's first draft-motivated volunteers. It also produced substitutes, who served in the place of those draftees who could afford to purchase their way out of service. Most importantly, it established, at least symbolically, the right of the federal government to induct men into national military service without the intervention of the militia.

The Confederate forces surrendered at Appomattox Courthouse in 1865. In the year after the Grand Army of the Republic had marched triumphantly down Pennsylvania Avenue in Washington, hundreds of thousands of volunteers were mustered out of the federal service, leaving a regular army of six cavalry regiments, five artillery regiments, and nineteen infantry regiments. As we will see in chapter 4, the veterans of the Union army were to become a major political force in the development of benefit programs that were to expand beyond the veteran population and affect both military expenditures and military accessions in the late twentieth century.

George Armstrong Custer lost a battalion of cavalry at the Battle of the Little Bighorn in 1876, and in 1877, federal troops were called in to control striking railroad workers, who had the sympathies of local militia. But there were no large-scale military engagements during the 1880s, and while the states recognized the shortcomings of militia organization, there was no strong move to establish a large federal army. When the Spanish-American War began, the army consisted of about 28,000 soldiers scattered around the country.

President William McKinley called for 125,000 volunteers in April, 1898;

and National Guard units, expanded by recent and untrained volunteers, answered the call, as they did the following month when Congress authorized an additional 75,000 troops. Of between 200,000 and 300,000 troops who served in the war, the great majority were volunteers from the militia. Two-thirds of them never had to leave the United States, and only a few were killed. Conscription was never considered. After the war, the volunteer force was demobilized, leaving the remaining federal forces in garrisons. However, as a result of the war, the garrisons included strategic locations outside the continental United States.[20]

At the dawn of the twentieth century, in terms of both principle and organization, an interesting foundation had been laid for the military manpower debate that was to follow. There was general agreement with the principle that had been espoused by George Washington regarding the responsibility of citizens to contribute to the common defense. The doctrine of states' rights still required that this contribution be primarily through participation in the militia, although the Militia Act of 1792 was ultimately to be a casualty of the Spanish-American War. There was recognition that in the absence of a large standing army in peacetime, mobilization of the militia for war was neither as smooth nor as socially representative as the principles of militia organization suggested that it should be. For the first time, Americans had attempted a national draft. It had violated the principle of equity, and it had produced riots. All of our wars had been fought primarily by volunteers, many of whom had served no longer than three months and most of whom had expected to return home at the end of hostilities. And Americans had committed themselves to continuing overseas responsibilities. This was the situation when, in 1899, President McKinley asked Elihu Root to become secretary of war.

Root understood the organizational problems of the military establishment, and in an attempt to deal with them, he brought to the military many of the principles of scientific management that were then being developed in American industry. The implications of this approach will be discussed at length in the next chapter.[21] Part of his organizational reform was intended to provide the federal government with a military force that would not be controlled by the states. This was accomplished by the Dick Act, which finally repealed the Militia Act of 1792 and gave the federal government much firmer control over the National Guard, making it a training ground for volunteer soldiers and, it was hoped, the nation's first-line military reserve, at the cost of sacrificing "all but the ghost of the universal military obligation."[22]

THE TWO WORLD WARS

In 1910, in Europe, massive armies were being raised on the basis of universal military obligation, although Britain was still clinging to the principle of voluntary service. The United States attempted to assume a posture of neutrality and mediation in the evolving conflict in Europe. However, neutrality became an increasingly elusive posture after the sinking of the *Lusitania* in April 1915. President Woodrow Wilson and the Democratic party attempted to avoid the expanding of United States military forces, but the Republicans increasingly preached preparedness. The justification of preparedness, however, was to repel an invading European army from North America should the need arise, not to intervene in the European war.

In moving toward the goal of preparedness, Congress in June 1916 passed the National Defense Act, which established a four-component land force, consisting of an expanded peacetime Regular Army of 175,000 troops; the National Guard, which carried an obligation for federal service; a reserve force, consisting of men who were to complete their active duty enlistments with the regular army and of officers from reserve-officer training programs in colleges; and a volunteer army, to be raised in time of war. The efficacy of the act was tested during the summer of 1916, when virtually the entire National Guard was federalized in support of Gen. John J. Pershing's punitive expedition into Mexico in pursuit of Pancho Villa. The guard was not able to bring itself to full wartime strength through voluntary enlistments, and in many cases, guardsmen who were mobilized made it clear that when they had enlisted in the National Guard, they had not considered the possibility of a real mobilization. The Mexican experience demonstrated that voluntarism would not bring either the Regular Army or the National Guard to full wartime strength. The years that led up to United States involvement in the First World War were punctuated by national debate on America's role in the international system and on the nature of the United States military.

President Wilson tried to keep the United States out of the European war, but he also told his defense secretaries to plan for the expansion of the armed forces. In April 1917 the United States declared war on Germany in the wake of German torpedoing of United States ships. In recognition of the lessons learned from the Mexican experience, on the day after war was declared, the selective-service bill was presented to Congress. The bill stimulated considerable debate in Congress, but it was signed into law on May 18, thus establishing local civilian boards to administer the registration of young adult males.[23]

While the weaponry of 1917 required larger armies than had participated in the wars of the nineteenth century, technologies of communication and transportation allowed the luxury of a mobilization that, by contemporary standards, would be regarded as leisurely. The first registration was held on June 5, and about 9.5 million young men registered immediately. During the course of the war, about 24 million Americans registered. The first lottery drawing to establish the order of selection was held on July 20. The first inductions took place almost four months after the declaration of war. By the end of 1917, half a million young men had been inducted. During the course of the war, nearly 3 million men were inducted: roughly two-thirds of the United States armed forces. The utilization of a conscripted mass army in the European war played a central role in establishing the United States as key participant in the international political system.

About 300,000 people evaded the World War I draft, and prosecution of them was pursued through the civilian court system. Substitutes and commutation fees were not permitted in this draft, but about 145,000 students under the age of twenty-one were allowed to defer service by enrolling in the Student Army Training Corps for three years. When the age limit for the draft was reduced to eighteen, the period of deferment was reduced to nine months. The first students were activated in October 1919, but the Armistice was signed in November, and all trainees had been demobilized by the end of the year. The draft was allowed to lapse at the end of the war, establishing precedents not only for a national draft and for student deferments from that draft but also for those deferments to expand into exemptions from service.

From the end of 1919 until 1940, the United States had an all-volunteer armed force. Congress considered a system of universal military training, but a nation that believed it had won the war to end wars did not see as a pressing issue a military manpower policy that would guarantee a large mobilization base. The National Defense Act of 1920 reaffirmed that the armed forces and the nation would rely on voluntary recruitment. The Joint Army and Navy Selective Service Committee was convened in 1926, and the foundation was thus set for a conscription system, but no action was taken. In 1933, members of the National Guard were granted dual enlistment in the federal forces. In 1936, Maj. Lewis B. Hershey was assigned to that committee.

During the early 1930s, in the face of the Great Depression and with hostilities erupting in Asia, Europe, and Africa, the United States responded—as it had prior to the World War—by retreating into neutrality. In late 1939, however, President Franklin D. Roosevelt proclaimed a "limited national emergency" and authorized immediate increases in the armed forces. By that time, the Joint Selective Service Committee had developed a proposed conscription law. In early June, 1940, Roosevelt requested the authority to call the National Guard into federal service. Late that month, France fell to Germany. Neither the president nor the War Department seemed to want to initiate conscription, but a pro draft movement among private citizens brought the selective-service bill before Congress.[24] Again the nation had the luxury of time to mobilize for war. Two years passed between the declaration of a limited national emergency and the declaration of war. More than a year before the declaration of war, local selective-service boards were being appointed, men were being registered, and lotteries and inductions had started.

In late August 1940, the president was authorized to federalize the National Guard, and the Selective Service Act was passed in September. Taking effect before America entered the war, the Selective Service and Training Act of 1940 might be regarded as our first peacetime draft.[25] It called for the registration of all males between the ages of twenty-one and thirty-five. In the first registration in 1940, more than 16 million men registered. Induction began in November, with Clarence A. Dykstra, president of the University of Wisconsin, serving as the first director of the Selective Service System. Dykstra commuted between Washington and Wisconsin for six months and presided over a system that called young men into service for a training period of a year or less, with service beyond the Western Hemisphere being limited to United States territories and possessions.

Dykstra resigned after six months, and Lt. Col. Lewis B. Hershey was appointed as the second director in July 1941. Congress had initially limited the number of draftees to 900,000 serving at any one time, but the limitations on the number, time, and location of service were subsequently modified to meet the needs of the war. By the time the United States entered the war in December 1941, about a million men had been inducted. Between November 1940 and November 1946, nearly 50 million men had registered, and more than 10 million had been inducted. The Selective Service System provided more than two-thirds of United States military manpower during World War II.

President Truman recognized that new technologies of warfare and transportation and the already evident hostility of the Soviet Union would preclude complete demobilization after the war. Truman was not a proponent of conscription; he preferred a small voluntary active force, supported by a mobilization system that would be rooted in universal military training (UMT). In 1945 he attempted to get approval for a universal military training plan whereby at the age of eighteen, all physically qualified males would receive a year of compulsory military training. He was not able to generate consensus on the need for or the efficacy of such a program. Critics argued that a short period of military training, followed by return to civilian life, would not really prepare young men for war; that to the extent that the system worked, it would be most successful in producing ground combat soldiers, whereas the wars of the future would be decided by air power and atomic weapons; and that UMT did not address the only pressing military manpower problems of the day—the provision of occupation forces for Europe, Japan, and Korea. Truman shifted from arguments based on military manpower needs to those based on citizenship responsibility and opportunities for self-improvement. This moved the debate to the philosophical choice between liberty and equality as basic national values. Congress and the nation opted for individual liberty.

Induction authority under the 1940 Selective Service Act was to expire on May 15, 1945, but the army thought an extension of conscription was necessary in order to maintain a force-in-being, so Congress extended the draft for a year. In the wake of the Soviet invasion of Iran—the first crisis of the Cold War—the 1940 draft was further extended, to March 1947. In late 1946, Truman initiated a second campaign to adopt a program of universal military training, but again Congress did not act. Although Truman was committed to maintaining a peacetime force-in-being, he recommended that the Selective Service Act be allowed to lapse, and Congress concurred. Congress did, however, establish the Office of Selective Service Records, with Hershey, now a general, as its director. A nucleus of selective-service personnel was retained, in case the system should have to be recovered from its stand-by status for a mobilization. However, from April 1947 to June 1948, the armed services were to rely wholly on the recruitment of volunteers.

THE COLD WAR AND KOREA

During the postwar period, the world was anything but pacific. Relations between the East and the West became increasingly hostile. Dangerous conditions existed in Palestine, Greece, Italy, Korea, and China, any one of which might have precipitated major military problems. The navy and the air force, which had newly evolved from the Army Air Corps, were maintaining their authorized strength, or close to it, through voluntary recruitment; but the ground combat forces—the army and the Marine Corps—were experiencing significant manpower shortages. Because of the unstable international environment and because combat forces were below strength, the Communist coup in Czechoslovakia in February 1948 served as the catalyst for a change in policy. At the time when this last Central European democracy was drawn into the Soviet bloc, the United States had roughly 1.6 million active-duty military personnel, including a quarter of a million occupation troops in Europe who were not equipped, organized, or trained to go into combat.[26]

Three weeks after the coup in Czechoslovakia, President Truman again asked for a system of universal military training and for the reenactment of selective service.[27] Selective service was seen as a short-range program to strengthen all of the services, rather than just the army, because World War II had demonstrated the increased importance of air power. Universal military training was meant to eliminate the need for draftees in the long run by enriching the reserve pool. However, in contrast to selective service, this mobilization base was intended primarily for the army, and UMT was opposed by the air force, which many saw as the most important service.

In June 1948 a new Selective Service Act was passed, with a two-year limit, and General Hershey was again appointed as director of selective service. An active-duty force of 2 million men was authorized. All men between the ages of eighteen and twenty-one were required to register, with selections to be made by local draft boards. Students could defer induction, and the president was given the authority to defer persons whose activity was deemed to be in the national interest.

The existence of a draft tends to encourage voluntary service, and in the wake of the act, enlistments increased. Only a few thousand men were actually inducted under the act, and in June 1950, as the act was about to expire, there had been no inductions for about eighteen months. The Truman administration requested a three-year extension of the existing Selective Service Act, a request that the House of Representatives was not happy with, because the law had not been used in a year and a half. There naturally was concern about the fact that in 1949 the Soviet Union had broken America's monopoly of nuclear weapons. Many people felt, however, that air power, rather than a mobilization base for a land army, was the most effective counterforce to the Soviet threat.

In the debate over the extension of the Selective Service Act, questions were also raised about the ability of the president to begin inductions without congressional authority. Both houses of Congress passed bills that would limit the president's authority to induct young men. A conference committee met on June 22 to resolve differences between the two bills, and on June 24 the armies of North Korea crossed the 38th parallel. The conference committee quickly recommended and Congress then passed, a one-year extension of the Selective Service Act.

The Korean War experience demonstrated the efficacy of registration, as well as the problems of estimating compliance. The selective-service historical data show only the aggregate number of people registered in a given year; they do not show the year of birth of registrants. And the number of people who should register in any given year can only be estimated. Nonetheless, the data show that from 1950 to 1954, more men registered than were estimated to be in the population that was required to register. Indeed, 1972, which as we shall see below was a year of policy ambiguity, was the first year after 1950 that aggregate registration fell below the estimates of liability for registration.[28]

Young men were drafted to fill the divisions that the United States contributed to the United Nations force that was sent to Korea. In 1951 the Universal Military Training and Service Act extended the president's induction authority until 1955, granted him authority to recall reservists, and expanded the manpower pool by lowering the induction age from nineteen to eighteen, by lengthening the term of service, and by canceling deferments for married men without children. The UMT component of the act was studied, but Congress never approved putting UMT into effect.

President Truman had continued to regard selective service as a transitional measure until universal military training could improve America's mobilization posture. When UMT failed to pass, however, selective service had to be institutionalized. During the Korean War, more than 1.5 million young men were inducted through selective service. In 1955 the Universal Military Training and Service Act was extended to 1959. In addition, the mobilization base was enriched through the Reserve Forces Act of 1955, which provided a means of adding men who had critical skills to the reserves.

The Eisenhower administration furthered the institutionalization of selective service. While Dwight D. Eisenhower was more strongly oriented toward air power as the key deterrent than Truman had been, he also favored a large standing army. Universal military training and volunteer service were both deemed to be too expensive as means of meeting our perceived manpower needs. However, the Reserve Forces Act continued to strengthen the mobilization base, and the threat of conscription produced large numbers of draft-motivated volunteers, who enlisted to get their choice of service and time period, rather than leaving themselves at the mercy of local draft boards.

As voluntary enlistments increased, inductions under selective service dropped, from more than a third of accessions during the mid-1950s to less than 10 percent during the early 1960s. As fewer draftees were needed, the Selective Service System sought to expand the categories of young men who would not be called, so as to justify the relatively few selections that were made. At the end of the Korean War, fathers and men over twenty-six were deferred. During the postwar period, occupational deferments were eased, largely through the "channeling" program, which was intended to encourage people with scientific, engineering, and mathematical aptitudes to seek education and employment that would enrich the nation's ability to design and produce weapons.[29] Ultimately, even parenthood became a justification for deferment.

While conscription was sufficiently accepted to be periodically and routinely renewed without much debate, it was recognized that the deferment system was continuing to produce inequities. The system was maintained, not because it produced draftees, who were relatively few, but because it stimulated enlistments for all the services, in particular bringing high-aptitude young men into both the enlisted ranks and the officer-training programs, and because it supported the reserve forces. Ironically, it could only fulfill these nonconscription functions as long as the few conscription decisions that were made were perceived to meet some minimal criterion of equity.

The equity of the deferment system came under increasing pressure as the baby-boom generation reached the age of military eligibility. Although occupational deferments had been made more and more liberally, by the early 1960s it was clear that there would be more young men who would not qualify for any of the liberal deferment categories than the services could use. In late 1963, selective service began to defer all married men, which conceptually gave the system a tool for handling the increased pool of potential manpower but which increased the marriage rate and again raised questions in the media and Congress about the equity of the system.[30] Senator Barry M. Goldwater, who was seeking the Republican nomination for the presidency, announced in early 1964 that he intended to end the draft; and in response, President Lyndon B. Johnson ordered the Defense Department to study the draft. Had it not been for the Vietnam War, conscription might have been phased out in the United States a decade earlier than it was.

THE VIETNAM WAR

A study by the Department of Defense projected that by the early 1970s, a peacetime all-volunteer force would be feasible. However, by the spring of 1965, when Defense Secretary Robert S. McNamara expected to act on the study's recommendations, United States involvement in Vietnam had intensified, and draft calls, which had been low during the early 1960s, had increased, as had opposition to the draft. The opposition was manifested in a variety of ways: for example, sit-ins at selective service offices, the burning of draft cards, demonstrations on college campuses, and weddings to take advantage of marital deferments. Reactions to the opposition were also varied. Legislation prescribed severe penalties for the burning of draftcards; draft resistors were prosecuted; the Justice Department investigated antidraft groups for Communist involvement; General Hershey ordered local draft boards to reclassify antidraft demonstrators 1-A (that is, immediately available for the draft); and President Johnson ordered an end to deferments for married men.

Pressure for the reform of the system was widespread. Secretary McNamara spoke in favor of civilian alternatives to the draft, and former Secretary of Defense Thomas S. Gates spoke in favor of a more broadly based national service system. A national lottery was proposed to alleviate the inequities caused by the decentralized conscription decisions made by local draft boards, a proposal that General Hershey strongly opposed.[31] Public support for conscription decreased markedly, as a large majority eventually came to favor a change in the system.[32]

The pattern of bias that existed in the conscription process during the Vietnam era was a complex one. In general, the poor were overrepresented among draftees.[33] However, because advanced technology had led to higher standards for induction, large numbers of young men who were judged to have less than the minimum required mental aptitudes were found to be not qualified: from 1950 to 1965, for example, almost as many young men were rejected on mental grounds as on physical ones.[34] Since mental aptitude tends to be correlated with socioeconomic status, many poor young men were found to be unqualified.[35] In sum, the poor were more likely to be found unqualified for service, but among those who were found to be qualified, the poor were more likely to be drafted than were men of higher social status. As a result of this process, blacks were overrepresented in the draft, not because they were black, but because they were poor. The selection process was consequential. Once people from lower socioeconomic backgrounds had been drafted, they were more likely to be channeled into the ground combat forces than into branches that required technical aptitudes. They were therefore also more likely to be wounded or killed than were persons who had backgrounds of higher socioeconomic status.[36] Again, blacks were overrepresented in these strata and, because of socioeconomic rather than racial discrimination, were overrepresented among casualties.

The Vietnam War came in the wake of the civil-rights movement and the War against Poverty in America, and conscription seemed to discriminate against those whom these efforts had been meant to help—poor people and blacks.[37] By 1966, there were widespread student demonstrations against the draft and its inequities.

In the summer of 1966, President Johnson appointed the National Advisory Commission on Selective Service (the Marshall Commission), which was supposed to consider the reform of the existing system and to make recommendations prior to the expiration or the renewal of the existing legislation in June, 1967. A number of conferences on the draft were held in late 1966, the most important of which was held at the University of Chicago in December 1966—a conference on selective service and its alternatives.[38]

Two major debates emerged at the Chicago conference. The first was between the economists Walter Oi and Harold Wool.[39] The former had been on the staff of the 1964 Defense Department study on conscription, but his analyses of the feasibility of an all-volunteer force had not been included in the report of the study issued to the Marshall Commission. The latter was at the time director of procurement policy in the Office of the Assistant Secretary of Defense for Manpower. Wool doubted the feasibility of a volunteer force.

Whereas the first debate concerned two economic models of military manpower, the second involved the juxtaposition of sociological and economic models. The first model advocated a system of national service that would integrate the armed forces into the broader institutional structure of American society and provide a nexus of commitment between the individual and the state.[40] The second favored an all-volunteer force that would preserve the freedom of individuals to decide whether or not they would serve and would produce an armed force through labor-market processes.[41]

The Marshall Commission met only occasionally.[42] However, its executive director attended the Chicago conference. No general consensus emerged from the conference, but national service and an all-volunteer force were clearly emphasized as alternatives to the draft. The commission's January 1967 report to the president reflected the issues that had been discussed in Chicago, and these issues were reflected again in the president's subsequent message to Congress.[43]

While both the Marshall Commission and the president endorsed a continuation of the draft, their positions differed markedly in tone. The commission was critical of the concept of a volunteer force, because it feared that such a force would be too expensive, would lack flexibility, and would become a mercenary one. The president, on the other hand, stated a preference for an all-volunteer force, and although he pragmatically saw a need to extend the draft, he sought major reforms in the system of conscription, including the development of a national lottery, the elimination of student deferments, and a reduction in the autonomy granted to local boards in making decisions about deferments. Congress rejected all substantive reform proposals and passed the Military Selective Service Act of 1967, which extended the draft for four years. While Congress refused to eliminate student deferments completely, eligibility for such deferments was reduced to the age of twenty-four or four years of study, whichever occurred first, thus denying young men the opportunity to avoid military service through long-term student status.

The failure of the Johnson administration and Congress to reform the Selective Service System in the face of high draft calls and continuing opposition to the draft probably contributed significantly both to the draft's becoming a major issue in the 1968 presidential campaign and, ultimately, to the end of the draft and the advent of the all-volunteer force.[44]

In 1968, deferments for all graduate study except medicine and allied fields were ended. The channeling system was being wound down. During the 1968 presidential election campaign, Richard M. Nixon promised to end the draft once the Vietnam War was over. Within three months of his inauguration, against the advice of Secretary of Defense Melvin R. Laird, Nixon appointed the President's Commission on an All-Volunteer Armed Force (the Gates Commission). The commission was chaired by former Secretary of Defense Thomas Gates, who had been an advocate of national service. Among the members of the commission were two former Supreme Allied Commanders in Europe, the retired generals Alfred Gruenther and Lauris Norstad. Milton Friedman was among the academic scholars on the commission.

The charge of the commission was to develop "a comprehensive plan for eliminating conscription." The commission's staff included four research directors who had worked on the Defense Department's 1964 study of the draft. Among them was Walter Oi, who was made responsible for estimating the demand for manpower.

The commission's studies and analyses were conducted during 1969 and early 1970. There was considerable disagreement among the members of the Gates Commission: Generals Gruenther and Norstad in particular were skeptical about the all-volunteer force, and Professor Friedman was strongly in favor of it. Chairman Gates, however, was able to get unanimous agreement from the commission members to the principle that an all-volunteer force, supported by a stand-by draft, was preferable to a mixed force of conscripts and volunteers and to the proposal that entry-level military pay must be raised. These principles became the first part of the commission's report— the part that was most widely read and that had the most influence on the policy debate. The dissent and disagreement were confined to later sections of the report. The report reflected a stronger sense of unanimity than characterized the commission.[45]

The issues that were addressed by the Gates Commission focused primarily on economic concerns. Would the United States be able to afford an all-volunteer armed force? The commission concluded that an all-volunteer force was feasible. Critics claimed that an all-volunteer force would weaken patriotism, would attract primarily the economically disadvantaged segments of society, and would therefore attenuate the relationship between the soldier and the military and between the armed forces and civilian society.[46] In the absence of a sense that was a citizen's duty to serve, employment in the military would lack personal meaning for the serviceperson, and the connection between civilians and the military would be similarly impersonal, particularly in those strata of society whose young adults would elect not to serve. The commission considered these objections, but decided that ending conscription would not fundamentally change either the composition of the force or the relationship between the armed forces and society.

In 1969, with the conduct of the war in Asia being turned increasingly over to Vietnamese military personnel, draft calls were drastically reduced. In 1970, much of the discretionary power of local selective-service boards was eliminated by the establishment of the national draft lottery, which General Hershey had opposed. The lottery assigned priorities to selective-service registrants on the basis of their birth dates. The reductions in student deferments and the introduction of a lottery increased the likelihood that males from higher socioeconomic backgrounds would be drafted. At the same time, the reduction in categorical deferments meant that only a small proportion of those who were liable for service would be called. This raised anew the issue of equity, unless one assumes, as the administration appears to have done, that randomness is equivalent to equity.

Nineteen seventy and 1971 were years of debate. In a message to Congress in April 1970, President Nixon stated that his objective was to reduce draft calls to zero, and he outlined a series of military pay increases and other steps that were designed to reach that objective. He addressed Congress again in January 1971, when he proposed further steps to move toward an all-volunteer force but also requested an extension of the draft. The issue of extending the draft was debated vigorously, but in September 1971, the final two-year extension of the draft was passed, along with a major increase in entry-level military pay. The 1972 defense appropriation, which was also passed in 1971, provided the funds for the all-volunteer force. Draft calls were low during the two-year extension of selective service, and in January 1973, six months earlier than Congress had required, Secretary of Defense Melvin Laird announced the end of peacetime conscription.

THE ALL-VOLUNTEER FORCE

The blueprint that the Gates Commission had set out for the all-volunteer force was rooted in economic behavior. It assumed that by making entry-level military compensation competitive with civilian wages, sufficient numbers of high-quality personnel would be attracted to military service, that the racial composition of the force would not be significantly altered, and that the people brought into the military could be molded into an effective fighting force. In 1973 the American economy was in trouble, youth unemployment was high, and entry-level military pay was roughly competitive with civilian wages, thanks to increases granted during the last years of conscription. In the absence of employment alternatives, the all-volunteer force appeared to be an immediate success. With unemployment particularly high among young black males and with the women's movement coming to regard the military as a channel for mobility, enough people were brought in. Contrary to the expectations of the Gates Commission, however, the social composition of the force did change. It became increasingly dependent on the poor, the black, and, to a lesser extent, women.

From the outset of the all-volunteer force, an alternative to the economic model was put forward. Echoing the discussions of the University of Chicago conference, Morris Janowitz, in particular, argued that even in the all-volunteer context, the military manpower system need not be driven solely by pecuniary considerations.[47] Having recognized that Congress would not support a national service system, he argued for rooting citizen participation in the all-volunteer force in the conception and traditions of public service. In the absence of such institution building to forge links between the roles of citizen and of soldier and between military and civilian institutions, he envisaged an all-volunteer force that would become increasingly dependent on less advantaged segments of society for manpower, that would become less socially representative of American society, and that would progessively become more estranged from other social institutions and social strata.[48]

Throughout the 1960s and until the decision to end the draft was made in 1971, debate on military-manpower policy was concerned with whether we could afford such a force, more than with the implications of having such a force even if we could afford it. Between 1971 and the end of the draft in 1973, attention shifted to the implications of such a force, particularly in terms of its social representativeness. Since the advent of the all-volunteer force, it has been subjected to almost continuous scrutiny and evaluation.

The sociological critique of the all-volunteeer force has focused on changes in the composition of the force, the ideological nature of the force,[49] and the relationship between the citizen and the state.[50] The economic defense of the all-volunteer force—which is represented by the Office of the Secretary of Defense and by defense contractors who are funded by that office—has focused on whether manpower goals were achieved, on the costs of achieving them, and on the quality of the people who have been brought into the services.[51]

The Gates Commission's projections of the quality and the quantity of personnel had been based upon the assumption that entry-level military pay would be competitive with entry-level civilian pay. Military pay had been tied to the general schedule of federal civil-service pay, and a series of caps on federal civil-service pay during the 1970s led to a violation of this assumption. By the end of the decade, entry-level military pay began to lag behind what high-school graduates were earning upon entry into the full-time employed civilian labor force, and indeed behind the federal minimum wage. The pay of first-term junior enlisted personnel, which had been 115 percent of the federal minimum wage in 1972, had fallen to 84 percent by 1979.[52] Not surprisingly, the services, which had been achieving more than 100 percent of their recruiting objectives in the middle of the decade, were achieving only 93 percent in 1979—a shortfall of more than twenty thousand recruits.

One would have expected the success of military recruiting to decline in quality as well as quantity. As military compensation became less attractive, those recruits who had the greatest access to other alternatives—that is, high-school graduates and people with higher levels of mental aptitude—should have been the first to disappear from the recruiting stations. The research done by and for the Office of the Secretary of Defense, however, indicated that this had not been the case. The research showed that the social composition of the all-volunteer force had not changed and that, indeed, the mental quality of the force had gone up.[53] In the army, which historically has had the greatest problems attracting high-quality enlisted personnel in large numbers, Clifford Alexander, secretary of the army under President Carter, ultimately banned discussions of quality, which he took to be racist. Young blacks had become markedly overrepresented among recruits during the late 1970s, and although black recruits on average had higher mental aptitudes than white recruits during this period, the secretary felt that concerns about quality were simply disguised complaints about the racial composition of the force.

Soldiers in the field, particularly those responsible for training new personnel, on the other hand, maintained throughout the decade of the 1970s that there had been a real decline in personnel quality. When, by the end of the decade, it had become impossible to deny that there were indeed important personnel problems tied to compensation and to the fact that a new personnel selection test, which had been implemented in 1976, had been miscalibrated, leading to an unintentional decrease in quality, there were straightforward psychometric and economic solutions: fix the tests and return to the Gates Commission's blueprint.[54]

Economic analyses disagree on the extent to which recruitment in the volunteer force has been responsive to the domestic economy and particularly to youth unemployment. They do not disagree that at least throughout the early 1980s there was such a response.[55] The recruiting successes of the all-volunteer force at its inception during the years of high unemployment were followed by reductions in resources. Between 1973 and 1976—years in which the age-eligible population was increasing and youth unemployment was generally increasing as well—funding for recruiting was cut back, the purchasing power of the average enlisted man was declining, and in 1976 the GI bill ended. Not surprisingly, recruiting became more difficult. The late 1970s constituted a second phase in the all-volunteer force.

As I mentioned above, the recruiting picture was confounded by an error that was made in a new selection and classification test introduced in 1976. In that year, the Department of Defense specified the Armed Services Vocational Aptitude Battery (ASVAB) as the single selection test to replace the various test batteries then in use by the various services. In order to maintain consistency over time, the scores of four subtests in the battery were combined into an Armed Forces Qualification Test (AFQT) score and were calibrated to previous selection tests, so that, for the period beginning with World War II, the meaning of the percentile score would be standardized.

A major error was made in calibrating the 1976 AFQT to earlier selection tests, thus inflating the scores of enlistees at the lower end of the mental-aptitude distribution. The error was discovered and corrected in 1980.[56] In the interim, while commanders in the field were complaining about the quality of the personnel being assigned to them, military manpower managers in Washington were taking pride in the levels of mental ability that the tests were reflecting. In 1976, when the services believed that they had admitted only about 5 percent in Category IV (the lowest acceptable mental category) personnel, almost 30 percent of the accessions in that year were Category IV. In 1980, when accessions were thought to be about 6 percent in Category IV, the actual figure was closer to 32 percent. Going into the 1980s, after upward adjustments had been made in military compensation, youth unemployment had increased, and the norming of the AFQT had been corrected, recruiting efforts produced both the quantity and the quality of recruits desired. If the all-volunteer force is to be judged on the basis of the number of people in the active force and their average mental ability, the force would have to be judged a success in the early 1980s—a third phase in the all-volunteer force.

The inclusion of sociodemographic representativeness as a yardstick against which to measure the force would temper that success. While the all-volunteer force has in recent years gotten at least its fair share of non-college-bound youth from the upper working class and the lower middle class, the force has become increasingly dependent on racial and ethnic minorities, and throughout the early 1980s, it has decreased in its representation from the higher socioeconomic and mental-aptitude strata. This latter, in particular, had implications for performance in using more and more sophisticated weapon systems. When the ability of the force to operate its equipment reliably was added as a criterion for evaluation, the outcome became even more questionable.[57] And given that the greatest decrease in strength was in the reserves, if the state of the mobilization base were to be added to the equation, a negative prognosis would be drawn. President Reagan's military manpower task force reported in late 1982 that the army's individual ready reserve (IRR), which is the most important source of pretrained manpower in an emergency, was short by 180,000 men in 1981 and projected that the shortage would be 240,000 by 1988, all of whom would be enlisted personnel with combat skills.[58] The task force also judged that the all-volunteer force was a success.

Success did improve in the late 1980s, with the implementation of a new GI bill. Enlistment rates were dissociated from youth unemployment, and the accession of college-oriented youth increased. This fourth phase of the all-volunteer force will be discussed more fully in chapter 4.

SELECTIVE-SERVICE REGISTRATION

The mobilization problems that continue to characterize the all-volunteer force have been recognized from the outset. Although conscription ended in 1973, selective service continued to register young men until 1975, when President Gerald R. Ford put it in "deep stand-by," to be resurrected in an emergency. In 1976 the Defense Manpower Commission called for a resumption of peacetime registration.

In 1978 the Defense Department conducted a mobilization exercise, called Nifty Nugget, to determine whether the reserves could be called up in an emergency. The worst fears of the mobilization planners were realized: they staged a practice war, and virtually nobody came. Analyses of Nifty Nugget by the Joint Chiefs of Staff, the Congressional Budget Office, and the General Accounting Office all agreed that the mobilization mission could not be fulfilled.

In December 1979, the Soviet Union invaded Afghanistan, and in the following month, President Carter announced in his State of the Union Address his intention to reinstate draft registration. The president had the authority to order registration, but he was dependent on Congress for the funding to do so. The issue of registration for a potential draft was no less controversial in January 1980 than it had been at other times in American history. Congress did not authorize the funds until June, and the first registration took place in July. Four months later, Ronald Reagan, who had taken a position against registration during the course of his election campaign, was elected president.

For a year, in the face of ambiguity about policy, compliance with registration requirements was low, and no attempt was made to prosecute noncompliers. However, on July 1, 1981, the president established the Military Manpower Task Force, under the chairmanship of the secretary of defense, and in January 1982, Reagan announced that on the basis of the report of the task force, he would continue registration and that after a grace period, noncompliers would be prosecuted. The current law requires young men to register within thirty days of their eighteenth birthday.

During late 1981 and early 1982, compliance was elicited primarily through publicity that attempted to remind young men what the legal requirements of registration were. The actual enforcement of the law was "passive": that is, it was limited to nonregistrants who were reported by others or who brought themselves to the attention of the authorities. In December 1981, Congress authorized a more active enforcement program. In addition, attempts have been made to link citizenship rights to the obligation to register. New York State, for example, denies state employment to nonregistrants, and since July 1983, registration compliance has been required of students who are seeking federal education loans, grants, or employment assistance. This requirement has been one of the most controversial aspects of the system.

Compliance with the current registration system seems to be comparable to the experience of earlier selective-service registrations: more than 93 percent of those who are required to register eventually do so, although many do not do so within the time interval required by law.[59] Whereas the rate of compliance appears to be high, literally hundreds of thousands of young men become criminals because of noncompliance. The registration system is not without its critics.[60] The degree to which it will in fact expedite mobilization is still in question. It does not involve classification, and in a highly mobile society, a large proportion of its address file will become outdated each year. Its most important characteristic may prove to be its assertion that in the United States, citizenship rights are associated with responsibilities.

OVERVIEW

The history of military manpower policy in the United States has been marked by major discrepancies between principle and reality. The militia principle, adopted from the British and put into law in the Militia Act of 1792, asserted the responsibility of citizens to serve in the military—a principle that was frequently enunciated by George Washington. While universal service thus became an ideal, neither the forces that resulted from the mobilization of the militia nor the volunteer forces that served on the frontier were broadly representative of society; rather, they were dependent on the lower social strata. Many of the inequities of the militia derived from their control by the states.

From the colonial period through the Civil War, as the United States was evolving as a nation, attempts to draft military personnel were no more equitable, and they produced popular opposition and domestic unrest. The first federal draft, during the Civil War, did establish the right of the federal government, as contrasted to states' rights, to induct men into military service; but as in earlier conflicts, the draft was not a major source of manpower in the Civil War. Rather, the war was fought primarily by volunteers.

At the beginning of the twentieth century, the Dick Act, which sought to establish the effective federal control of the armed forces through the repeal of the Militia Act of 1792, repealed the principle of a universal military obligation as well. World War I was the first war in which the United States was actually dependent on a draft for military manpower, and the draft was an equitable one. But the postwar National Defense Act of 1920 reaffirmed the nation's reliance on voluntary recruitment in peacetime, despite the fact that the United States had assumed a new international role.

Conscription was reinstituted in World War II, and again, with a major mobilization, the draft was generally equitable. In the absence of support for universal military training or universal service during the postwar years, conscription was continued, with only one fourteen-months lapse. Relatively little opposition was expressed during periods of major mobilization or periods when virtually nobody was drafted. However, during periods when large numbers, but not majorities, of the eligible population were drafted, as during the Vietnam War, opposition on the basis of inequity grew. There is perhaps a lesson to be learned here from the country's allies. Those that have volunteer forces, such as Canada and Great Britain, bring very small proportions of their young adults into the military. Those that have conscription, such as Germany and France, bring majorities or substantial minorities of their youth into the military. The absence of selective conscription of small proportions of the eligible population on a cross-national basis indicates a potential structural instability consistent with America's experience during the Vietnam era.

The experience of the all-volunteer force, particularly in its first and third phases during the early 1970s and the early 1980s, demonstrates that under conditions of high unemployment, with military compensation favorable relative to civilian pay levels and with a willingness to invest resources in recruiting, enough people can be recruited, at desired levels of education and mental aptitude, to staff the force on a peacetime basis, as well as to provide elite combat troops for simultaneous operations in the Sinai, Lebanon, and Grenada, in a roughly ascending order of the intensity of the conflict. The ability of the all-volunteer force to mount a larger-scale military operation short of a full mobilization, however, has not been tested.

The consequences of having the low-aptitude personnel who were recruited between 1976 and 1980—the second phase of the all-volunteer force—under a misnormed aptitude test stay in the force and of having them increasingly staff the noncommissioned officer corps have not yet been fully explored, nor have the implications of whether the attachment to one's unit and to the nation—which have historically been shown to be important components of combat effectiveness—can be developed in personnel who are motivated by pecuniary considerations, an issue that the army has addressed during the fourth phase of the all-volunteer force in the late 1980s. Perhaps most importantly, no major strategic analyst has argued that the all-volunteer force would be enough to sustain a major confrontation between the NATO nations and the Warsaw Pact. These issues will be addressed in the chapters that follow.

3
Changes in United States
Social and Military Organization

The changes in military manpower policy and organization that have taken place throughout American history have both reflected and been accompanied by basic organizational changes in United States society and its constituent parts as Americans have achieved nationhood and a central role in the world political system. These organizational changes, in turn, have been shaped by technological advances, and shifts in the world political climate, in definitions of military mission, in the structure of civilian organizations, and in values in American society. Over the course of American history, these changes have contributed to a redefinition of military service from being an obligation of citizenship in a community to being an obligation of national citizenship and, most recently, to being a job. The armed forces, in turn, have been transformed from a local to a national institution and, most recently, to an employer—perhaps, as noted earlier, an employer of last resort. As we shall see in the next chapter, these categories have not been mutually exclusive. However, the changes that have taken place have led to a definition of military service that is both increasingly devoid of a sense of citizenship responsibility and increasingly impersonal in the treatment of the service member.

These changes have implications for military manpower policy and for military effectiveness. The decreased sense of citizenship obligation may influence our ability to raise a military force, and the increased impersonality of the military may raise obstacles to military victory in the event of war. The effectiveness of military units can be altered by the nature of the relationships that exist among personnel—such as cohesion among peers or respect and trust between superiors and subordinates. It can also be affected by the degree to which soldiers, both individually and as units, understand and are committed to the relationship between their responsibilities and broad national goals. The tides of social change seem to mitigate against cohesion among soldiers, trust between soldiers and their officers, and an affective commitment of the soldier to the state. As a consequence, military effectiveness may have been harmed. Steps are now being taken to address these issues in the United States military, but their success has yet to be demonstrated.

THE RATIONALIZATION OF SOCIETY

One of the major themes of sociological and economic analyses of social change is that of increasing rationality.[1] Societies are seen as becoming more urbanized, secularized, commercialized, impersonal, and dependent upon formal legal systems and scientific technology and as placing less importance on traditional informal customs. The world of work in such societies is itself presumed to become more impersonal, more bureaucratic, and more professionalized. Individuals in such societies are seen as less embedded in social networks based on affective ties and as increasingly motivated by calculated self-interest. These trends in social development may be counterproductive for the military because, at least for land warfare, it has been demonstrated historically that strong affective ties in military units are essential for combat effectiveness. Thus the interpersonal relationships required for effective operation within small military units may be at variance with the value systems and the institutions of preservice socialization in an impersonal urban industrial world that have shaped the perspectives of their personnel. Indeed, formal military organization itself may interfere with the development of cohesion in small units.

That the United States manifests the characteristics of a bureaucratized and rationalized society is a frequent theme in sociological analyses of American life. The sociologist David Riesman, for example, while he noted the trend toward increasing "other-directedness," did not see this as a quest for the fulfillment of collective goals; rather, it was a quest for the recognition of individual achievement as measured against consensual standards.[2] Maurice R. Stein has documented the change in the nature of social relationships within communities as well, extending in particular to the military, where the bureaucratic aspects of organization and the castelike aspects of the rank structure preclude the development of a collective sense of community. Indeed, in Stein's view, even interpersonal attachments among groups of buddies, which military sociology made much of at the end of World War II, were seen as relatively unimportant.[3]

This is not to argue that American life has become wholly individualistic and impersonal. At the birth of the Republic, as Seymour Martin Lipset has noted, the themes of individualism and achievement coexisted with those of equality and collective concern.[4] While other analysts such as Riesman have seen a trend in the direction of increasing individualism, Lipset has seen a continuing interplay between individual and collective priorities. The pendulum seems to have swung far in the direction of individualism, but it is impossible to deny the reality of expression of collective sentiments and commitment when the United States has been faced with national tragedies, such as the taking of hostages at the American Embassy in Teheran in the winter of 1980 or the bombing of the the marines' headquarters in Beirut in October 1983. Such sentiments have also been expressed in the wake of perceived national triumphs, such as the invasion of Grenada in October 1983. Over the long sweep of history, the United States may have become more individualistic as it has evolved as a nation, but nationhood itself has also served as a basis for collective identification.

THE RATIONALIZATION OF THE MILITARY

The German sociologist Max Weber, whose work forms the basis of contemporary analyses of societal rationalization, believed that organizations within modern societies were also being rationalized. This included military organization. Like rationalized society, rational-legal bureaucratic organization was characterized by a division of labor based on laws and regulations, by a clear hierarchy, by management based upon written documents, and by specialization based on training. Weber thought the military was becoming bureaucratized as the obligation and the right to serve in the military were being transferred from the "shoulders of the propertied to those of the propertyless";[5] thus he anticipated criticisms of both conscription and the all-volunteer force in the United States. Weber also thought that emerging military technologies would necessitate the growth of military bureaucracies.

The growth of impersonal military bureaucracy in the United States, which paralleled the growth of industrial bureaucracy, was reflected in Elihu Root's program to modernize the War Department at the beginning of the twentieth century. Root felt that despite the United States victory in the Spanish-American War, the army had made a large number of mistakes, which had been caused by basic organizational problems. During the early years of the century, American industry was being influenced by Frederick W. Taylor's mechanistic approach to "scientific management,"[6] and Root sought to bring this new approach to management into his War Department. On the assumptions that military organization was more similar to civilian corporate organization than had previously been realized, that such organizations were like machines, and that the American soldier was simply a cog in the machine, Root brought impersonal, rational, quantitative management to the War Department.[7]

Root sought to establish staff agencies to develop war plans and to evaluate new technological developments. He sought to develop a rational system for the selection and promotion of officers. And he sought a training system that would prepare officers for the large-scale maneuvers of future wars. From Root's initiatives came the organization of the army staff—a structure that persisted throughout the century without any major overhaul.[8] The staff organization that he developed, the establishment of a War College, and the beginning of a national mobilization base should all probably be regarded as positive contributions to national security in the long run. The depersonalization of the American soldier through the advent of scientific management, however, has remained a controversial and counterproductive innovation of major proportions. The advent and implications of corporate management techniques in the United States military will be examined at greater length later in this chapter.

The adoption of Taylor's "scientific management" was a step in the direction of organizational rationalization, as was the continuation of this tradition later by Defense Secretaries Gates and McNamara. In civilian work places, this mechanistic approach produced problems of alienation, disaffection, and low productivity. By mid-century, it was being replaced by a more "human relations"-oriented approach to personnel management.[9] In turn, this moved civilian organizational models beyond the rigid Weberian bureaucracy and toward more adaptive organizational forms.[10] Early in the twentieth century, American industry frequently borrowed managerial technologies from the military. Tests for the selection and classification of personnel, for example, were most extensively pioneered by the War Department. Elihu Root, however, had established the opposite pattern as the dominant one: the flow of management technologies from the civilian sector to the military. This pattern has persisted into the second half of the century.

Organizational and budgetary changes go hand in hand, and from this perspective, the National Defense Act of 1916 must be seen as a way station in the organizational evolution of America's defense establishment. It laid the groundwork for a "total force" land army of four components: a regular standing army, a federally obligated National Guard, a reserve component, and a "volunteer army," to be raised only in time of war. It laid the groundwork for a navy oriented toward large, expensive warships—battleships in this case. It set the stage for a continuing budgetary competition between the army and the navy. It also established the Advisory Council of National Defense, to deal with problems of industrial mobilization. If one were disposed to see the United States as a garrison state dominated by a military-industrial complex, here was the seed beginning to take root.

The advent of aviation technology tightened the bonds between industry, which manufactured aircraft, and the military, which used them. Aviation, like naval warfare, is capital intensive, and its machinery must be maintained even in peacetime, as must the skill levels of its personnel. Recall that the navy, which was regarded as a major instrument of foreign policy and defense, had been our first peacetime force-in-being. The fact that contemporary discussions of military manpower policy are couched primarily in terms of army personnel is no accident or oversight. It is a reflection of the historical fact that the mobilization model was applied most importantly to the ground forces. The navy evolved earlier as a standing peacetime military force, and the air force joined it.

Throughout the 1920s and the 1930s, practitioners of the newly developed art of aviation in the army worked to define their appropriate niche in modern warfare. They sought autonomy from army generals who thought in terms of warfare on the ground. These aviators sought to develop a doctrine for strategic bombing. And they sought to prove that air power was useful in sea warfare as well as land warfare, both as a threat to hostile ships and as a weapons platform to be launched from friendly ships. Great progress was made on all these fronts. The apparent successes of the air war in World War II,[11] the growth of the Army Air Force, and rapid developments in aircraft and weapons technology (including the advent of nuclear weapons)—all led to the establishment in 1947 of an independent air force that was equal with the army and the navy. The army was concerned, probably correctly, that given the tradition of post-war demobilizations, it would suffer in budgetary allocations relative to the capital needs of the navy and the air force.[12] It thus pressed for a unitary budget under a single Department of Defense.

The three services were made subordinate to a secretary of defense and to the now formally constituted Joint Chiefs of Staff. Thus there were now three services, rather than two, and one new federal bureaucracy—the Department of Defense.[13] The advent of air power and the emergence of an independent air force affected military manpower policy to the extent that advocates of air power felt that this new medium of deterrence and warfare reduced the need to maintain large ground forces. Military manpower became less central to our conception of national security, and weapons systems became more central.

The move to consolidate authority for defense in the hands of the secretary of defense, which began under President Truman in the 1940s, was completed in the late 1950s and 1960s. The stage was set by the Department of Defense Reorganization Act of 1958, which allowed Thomas S. Gates, Jr., who was appointed secretary of defense in 1959, and Robert S. McNamara, who followed him in 1961, to continue the process, which had been started by Elihu Root, of bringing rational corporate management techniques to the military. Gates, it will be recalled, was later to chair President Nixon's commission on an all-volunteer armed force and to elicit from that commission its support for the economic viability of such a force.[14] It was during Gates's term as secretary that the ideas of substituting functional for line-item budgeting procedures and of introducing systems analysis as a means of evaluating the cost-benefit trade-offs of competing systems were raised in the defense community. Both instruments increased the secretary's control.

Secretary McNamara achieved the goal of functional budgeting with the establishment of the Planning, Programming, Budgeting System (PPBS), which allowed budgeting by program and mission, rather than by service. Program priorities were established in the Office of the Secretary of Defense. McNamara also instituted systems analysis as a means of evaluating the costs and benefits—or at least the economic costs and benefits—of alternative programs. One of the long-term consequences of this approach was that it limited program evaluation to criteria that could be measured in standardized units—usually monetary units—whether or not these were the most important criteria. Less tangible factors, such as morale, leadership, and cohesion—components of the military personnel system—were not evaluated as costs or benefits, because they are not easily quantified and therefore could not be included in the analyses.

QUALITY OF LIFE AND
ORGANIZATIONAL DEVELOPMENT

The early history of American industrialization was one of domination by management. Taylor's scientific management was based on this structure, which defined workers in impersonal terms. However, civilian industry has increasingly accommodated itself to the desires of the workers. The most traditional manifestation of worker representation has been the routinization of the adversarial relationship between labor and management through unionization and collective bargaining.[15] The impetus for labor organization and an institutionalized labor-management relationship came from workers' demands for improved compensation and working conditions, although management has increasingly recognized the union as a mechanism for social control as well.

More recently, a broader societal concern with the quality of American life has led to efforts on the part of industry to improve the lot of the worker. The belief was not only that happy workers would be more productive but also, to a lesser extent, that an improved quality of life is a worthwhile end in itself, even if it does not yield greater productivity. In both the military and the civilian sectors, the quality of work life and job satisfaction have become central concerns.[16]

The "humanization of work" has become an important area of technology transfer. American business has sought to learn lessons from experiments in Scandinavia and Japan,[17] and the armed forces have sought to learn lessons from the experiences of industry.[18]

Concern for the quality of life in the military has been most dramatic in the voluntary, rather than the conscription-based, armed forces and has been of greater concern in nations at peace than in those at war. Although the United States military has been influenced by civilian industrial-management strategies since the early implementation of scientific management and although the measurement of job satisfaction in the army was a concern even during World War II, there was a considerable lag between the development of the human-relations orientation in industry and its adoption by the United States armed forces.

Because (1) the United States military, under the mobilization model, was not accustomed to maintaining a large force in peacetime; (2) in peacetime it was difficult if not impossible to measure military "productivity"; and (3) under conscription it was not necessary to improve the quality of military life in order to get personnel, United States armed forces came relatively late to the game of management based on human-relations principles. However, influenced by the Vietnam War and the conversion to an all-volunteer format, the United States armed forces have in recent years introduced a range of organizational development strategies that are aimed at improving organizational functioning and that reflect techniques used in civilian industry.

During the Vietnam War, the armed services were faced with major problems in the management of human resources, particularly in the areas of illicit drug use, racial tensions, and attrition due to a variety of causes, including desertion. Under the pressure of wartime conditions, these were dealt with on a piecemeal basis; programs were aimed at specific problems, such as drug-education programs and racial-awareness programs.

In the early 1970s, a realization that drug and racial problems were continuing at the same level, that personnel were coming into the services with work attitudes similar to those of their civilian counterparts, and that the emerging all-volunteer force was going to require an improvement in the quality of military work life, if the services were to compete effectively in the labor market, led the services to seek broader techniques of personnel management in the human relations tradition. The services adopted a range of organizational-development (OD) intervention strategies that had been developed by industrial psychologists in civilian work settings.

The form that OD took in the armed services reflected basic organizational differences among the services themselves. The air force is probably more similar to a civilian work setting than are the other services in terms of the high level of technology, the small proportion of the force that is involved in purely military or combat tasks, and the impersonal nature of modern air warfare. Moreover, it is a relatively decentralized organization, whose major commands have a high degree of autonomy. Thus, one might expect OD in the air force to take on the forms that tend to appear in large civilian corporations that have divisional organization.

Organizational development did in fact take place in the air force as a highly decentralized, relatively diffuse, and relatively low-cost operation aimed at improving the quality of work life. Local commanders were given broad discretion to call in consultants from, for example, the Air Force Institute of Technology. The consultants would discuss organizational problems, diagnose the local situation, recommend one or more OD intervention strategies, and depart. This approach to OD might be called the Lone Ranger model, because of its dependence on outside intervention—an approach common in civilian industry—and a "silver bullet" strategy to solve the problem.[19] In 1975, coordination of the air force's OD efforts increased with the establishment, in the Directorate of Personnel Plans, of a deputy for human-resource development. This coordination did not impose standardization on the air force's effort; rather, it set general policy in the OD area by legitimizing past practices, and it facilitated communication about techniques that had been tried in one or more air force settings.[20]

The navy is also a relatively high technology service, but it has a large force of unskilled labor and a long tradition of centralized control and coordination. OD developed in the navy as a less voluntary system, with a more standardized approach. The program was executed by a series of Human Resource Management Centers and Human Resource Management Detachments, which operated in a sense as franchise concerns, dispensing a standardized OD package. This is the "McDonald's" model of OD.

The navy's approach was survey-guided development, which used a survey feedback instrument adapted from an organizational diagnostic tool used widely in civilian settings. Teams of active-duty navy personnel, trained in OD techniques, worked with navy units as part of their routine operational scheduling. The units were put through a "human-resource management cycle," which involved preliminary meetings between consultants and command personnel, the administration of the survey, the feedback of data to the command, the identification of potential areas of improvement, and the suggestion of ways in which those improvements might be accomplished.[21]

The army, probably more than the navy, has a traditional military view of organization and has shown a marked propensity to define personnel-management problems in terms of "leadership"—a term that is more a valued symbol than a concrete concept. Nonetheless, the organizational perception seems to be that if army leaders were doing their jobs correctly, there would not be personnel problems. It is to be expected, therefore, that OD interventions in the army would be aimed at improving the quality of leadership.

Because of needs to adapt to a variety of situations and to perform a wide range of missions, the army is both less centralized (in terms of control) and less standardized (in terms of procedures) than is the navy. These factors moved OD in the army in the direction of what might be called the "missionary model."

Like the navy, the army during the 1970s trained specialized personnel in OD techniques at its Organizational Effectiveness Training Center. While a variety of OD techniques were introduced, the army emphasized those that are aimed at improving the skills—including interpersonal skills—of the commander, as well as the effectiveness and cohesion of his staff: in other words, leadership development and management-team building. Having success-fully completed their training, organizational-effectiveness staff officers and NCOs were assigned to the staffs of large army units in the field to spread the gospel. In contrast to the navy case, the utilization of the OD specialist's skills by the commander was voluntary. And in contrast to the air force, the presence of the OD specialist as a member of the unit, rather than as an outside consultant, was not voluntary.

The success that OD interventions in the armed services had in improv-ing organizational effectiveness and organizational climate is at best dif-ficult to assess. The major criterion for evaluating the effectiveness of a military organization has historically been victory in battles and wars. This criterion obviously does not apply to a peacetime force-in-being.

A general criterion used in evaluating the effectiveness of organizational interventions is job satisfaction, and here all three services noted a decline between the early 1970s, when OD was introduced, and the late 1970s.[22] This is not to say that the human-relations approach to management was responsible for the decline. Indeed, the decline might have been greater in the absence of intervention efforts. Moreover, job satisfaction in the United States military has improved somewhat during the 1980s. Nonetheless, organizational development cannot be credited with improving job satisfac-tion. What it did accomplish was a dramatic demonstration of the willingness of the armed services to adopt management strategies from commerce and industry, which reflected a definition of military personnel as employees.

The effects of OD in the armed forces were mixed. They reflect a clear attempt to substitute the human-relations approach to management in place of scientific management, at least insofar as personnel issues are concerned. Both approaches, however, substitute impersonal management for leader-ship. Leadership, a more personal and affective tie between commanders and their subordinates, has repeatedly been shown to be an important fac-tor in combat effectiveness. By the late 1980s, all of the services had de-creased their utilization of OD techniques.

LEADERSHIP AND MANAGEMENT

No other factor signals the increasing impersonality of the civilian work place and the military unit in the United States as dramatically as does the progressive displacement of processes that involve the leadership of people by processes that involve the management of resources, some of which are people. One disquieting reflection of the rationalization of organizations in modern America has been the tendency in the armed forces, in corporate enterprise, and in colleges of business and management to use the terms *leadership* and *management* as if they were synonymous.[23] This obscures the fact that the two concepts come from different perspectives in social philosophy and are rooted in different assumptions about the essence of human nature and of human organization. They have been developed, tested, and refined in the context of different scientific disciplinary traditions. Most important, they both refer to processes in the real world that are essential to the effective performance of the task of a large collective enterprise such as an armed force. To the extent that the terms become confused with each other, we risk losing at least a part of what is central and unique to each, as well as what is essential to the effective functioning of a modern military organization.

The concept of leadership is grounded in theories of social organization that derived from nineteenth-century social thought in France and Germany. In France, for example, it was reflected in the collectivistic orientation of Auguste Comte.[24] From this perspective, the emergence of leadership—defined largely as a process of coordination—is a manifestation of the cooperative distribution of functions in an organization or in a society in order to achieve shared goals. Some people assume command, while others are willing to defer to those who are willing to take on the burden of leadership. The basis for this agreement is the existence of a consensual normative order. Comte's focus was on social structure, but this concern was gradually transformed by others who worked in his tradition—most notably Emile Durkheim, who moved away from the assumption that social structure was given and toward a concern with the relationship between the individual and the collectivity.[25]

In Germany, theoretical work that was ultimately to have a major impact on modern theories of leadership was done by Georg Simmel and Max Weber. To the study of social organization the former brought a concern with the forms and consequences of social interaction and a recognition that social structure was a reflection of these interactions.[26] Weber, whose work on rationalization we noted earlier, similarly recognized that the major structures of society reflect interactions among people.[27]

In the United States, these perspectives found their counterparts in emerging theories of group dynamics, most notably symbolic interactionism and role theory, which, like the European theories, came to focus on social groups rather than on abstract structures and on interaction rather than on formal organization. From this perspective, leadership came to be defined in terms of roles that exist in social groups to help group members achieve collective goals. Methods for the study of leadership came to focus on interaction within the group.

The field of group dynamics developed in the United States during the 1930s. This development was itself supported by the trend toward increasing rationalization: a societal commitment to science, the emergence of human-service professions that could legitimize and utilize the theories and methods that were developed—the harbingers of the welfare state—and the existence of established social sciences that had already demonstrated the importance of studying social groups and had designed at least preliminary research methods to contribute to the new field.

Much of the early work in group dynamics focused on the importance of leadership. The landmark studies of Kurt Lewin, Ronald Lippitt, and Robert K. White demonstrated that the same group of people would behave differently under the direction of leaders who had different styles.[28] Although the accumulated evidence of research in group dynamics rejects the unicausal model of leadership quality accounting for group performance by itself, it is equally clear from this evidence that the degree to which leaders are supportive of their followers and of group integration has consequences for the performance of the group.

Recognizing that leadership was a microlevel process, much early work focused on the identification of the characteristics of good leaders, particularly in terms of personality traits. This line of research has not proven to be fruitful. Recent research has focused on the situational constraints on leadership and on the leadership functions that must be performed in the group. What remains constant in recent research is the recognition that the nature and the quality of the interaction between the leader and other group members are strong determinants of the effectiveness of the group.[29]

It is important and interesting to note that much of this social-science research on leadership used military personnel as subjects, and it was funded, at least in part, by the United States armed services. Indeed, the centrality of leadership in groups, as well as related small-group processes, which were concerns of the armed services during the 1940s, the 1950s, and the 1960s (the heyday of small-group research), is reflected in the fact that during this period, the major source of research support in this field was the United States Navy and that although it was a new institution, the United States Air Force was second among nonuniversity sources of funding. Equally impressive, while the largest number of researchers in the field of small-group processes were affiliated with universities, the second-largest number were in the United States Air Force.[30]

Military support for research on group processes virtually disappeared after the 1960s as rational management became increasingly entrenched in the Department of Defense. Even during the height of military concern with group processes, the army, which is the largest of the United States armed services, lagged behind the other services in the conduct and support of research on leadership in groups. While the army has traditionally recognized the importance of leadership, acknowledged the interpersonal nature of the leadership process, and sought ways to improve the quality of its leadership, it has not approached the concept with any degree of precision. Thus, a study done for the Department of the Army by the Leadership

Motivation Branch of the Personnel and Administration Combat Development Activity at Fort Benjamin Harrison, Indiana, in 1975 reported that *"The Dictionary of Army Terms*, AR 310-25, does not include the word 'leadership' " and that in both the *Officer's Guide* and the *Armed Forces Officer* (DA Pam 600-2) "the terms command, management, and leadership are used frequently interchangeably and always nebulously." The study did recommend that a definition of leadership be included in the *Dictionary of U.S. Army Terms*, but it suggested a phrasing that was general enough to cover virtually any application of authority within an organization: "Military Leadership is the process of influencing human behavior so as to accomplish the missions of the organization." This definition does not differentiate between affect and remuneration as incentives to perform.

During the 1980s the army replaced leadership concerns with an emphasis on "vertical cohesion"–affective bonding between superiors and subordinates. Cohesion had become the new fad in personnel management. There was little recognition that vertical cohesion had anything to do with what had previously been called leadership.

Whereas social theories about leadership had their roots in concerns about the pursuit of collective goals and the functioning of groups, the field of management has been more strongly tied to the individualism of Herbert Spencer and other social Darwinists[31] and to the utilitarianism of the classical economists Adam Smith, David Ricardo, John Stuart Mill, and Jeremy Bentham.[32] Rather than on a concern with having social groups strive together to achieve collective goals, the management orientation has focused on the desire of the individual to maximize payoffs, by making decisions based upon a rational calculus. For managers themselves, the motivation is the maximization of profit. Workers, in turn, are assumed to be motivated by an expectation that their participation in a collective enterprise will benefit them individually. Thus the traditional management model does not assume that individuals are committed to group goals; it merely assumes that they will have individual interests in the fulfillment of these goals. The managers need not themselves be participants in the group processes that are oriented toward goal attainment. The task of the managers is the more abstract one of allocating resources within the organization toward the fulfillment of organizational goals. The fact that scientific management has been displaced by the human-relations approach to management in the military and in civilian work places makes management no less individualistic. The human-relations approach focuses primarily on individual needs, rather than on organizational productivity.

Classic human-relations management has not been very successful in the civilian contexts where it was developed. Conflicts between labor and management, absenteeism, and the quality of work continue to be problems in civilian organizations. Organizational-development techniques, such as those discussed above, grew out of the human-relations approach and sought to incorporate into the repertoire of management concerns the individual's drives toward personal growth and toward an ability to contribute to the organization; the importance of peer-group influences; and the interactive processes of leadership and followership. In short, this approach attempted, not to distinguish leadership from management, but to incorporate leadership into the matrix of resources that are being rationally managed.[33] More recently the focus on vertical cohesion has been a further extension of this thinking, which is embedded in a rediscovery of the cohesion that characterized militia units and in a belief that this cohesion is a resource that can be managed. The question remains as to whether emergent group processes, such as leadership and cohesion, which are essential for combat effectiveness, can in fact be rationalized.

COHESION IN MILITARY UNITS

Within modern military organizations the basic conflict between the traditional solidarity of the community and rational integration, as reflected in bureaucracy and professionalism, is manifested in Janowitz's classic study of the professional soldier.[34] Janowitz has noted that the style of life of the traditional military community enhanced group cohesion, but he also has pointed out that (1) social relations within the military community had been changed by the "organizational revolution," (2) military life had become more impersonal, and (3) social cohesion had been weakened. Leadership reflects one form of such cohesion—cohesion between superiors and subordinates, or vertical cohesion.

Janowitz thought a change in the nature of organizational authority underlay this trend—a change from "authoritarian domination" to "greater reliance on manipulation, persuasion, and group consensus." The era of authoritarian domination had been characterized by the heroic leader. The hero was seen as having been replaced over time by the military manager, who was responsible for a more complex military technology than the mounted warrior had been. Whereas Weber saw the decline of personalistic leadership as a necessary condition for the development of more complex military technologies, Janowitz thought that technological change, as well as changes in scale, had major effects on the nature of organizational authority.

Regardless of the causal sequence, both Weber and Janowitz saw the same trend emerging in the military and in modern society at large: increased rationalization, less commitment to the collectivity, greater impersonality, less emphasis on traditional leadership, and more emphasis on modern management. These trends have effects on interpersonal relations other than those between superiors and subordinates. They affect the relationship between peers within military units, as the military attempts to manage these units rationally.

During the early years of the United States military, cohesion was enhanced by the militia model and later by the National Guard. The National Guard had shortcomings as the military mobilization base of a democratic nation. During the 1840s, as the militia system was dying out, volunteer units were emerging within it that were recruited from the social elite, attractively uniformed and well equipped. Among these was New York's 7th Regiment of "National Guards." This designation, which became the common name for this type of unit, was meant to honor the marquis de Lafayette's 1824 visit to the United States. The states, by encouraging these elite volunteer units and by neglecting the more general militia, essentially made the National Guard the country's reserve for ground combat troops during the second half of the nineteenth century, thereby substituting voluntarism for universal obligation. The guard granted itself a national embodiment that transcended state boundaries in 1879, when the National Guard Association was formed.

Despite the elitism, the politicization, and the absence of a sense of obligation in the National Guard—or perhaps because of them—the guard was able to continue a tradition of cohesion that had characterized the geographically based militia. The guard established units on a territorial basis. Soldiers who served together usually came from the same community, knew each other outside of their military roles, and increasingly came from similar social backgrounds. The cohesion resulting from the fact that military service was embedded in a broader community-based social fabric was an important factor in producing high morale—a dimension that is usually omitted from cost-benefit analyses of the military.

More than a century ago the French military analyst Col. Ardant de Picq had recognized that rational analysis of military organization and combat formations tended to be wrong, because it neglected intangible factors that are difficult to objectively measure but that are nonetheless imperative to effective military operations.[35] The cohesion and morale that characterized the geographically based units of the militia and the guard were such factors. The loss of this geographic base was one of the consequences of a system of national conscription.

After World War I, the United States Army differed from its European counterparts in its policy of training and replacing soldiers as individuals rather than as units or as groups; the result was high turnover rates in small units. Thus, personnel did not have the opportunity to build cohesive bonds with their comrades in the same sense that personnel in other armed forces had. In the American forces in World War II, S. L. A. Marshall rediscovered the principle that morale, rooted in a feeling of unity among soldiers, is what gives soldiers the courage to fight.[36] Marshall's findings, based on after-action combat interviews, were confirmed by Samuel A. Stouffer and his team of researchers in the War Department.[37]

In contrast to the United States policy of replacing individuals, the German Wehrmacht maintained a unit rotation and replacement system until very late in the war and, as a result, maintained a high degree of organizational integrity and fighting effectiveness. Edward A. Shils and Morris Janowitz have found, on the basis of interviews with German prisoners of war, that "when the individual's immediate group . . . offered him affection and esteem from both officers and comrades . . . the element of self-concern in battle, which would lead to disruption of the effective functioning of his primary group, was minimized." Once the primary group structure had been disrupted, however, there was a loss of leadership, and physical survival took priority over military resistance.[38]

The recognized importance of unit cohesion notwithstanding, the logistics of maintaining a force-in-being based on a national conscription system that started with World War II moved military personnel policy increasingly in the direction of an individual-based, rather than a unit-based, system of rotation and replacement. The disappearance of solidary primary groups in the army is generally identified as having started with the Korean police action, in which the spatial dispersion of personnel and the individual-rotation system mitigated against the maintenance of group ties among combat soldiers. The major source cited for this inference is Roger W. Little's research on buddy relations, which at one level seems to suggest that the primary group was replaced by the dyad in that conflict.[39] As John H. Faris has noted, however, even though the individual-rotation policy then in effect was disruptive of primary-group relations, such relations did persist as networks of interpersonal linkages.[40] Moreover, an experimental unit-replacement system was introduced in three infantry companies in Korea, with four-man teams being trained and assigned to the field command as units. Morale was found to be higher in these experimental replacement teams than among infantrymen who were assigned individually to units as a control group, and the experimental teams seemed to perform somewhat better in combat situations, thus strengthening the case for a team-replacement system.[41]

In the years after the war, the army recognized the importance of solidary ties, and experimented with a number of programs to enhance group cohesion through unit rotation.[42] From 1953 to 1955, infantry platoons were shipped intact to Europe. Between 1955 and 1959, under a program called Gyroscope, units from company to division size were rotated between the United States and Europe. The men who volunteered for Gyroscope knew that they would stay with the unit for a complete tour, and draftees who were assigned to these units knew where they would be for their tours. In many cases, the unit returned to a "home" station. In 1957, the adjutant general conducted an evaluation of Gyroscope for the deputy chief of staff for personnel. A survey of the attitudes of troops who had participated in the program showed, among other things, that three-fourths of the participants favored unit rotation over individual rotation and that three-fourths favored small-unit rotation over the larger-unit Gyroscope system.[43]

Gyroscope was followed by OVUREP, an overseas unit-replacement plan that deployed seven infantry battle groups to Korea. The OVUREP units were put together at basic-training centers, where officer and NCO cadres were responsible for individual and unit training of recruits prior to deployment. OVUREP was apparently a success, but it lasted for only a year. Analysts disagree about whether its demise was due to a diversion of resources to meet the army's expansion needs following the Berlin crisis or whether it was simply cannibalized in Korea, as its officers were pulled out to staff the 7th Division Headquarters, its tall soldiers were assigned to the division's honor guard, and its musicians where assigned to the division's band.[44] Both processes probably contributed.

OVUREP was followed almost immediately in the early 1960s by Rotaplan, under which battle groups were rotated between Europe and the United States on a six-month basis; by Long Thrust, under which battle groups were rotated from the United States to Europe on a ninety-day basis; and by a platoon-replacement system, which was established to man the Davy Crockett weapon system being deployed in Korea. Each of these programs disappeared rapidly.

Despite this series of unit-rotation programs, which suggest that the army was sensitive to the importance of unit cohesion, logistical costs came to outweigh morale gains in the policy process, and the personnel-rotation system used during the Vietnam War was an individual one, which hindered the development of cohesive ties and almost guaranteed that the ties that did develop would neither be rooted necessarily in one's own unit nor support the purposes of the army. Charles Moskos has seen this policy as producing behavioral patterns that were motivated primarily by self-interest among combat troops.[45] Paul L. Savage and Richard A. Gabriel, in turn, have interpreted Moskos's observations as evidence that the primary group was destroyed as a social form in the United States Army in Vietnam.[46] This interpretation, however, runs counter to Moskos's further observation that self-interest in fact produced solidarity in combat squads.[47] The emergence of primary groups is not a product of the army's personnel policies; it is a normal process of social organization. In organizations like the army, such groups may crystallize around goals that run counter to the norms of the organization, as John Helmer has noted in his analysis of drug and alcohol cultures in the army in Vietnam.[48] Thus, cohesion itself is not enough, and naturally emergent cohesive groups may be counterproductive in terms of organizational goals. Organizational policies aimed at achieving and structuring cohesion, however, can increase the likelihood that the emergent groups will support organizational goals.

After the war, during the early years of the all-volunteer force, partially in recognition of the dysfunctions of the individual-rotation policies pursued in Vietnam, the army began a series of additional programs to reassert the importance of unit cohesion. In 1974 the army announced that it was going to train and rotate intact M60A2 tank crews to Europe, rather than training and rotating individual members of armored crews. The rotation program was expanded to Brigade 75 and Brigade 76. The conceptualization of these latter programs was reasonable in terms of its sociology. The units were to be brought to full strength; undergo at least ninety days of unit training in the United States; be deployed as intact companies from Fort Hood, Texas, to Germany for six months, where they would find waiting for them equipment similar to what they had been training on and where they would be stationed together; and then return to the United States, to be replaced by another brigade-sized unit.

Unfortunately, the management of the program was not up to the level of its conceptualization. Personnel turbulence characterized the unit until very shortly before its deployment. The United States had not been able to negotiate with the German government for a location that the brigade could call its own, so it was split up on its arrival in Germany. The tanks that were waiting for it in Germany were a different model from the ones that the troops had trained on at Fort Hood. It was not a successful experiment, and the second test of it did not iron out the problems. It was discontinued after one year.

More recently, as a reflection of the belief in the importance of cohesion held by Gen. Edward C. Meyer, army chief of staff during the early 1980s, a series of initiatives has been undertaken to maximize stability and reduce turbulence through programs of unit rotation and home basing within the context of a regimental system.[49] In mid-1980, the Army Cohesion Study (ARCOST) developed a plan for a company-level replacement/rotation system and for the establishment of a regimental system. A test during the summer of 1980 involved three thousand new recruits, who were kept together in training and in operational platoons; they were judged to have higher morale and performance than did recruits who were trained and assigned as individuals.

By the end of 1980 the chief of staff had approved the COHORT (cohesion, operational readiness, and training) program, in which company-sized units were to be recruited, trained together, and assigned as units for their first three-year tour, in an attempt to judge whether their operational readiness was in fact greater than that in units based upon individual rotation. The last of the initial COHORT companies began initial active-duty training in March 1981; and in mid-1981, expanding the COHORT concept, the army started phasing in a new regimental manning system, in which the companies were assigned to the administrative regiments to which they would belong whether they were located in the continental United States or were rotated overseas. According to this new system, rotation was to take place on a battalion basis, with the battalion having a home base in the United States to which it would return after foreign tours of duty. This regimental system would both keep soldiers and their leaders together in units longer and, through the home-basing characteristic, help establish ties between army units and host civilian communities. Newly enlisted soldiers would serve in the same unit from the beginning of initial-entry training through the end of a three-year cycle. In the mid-1980s, the army began to experiment with battalion-sized, rather than company-sized, COHORT units, apparently on the assumption that bigger is better but forgetting that the goal of the COHORT system was to produce small, highly cohesive interpersonal networks. The battalion COHORT system proved to be logistically untenable, and by the late 1980s the army was again backing away from the concept of cohesive units.

CIVIC CONSCIOUSNESS AND THE SOLDIER

If concern for unit cohesion—a soldier's attachment to his peers and leaders—was a casualty of rational personnel management in the military during much of the twentieth century, concern for the attachment that the soldier felt to the nation was almost a fatality of the more general rationalization of society—a war in which organizational rationalization was but one battle.

The history of United States military manpower policy is replete with manifestations that as a nation, since the time of George Washington, Americans have generally subscribed to the principle that military service was an obligation and a right of citizenship. While this principle was breached more frequently than it was realized, the early militia acts and the definition of conscripts and reservists as "citizen-soldiers" reflected the principle of associating military service with attachment to the symbols of nationhood. However, while the social-science research during World War II pointed to both the importance of primary groups and the importance of national symbols, the latter concern has been largely ignored even by the social-science community. The principles and traditions of military service as being a manifestation of citizenship have been eroded by time and by social change. These principles had been reinforced by the traditions of cohesive military units and, in turn, had reinforced their cohesion. It is not clear, however, that in recent years the recognition of the importance of cohesion as a characteristic of the form of effective military units has been accompanied by a recognition of principle and tradition as part of their content.

Janowitz has argued that the morale studies conducted by Stouffer and his research team, which played such a major role in pointing out the importance of cohesion, subsequently gave military leaders a justification for *limiting* the political, or citizenship, content of their training.[50] This perspective has appeared in the social-science community as well. Thus, Savage and Gabriel, in their analysis of the United States Army in Vietnam, have suggested that "we know that military cohesion exists quite apart from politics and ideologies in the civilian political systems . . . a continued sense of 'cause,' at whatever level of saliency, is not vital to military cohesion . . . this literature degrades any sense of mission on the part of soldiers transcendent of the immediate tactical mission."[51]

Such a reading of the literature mistakes primacy for determinism. Shils and Janowitz, in their study of the Wehrmacht, clearly have emphasized the importance of primary groups and, in fact, noted the apolitical attitudes of German soldiers. However, Shils and Janowitz have also pointed to the deep devotion of German soldiers to their national leaders: "There could be little doubt that a high degree of identification with the *Fuhrer* was an important factor in prolonging German resistance."[52] Similarly, in the case of the United States forces, Shils has noted that the "tacit patriotism" of the American soldier contributed to combat motivation.[53] Along similar lines, Moskos has pointed out the importance of "latent ideology" for American troops in Vietnam.[54] Indeed, Moskos has viewed ideology as more important than group cohesion for combat motivation in World War II, Korea, and Vietnam.[55]

Throughout the last two decades of debate on the draft and the all-volunteer force, sociologists have argued for the citizenship component in military service.[56] However, with the advent of the "welfare state" and with a concern for the benefits that society should provide to the citizenry, citizenship *rights* have received much more attention than have citizenship *obligations*. The provision of a good job came to be regarded as a citizenship right, and people who went to work for the all-volunteer force as uniformed federal employees turned out, in the early years, to be looking for the same characteristics in their jobs as were civilians working in the private sector. During the mid-1970s, the preferred job characteristics of enlisted men in the army and the navy were good pay, favorable fringe benefits, and opportunities to control one's personal life and to avoid bureaucracy. The same pattern held for employed civilian men.[57]

The military services were seen as less able to provide these—particularly the latter two—than were civilian employers, but the similarity in preferences was clear. Of fourteen job dimensions that were explored, the opportunity to serve the country ranked tenth; and again, military personnel did not differ from civilian employees.

A survey of the attitudes of high-school students toward military service, conducted in the early 1980s, mirrored these findings closely. Among students in the highest mental category, service to the country ranked ninth out of fifteen reasons that were explored for enlisting in the army.[58] Educational, medical, dental, and retirement benefits; salary; work experience; and opportunity to travel—all ranked higher. The optimistic note, of course, is that attachment to the nation did not rank last or did not disappear entirely, according to these studies. However, a sense of citizenship obligation to serve the country was clearly not strong among military personnel, their employed civilian peers, or the youth who were about to enter either the military or the labor force. Within reason, civilian workers can afford to be indifferent to what their employers require of them in exchange for wages. Military personnel are not likely to be equally indifferent to requirements that they risk their lives in the event of war on the basis of the market mechanism, although the market may well induce them to join the military during peacetime. If Shils, Janowitz, Moskos, and others are correct in noting the importance of symbolic attachments for combat motivation, what is more important is that little is being done to ensure that this factor will be inculcated.

With the advent of the all-volunteer force, the historical policy of maintaining a balance between citizen-soldiers—who manifested the principle of citizenship obligation—and professional soldiers was replaced by an emphasis on the latter.[59] Only recently has there been a return to the inclusion of obligations in the conceptualization of citizenship,[60] as well as a recognition that in an era of deterrence and constabulary military operations, the concepts of citizenship and patriotism in both the nation-state and the world community have consequences for military organization, because economic incentives alone are not a sufficient basis for maintaining an effective all-volunteer force. Janowitz has reminded us that research on World War II suggested that it was the articulation of attachment to secondary symbols and the structure of primary groups that produced effective combat units, and he has argued for the development of civic consciousness— not rigid ideology or simple patriotism, but self-critical commitment and attachment to the nation-state, recognizing and supporting both the traditional national and more recent international responsibilities of citizenship.[61]

Empirical support for the principle that the population will support a conceptualization of the military establishment that includes a citizenship component comes from survey data that show growing support for registration and for a military draft, as well as a willingness among a plurality of young American males to volunteer for service in the event of a necessary war.[62] Perhaps more impressive, feelings among first-term army personnel that "everyone should have to serve his or her country in some way," which never exceeded 65 percent during the 1970s, approached 80 percent during the early 1980s.[63] One of the emerging issues that faces the nation is how citizenship education and military service are to be articulated. The United States has never done a particularly good job of citizenship training within the military, which frequently has resisted such a role. Nor has it done so in recent years in the civilian sector, where the responsibility for such education properly resides. The World War I mobilization had required the development of courses to sensitize young Americans to the reasons for the nation's involvement, but those courses were conducted primarily by civilian educational institutions. The War Department did not undertake a political training mission until 1918, even though it recognized the importance of a commitment to national ideals for combat effectiveness.[64] During the inter-war period, concerns with contributing to combat morale through citizenship education were replaced by concerns for troop welfare, and resources that had previously been used to support patriotism and ideals were turned to post libraries and recreational facilities. What remained of political training was superficial and ineffective.

At the outset of World War II, the low level of morale of American soldiers was quickly recognized, and citizenship education was quickly and effectively resurrected as the Army Orientation Program, which was intended to sensitize soldiers to the political dimensions of the war. At the end of the war, however, rational management concerns dictated that resources spent on political-education be redirected to supporting the demobilization effort.[65]

The debate on Universal Military Training and the advent of the Korean War rekindled efforts at citizenship education in the armed forces. However, Senator Joseph R. McCarthy's attack on the program for being "soft on communism" led to another redirection of the program in the mid-1950s, away from citizenship education and toward anti-Communist indoctrination. The army in particular was not comfortable with this role, and the firing of Maj. Gen. Edwin A. Walker in 1961 for indoctrinating his troops in his own irrationally rabid form of anticommunism (including his accusation that top officials in the Department of Defense were in collusion with the Communists) led to the dismantling of the political-education apparatus by the mid-1960s. One result of this course of action was that the United States soldiers who were asked to fight, kill, and die in Vietnam were not effectively told the reason that they were there—a reflection that we had forgotten the lessons of the two World Wars.[66]

McCarthyism left its mark on citizenship training in the civilian sector as well. During the 1950s, many teachers in public schools were fired or asked to resign on the basis of suspicions of disloyalty or softness on communism. In the short run, teaching about politics in America moved to the right ideologically. The subsequent reaction against McCarthyism left teachers less willing to present controversial positions of either the Right or the Left, for fear of negative sanctions from within the educational system.

The young generation has thereby been denied, to an important extent, the opportunity to analyze and debate the complexities of the modern political system.[67]

The change in citizenship education was no less pronounced in the teaching of the other social studies and social sciences than it was in the teaching of American history, but it was most dramatic in this last area—the common denominator that prepares the young generation for citizen participation. Critics of the "new history," which focuses on social issues rather than on historical events and which seems to be embarrassed by America's past, have suggested that for decades the history curriculum has been weakened, in terms of both substance and standards.[68] The problem seems to be as deeply embedded in the discipline of historical research as in the teaching of history and, again, is probably as severe in the other social studies. The historian Gertrude Himmelfarb has reported on a conversation with a scholar engaged in a historical study of living and working conditions and interpersonal relations in a New England town during the late eighteenth century, basically a study in the quality of life:

I asked him whether his study . . . had any bearing on what I, admittedly not a specialist in American history, took to be the most momentous event of that time and place . . . the founding of the United States of America. . . . He conceded that from his subjects and sources . . . he could not "get," as he said, to the founding of the United States. But he denied that this was the crucial event I took it to be. What was crucial were the lives and experiences of the masses of people.[69]

Himmelfarb was seeking, not a repudiation of a concern with quality of life, but merely a recognition that "the lives and experiences of the masses of the people" are affected by events such as the founding of nation-states. Such a recognition was not forthcoming. Because in our view, the growth of nationhood was a crucial process in the shaping of our military manpower policy, neglect of the former is extremely important for our understanding of the latter.

During the 1960s, 1970s, and 1980s the definition of citizenship in the United States and other nations of the Western industrial world has been broadened so as to involve participation not only in the polity but in the work place as well. As noted, this broadening has been accompanied by an emphasis on citizenship rights rather than responsibilities.[70] Thus, although, for those who serve, military service has historically been associated with citizenship both because it has been viewed as a manifestation of citizenship obligation and because the military has served as an instrument of citizenship education,[71] issues of quality of military work life, rather than obligation to the nation, may have become the primary citizenship issues associated with military service.

That quality of life concerns are not the only issues has been demonstrated by Faris, whose analysis has shown that a sense of mission—a feeling that what the military does is necessary and important—while less powerful than quality-of-work-life factors in predicting reenlistment intentions in the all-volunteer force, is more powerful than feelings about pay and benefits.[72] This demonstration that a sense of mission is more important for reenlistment decisions than for initial-enlistment decisions suggests that the experience of serving in the military is having some effect on citizenship awareness. This should have salutary effects both on military effectiveness, as soldiers come to a better understanding of their role in a complex international system, and on more general citizenship participation. Nonetheless, the processes of civic education that are involved are currently largely informal, and we have yet to determine how to conduct citizenship training appropriately in such a welfare-state context in which citizenship itself is increasingly being defined in economic rather than political terms.

ORGANIZATIONAL CONVERGENCE AND THE REDEFINITION OF SERVICE

The rationalization of American society and that of the United States military—the latter accomplished partly through the adoption of civilian management strategies—has been accompanied by increased similarity between civilian organizations and the armed forces, or at least some elements of the armed forces. Prior to World War II and the formulation of Harold D. Lasswell's garrison-state model, there were important differences between the nature of civilian and military organizations, between the military and civilian work forces, and between the nature of military service and civilian employment. These differences mitigated against the fusion of military and civilian spheres.

Crucial technological differences between the two spheres were rooted in the fact that military personnel spent their time doing different things than did civilians. Warfare was a land-based event, with the infantry and, increasingly, tanks (which had only recently replaced the mounted cavalry) being the core of the army. The military world was overwhelmingly male, predominantly young, and predominantly single. The military work force was elastic, based on the mobilization model. For those who were mobilized, military service was seen as a short-term obligation to the state. Most importantly, for most enlisted soldiers, it was clearly different from civilian employment.

The mid-century changes that made the mobilization model obsolete produced a military organization increasingly dependent upon skills that were needed in the civilian economy as well. Many of these skills required costly training. If the military were to continue to bring young untrained personnel into service and to absorb the costs of their training, it would have to retain many of them in the expanded force-in-being beyond their initial obligated tour in order to get an acceptable return on its investment in training. Such retention involved competing with civilian employers for these trained personnel. For career personnel then, the military was in competition with civilian employers decades before the advent of the all-volunteer force, and it was beginning to shape organizational environments that were similar to civilian work places. By the 1950s and the 1960s, military sociology was stressing the increased similarity of military and civilian organizations. Janowitz, for example, has argued that "to analyze the contemporary military establishment as a social system, it is . . . necessary to assume that for some time it has tended to display more and more of the characteristics of any large-scale nonmilitary bureaucracy."[73]

Scholars quickly came to recognize that common technologies, which lead to common organizational forms, could not lead to the total elimination of the fundamental difference between the military world and the civilian world, given the unique military function of managing large-scale organized violence. By the early 1970s, some analysts were defining the convergence function between military and civilian institutions as an asymptotic one, with the two structures becoming increasingly similar but failing to reach a point of intersection.[74] In 1971, Janowitz pointed out that "the narrowing distinction between military and nonmilitary bureaucracies can never result in the elimination of fundamental differences."[75] Moskos took the extreme position, which he has since rejected, that in fact the trend had been reversed. "The over-two-decade long institutional convergence of the armed forces and American society is beginning to reverse itself . . . the military in the post-Vietnam period will increasingly diverge along a variety of dimensions from the mainstream of developments in the general society."[76]

The position that Moskos subsequently moved to became the basis for a more refined model of civil-military organizational convergence and of the transformation of the nature of military service in America. Rather than regarding convergence in gross organizational terms, Moskos has argued that some elements of the armed forces would be divergent and traditionally military, particularly the ground combat forces, whereas others would be convergent and civilianized, particularly clerical, technical, and administrative areas.[77] This theme of the differentiation of the force and its elaboration into a two-force structure—one convergent and civilianized and the other divergent and military—has been further developed by other analysts. Hauser, for example, has envisaged the United States Army of the future as consisting of a combat force, divergent from civilian society and maintaining traditional military values; and a support force, convergent with civilian society and serving as a buffer between civilian society and the combat formations.[78] More recently, Moskos has modified his own formulation somewhat; he is now advocating a two-tier personnel system based upon the differentiation of "citizen-soldiers" from "career-soldiers," rather than combat from noncombat personnel.[79] One means of reinstituting the role of the citizen-soldier is the establishment of a system of national service.

In addition to agreement among analysts that at least some parts of the United States military establishment are coming to resemble civilian corporate bureaucracies, there is an emerging body of theory that argues that at the level of the individual soldier, sailor, or airman, military service is increasingly growing to resemble civilian employment. Before the conversion to an all-volunteer force, the nature of military compensation, the conditions of service, and the system of traditional symbolic rewards in the armed forces caused military service to be defined as something other than a civilian job. Although military personnel were not well paid by civilian standards, they were involved in an activity that was as much a community as it was a work place. They shared a fraternal spirit with brothers-in-arms, and they received societal respect for their fulfillment of a responsibility of citizenship.

The Gates Commission rejected this definition and, by accepting both a labor-market model of military manpower and a human-relations orientation to management, assumed that if the all-volunteer force were to succeed in competing with civilian employers for quality personnel, it would have to adopt the most desirable attributes of those employers.[80] Among the recommendations of the commission were that military compensation be based on a salary system, similar to that of civilian industry; that the lateral hiring of trained personnel from the civilian labor force be increased; and that in general, the all-volunteer force compete with industry for quality personnel as similar, although not identical, entities.

During the transition to an all-volunteer force, efforts were made to make the military competitive with civilian employment in terms of pay. Between 1967 and 1975, Regular Military Compensation (RMC)—the sum of base pay, quarters and subsistence allowances, and tax advantages—increased by 87 percent, while general-schedule civil-service salaries increased by 55 percent. A 1974 survey of conditions of military service in the Western nations reported that while all of these nations had their military pay structured "in relationship to civilian employment," only the United States, Canada, and the United Kingdom—all of which had volunteer forces—indicated that their pay scales for the services were comparable to those for civilian employment.[81] During the late 1970s, United States military compensation was tied directly to general-schedule civil-service pay; and as noted earlier, caps on civil-service pay caused entry-level military compensation to dip below the federal minimum wage in the late 1970s, producing severe manpower problems for the all-volunteer force.

With the move toward equalizing military pay levels and civilian pay levels, and the attendant increases in direct personnel costs in the armed forces, there were changes in the structure of benefits that have traditionally been associated with military service. Some benefits that have traditionally enhanced the image of the military as a fraternal community that looks after its members, its past members, and its dependents began to decline. There were decreases in the availability of medical care to military dependents and retirees, and there were cutbacks in allowances for travel and the shipment of household goods. Postgraduate-education benefits for active military personnel were cut back during the late 1970s, as were educational benefits for veterans. Appropriated fund support for military commissaries has been under attack. Junior officers who had good service records and who desired military careers were discharged from the service through reductions in force before they could become eligible for retirement benefits. Indeed, the entire traditional military retirement system has been changed to conform more closely to the retirement plans of civilian organizations.

In sum, the conditions of working for the armed forces as a uniformed member of the service have increasingly come to resemble the employment conditions of a civilian occupation. Whether by design, intuition, or accident, the makers of military personnel policy have sought to compete with commerce and industry for workers by making military employment increasingly similar to civilian employment; but they have overlooked the fact that most civilian workers are not asked, as a central part of their job, either to risk their lives or to threaten the lives of others in defense of the state.

These organizational changes, in turn, may have changed the nature of military service at the level of the individual service person. At the 1973 annual meeting of the American Sociological Association, in a presentation that focused on enlisted personnel, Charles Moskos noted, almost in passing, an "organizational shift from a predominantly institutional format to one more resembling that of an occupation."[82] By the mid-1970s he had identified the definition of military service as a calling as the individual orientation associated with the institutional format and the definition of service as a job as the orientation associated with the occupational format.[83]

I do not mean to suggest that the notion of the military as a job was new in the 1970s. Indeed, it had been anticipated by Janowitz who, in discussing the officer corps in 1960, had noted that "those who see the military as a calling or a unique profession are outnumbered by a greater concentration for whom the military is just another job."[84] Neither is this hypothesized change unique to the military. Rather, it reflects the organizational rationalization and depersonalization common in American society. Nonetheless, it may be particularly consequential for the military if, indeed, affective and collectivist bonds are necessary for effectiveness in combat.

The distinction between a calling and a job parallels that between leadership and management in a way, and it reflects the rationalization of the military. The institutional conceptualization is embedded in the traditions of military sociology and military history, and it focuses on those aspects of the military that differentiate it from civilian organizations: engagement in combat operations during wartime, a willingness among peacetime soldiers to go to war if necessary, attitudes regarding obedience to authority, the role of force in international relations, and the appropriate role of the military in domestic politics. The orientation of the military as a calling is legitimized by institutional values.

The occupational orientation, on the other hand, is rooted in the perspectives of industrial psychology and management and is legitimized by the values of the labor market. In terms of this conceptualization, a member of the armed services comes to see his service in much the same terms as does an employee in a civilian organization. Instead of being motivated to serve his country and make the world a better place, he is concerned with pay, benefits, and the quality of working life. The nature of the individual's relationship to the organization is transformed, with the traditional implied contract of mutual obligations between the service person and the service being replaced by an explicit contract in which work and time are exchanged for economic remuneration. The military installation, base, or post is seen less as a community and more as a work place, in which the uniformed employee spends only his working hours. If the nature of the employment does not meet one's expectations, one does not feel bound to serve one's obligated enlistment period; instead one feels almost as free to seek a way out of the organization as does one's counterpart in the civilian sector. During the late 1970s, more than one-third of the services' enlisted volunteers left before completing their obligated tours.

This hypothesized transition of military service to an occupation has been manifested in the recruitment strategies used by the all-volunteer services. Recruitment advertising has stressed the benefits of service that make the armed forces look good relative to civilian employers: for example, pay, training in a skill, higher educational benefits, and travel in Europe. It has played down the very factors that make the military different from civilian employers: assignment away from one's family; military training and maintenance activities that are dirty, distasteful, or boring; and the likelihood of physical danger in the event of hostilities.[85] Only recently has recruitment advertising pointed out to prospective soldiers, sailors, and airmen that "We're not a company; we're your country." And this is still not the dominant theme used in recruiting.

If Moskos is correct, there are other correlates of the occupational model that must be attended to. If military personnel are in fact becoming more and more like civilian workers, they might well be expected to seek some control over the nature of their work lives by using the same techniques as other workers do, including unionization. The Defense Department has been sufficiently concerned about this prospect to issue a regulation prohibiting it, and Congress has manifested its concern by passing legislation against military unionization. There does not yet seem to be a great deal of support for unionization among United States military personnel, but if military service does come to approximate civilian employment, the prospect of unionization cannot be discounted in the long run.[86]

Undoubtedly, both soldiers and civilians believe that military service is more like a civilian job than it used to be. A 1978 army survey asked whether soldiers had always thought of their army service primarily as a job and whether contemporary soldiers thought of their army service primarily as a job. The respondents split about evenly on the issue of whether soldiers had always thought of their service primarily as a job. However, more than 86 percent of them believed that contemporary soldiers thought of their service primarily as a job. Along similar lines, a survey of the American civilian population, conducted by the Survey Research Center at the University of Michigan in the summer of 1974, asked respondents to agree or disagree with the statement "Life in the armed forces is more like civilian life than it used to be." More than 77 percent of the respondents agreed.[87]

If the convergence of military and civilian organizations in America has indeed produced more of an occupational orientation among military personnel, then the question must be asked whether this orientation can coexist with a sense of calling and commitment or whether the two orientations are mutually exclusive. The available data do not consistently support the change that Moskos hypothesized. Rather, the studies that have been done in the context of Moskos's model show a combination of the two orientations: a posture of "pragmatic military professionalism" that reflects concerns for both individual well-being and collective national security.[88] This research has clearly shown an occupational orientation in the attitudes of personnel in the all-volunteer force. However, this orientation seems, not to have replaced a sense of calling, but to coexist with it. While military personnel policy makers and Moskos himself seem to feel that a choice between the two models must be made, the more important task may be to understand how this combined orientation can best be utilized in the interest of national security.

Among the American services, the United States Air Force has conducted the largest effort to explore this issue. Michael J. Stahl, T. Roger Manley, and Charles W. McNichols, in their research on air force personnel, suggest that a respondent could score either high on both occupational and institutional dimensions or low on both. However, they stress conceptualizations that emphasize incompatibilities between the two orientations.[89] Research on the Canadian armed forces has shown that a mixture of institutional and occupational orientations is the modal pattern.[90] And research on United States soldiers has shown that institutional and occupational orientations covary in some army units, that high scores on both dimensions characterize the modal pattern, and that noncareer soldiers tend to be institutional, rather than occupational, in their orientations toward service.[91] The issue of whether military service is a calling or a job seems not to be a dichotomous choice; rather, it seems to have evolved to the degree to which these orientations are balanced among our military personnel as they seek both to assure their economic welfare and to serve the interest of national security. The contemporary issue seems to be not whether these orientations coexist—because they do—but whether they will continue to coexist in the future. The continuity of economic concerns is virtually guaranteed by the rationalistic trends in society, which the military can be expected to reflect. The continuation of a sense of civic consciousness, however, seems to be dependent upon a set of institutions of education and socialization that themselves may be waning.[92]

Probably more crucial than whether military personnel see their service in part as a job is the issue of whether and under what conditions such personnel will go into combat. Willingness to go into combat is not in itself an indicator of combat effectiveness, but this motivational factor is a component of such effectiveness. One of the distinctive characteristics of military service as a calling, in comparison, for example, with working on an assembly line in an automobile plant, is the nature of the commitment of the individual and the nature of the consequent sacrifice that he or she might be called upon to make within the normative expectations of his job.

Under a traditional model of military service, it was expected that a soldier might be called upon to risk his life in defense of his country, particularly because under the mobilization model, the great majority of military personnel served during periods of intense conflict. One could equally expect that if an automobile manufacturer asked its labor force to take up arms and go into battle, it would meet with widespread refusals. If indeed American soldiers, in their attitudes toward their job, are coming to resemble the assembly-line workers more closely than they resemble their conscription-era counterparts, then their willingness to go into combat becomes an empirical question. We need look back only as far as the Vietnam engagement to realize that the issue of whether American military personnel will go into combat when ordered to do so is a real one.

The question is not simply whether anyone will be willing to engage in dangerous activities such as combat. In a peacetime environment, in the civilian world, there are individuals who are willing to enter high-risk occupations in return for remuneration. Indeed, there are individuals who undertake great risks in their leisure-time activities for no remuneration and frequently at great financial cost. We might find the same motivations among some people in combat jobs in the armed forces. These motivations, however, are different from those that have traditionally led large numbers of Americans to be willing to go into battle in defense of national security. If the armed forces were to be dependent primarily upon people who were willing to take risks either for remuneration or for thrills, it is unlikely that we would be able to field a viable combat force when faced with a large-scale threat.

Concerns have been raised repeatedly during the post–World War II period about whether a peacetime force-in-being, in a deterrence posture, would be able to maintain its combat readiness[93] or whether its "fighting ethic" would suffer.[94] These concerns predated the all-volunteer force, but the move to voluntarism makes them more salient. The accumulating evidence is that many soldiers in America's all-volunteer force are willing to fight. Charles W. Brown and Moskos have found some resistance to combat, particularly in unpopular wars or wars very far from home, but the great majority of the soldiers they studied expressed a willingness to do their job. This was particularly true in elite combat units, such as rangers and paratroopers.[95] The willingness among soldiers in elite units to fight has been reflected as well in studies of marines by David Burrelli and myself[96] and in studies of paratroopers by William C. Cockerham and L. E. Cohen, and by Jesse Harris, Joseph Rothberg, David Marlowe, and myself.[97] These findings are particularly important because elite combat units were volunteer units even during the days of conscription. However, most of the troops in today's all-volunteer force are not in elite units.

Moreover, there is contrary evidence, from David Gottlieb's interviews with young soldiers in the all-volunteer force, that some soldiers who regard service in the all-volunteer force as a job have not thought about going into combat as part of that job. This seems to be true even among some troops in combat specialties.[98] Gottlieb's respondents, however, were at an early stage in their army service and had not completed their organizational socialization. It may be that occupationally oriented soldiers will fight well. Research does suggest that occupational orientation alone does not seem to undermine combat readiness.[99] To date, however, the combat performance of the all-volunteer force has not been reassuring.[100]

OVERVIEW

The long-term trend toward rationality in modern industrial societies and the fact that the pendulum of values in American society has been swinging toward an emphasis on individualism for several decades had made a marked impact on the American military, which is a microcosm of its host society. The trend toward rationalization has produced differentiation and specialization of the armed forces into different service branches, each of which has relatively unique needs for personnel and capital. The specialization of military technology, in turn, has contributed to the abandonment of the militia model of a nation in arms and has substituted a conception of the military as an important segment of the labor force for the ideal of the citizen-soldier.

Rationalization has also been reflected in the adoption of civilian management strategies to run our increasingly complex and capital-intensive military establishment, and from the outset, strategies of "scientific management" involved the depersonalization of the soldier. More of the military budget has been shifted to equipment rather than personnel, and the philosophy underlying personnel policy has shifted from one of equipping the man to one of manning the equipment. Under scientific management, the soldier has become a cog in an impersonal machine.

This philosophy and the quantitative management techniques that supported it—the planning, programming, and budgeting system (PPBS) and operations research—further discounted the human components of military service, such as leadership, unit cohesion, and a commitment to national ideals, because these were difficult to measure. The military suffered from this philosophy. With the end of conscription, it found itself short of tools to man and maintain the human side of the force, and it was dependent upon the assistance of a high youth-unemployment rate in the civilian economy at the advent of the volunteer force.

The era of the all-volunteer force has seen a shift away from pure quantitative techniques of personnel management and toward the adoption of a stronger human-relations orientation. This orientation, however, has been based on a labor market model of the force and has, until very recently, simply added quality-of-life incentives to purely economic incentives as vehicles for motivating people to join and remain in the armed forces. This incentive structure, to the extent that it is successful, may bring enough people into the military and may even contribute to improving the quality of the people at high-enough levels of compensation. It also contributes strongly to the redefinition of military service as a job, similar to employment in the civilian labor force. Without paying attention to the traditional intangibles of leadership, cohesion, and national commitment, however, the ability of the force to fight and win wars may in the long run be problematic. At present, the combination of an occupational view of the military—which reflects manpower policy—with a traditional view of the military mission—that, like all traditions, has an inertia of its own—have substituted in place of the citizen-soldier a pragmatic military professional who is willing to go to war.

The pragmatic component will continue to exist, reinforced by dominant social values and by the recruitment and reenlistment appeals used by the services. The continuation of the professionalism component, which reflects a sense of military mission, cannot be as easily assumed. The problem of developing a sense of national commitment is particularly acute, because this function is not primarily the responsibility of the military and because the institution that once performed it—the school system—now does so with less enthusiasm if at all.

Organizational-development strategies adopted from the civilian sector during the 1970s addressed primarily issues of management and job satisfaction, rather than leadership, cohesion, and commitment. That they did not improve these factors, then, is not surprising. Neither is there evidence that they improved management or job satisfaction. The latter dimension at best remained constant during the first decade of the all-volunteer force—a decade during which the defense establishment came under an unprecedented level of criticism for mismanagement. Recent initiatives within the military, which were not adopted from the civilian sector but which recognize the unique nature of the military institution, show initial signs of success.

Another manifestation of societal rationality—with positive as well as negative consequences for the military—has been the rise of the welfare state, to be discussed in the next chapter. While contributing to a more pragmatically individualistic and less cohesive military, these two trends have also contributed to the establishment of a military-personnel philosophy that during the era of the all-volunteer force, has been based more and more on the abilities of people and on the fit between those abilities and the needs of the services and less on the ascriptive characteristics of the personnel. Thus the racial integration of the military, which began during the early 1950s, made major gains during the 1970s and the 1980s. So, too, were there major changes in the patterns of utilizing female personnel, although here, social values and military organization have been slower to change. Constraints on gender-equal utilization seem rooted largely in traditional images of ground combat, and as warfare becomes more capital intensive and places opposing combatants at greater distance from each other, requires less physical strength, and in fact blurs the distinction between soldiers and civilians, the issue of gender may become moot. Certainly if we move toward a system of national service as a citizenship obligation, it will be difficult to maintain gender differentials without admitting that there are two classes of citizenship. In any case, the nation is likely to face increasing demands from economically disadvantaged segments of society for recognition that military employment is a right of citizens. These issues will be discussed in chapter 5.

4
The Welfare State
and Military Service

The single greatest institutional reconfiguration in industrial societies during the past century has been the advent of the welfare state: that is, the assumption by the state of responsibility for guaranteeing its citizens—and, increasingly, residents who are not citizens—certain "minimum standards of living in terms of income maintenance, health and nutrition, education, and housing."[1] Structurally, this has led to the development of new social institutions to fulfill this responsibility. Ideologically, it has led to the increased legitimacy of a sense of collective responsibility for the public good.[2]

The development of welfare states was a logical sequel to and was dependent upon the advent of nation-states. However, consensus has not been achieved on the legitimacy of the welfare state, the means through which its goals are to be achieved, or the degree to which the benefits of citizenship are to be tied to citizenship responsibility. A commitment both to the principle of the welfare state and to the institutions that it supports are issues of continuing policy debate.

As noted in chapter 1, most analyses of the modern welfare state see its precursor in the "liberal" programs of Otto von Bismarck in Germany during the 1880s—programs that can as easily be interpreted as conservative attempts to preempt more radically socialistic policies. The German initiatives were followed fairly quickly by governmentally assured programs of assistance and social reform in other European nations. From this perspective, the United States, in comparison to the nations of Western Europe, has been viewed as a laggard in the development of programs for national income, health, education, and housing. The very processes that hampered the development of a national armed force—the issue of states' rights and the high social value placed on individualism—were seen as obstacles to the growth of national institutions of social welfare as well.

From this critical perspective the conception of the welfare state in the United States is viewed as having taken place during the Great Depression, and its birth is marked as the Social Security Act of 1935. Its growth is then charted during the post–World War II period, during which major programs of income redistribution were established in the United States. This is consistent with Harold D. Lasswell's "garrison state" model—also discussed in chapter 1—which viewed income redistribution as essential to the reduction of opposition to an increasingly militarized and mobilized state from underprivileged segments of society.

In contrast, my thesis in this chapter is that the development of the welfare state in the United States predated by two decades the growth of welfare institutions in Europe, despite the fact that the United States had not attained the level of nationhood found on the European continent. In conformity with the value placed upon individualism in America, however, the welfare policies that were initiated in the United States were initially earned benefits, rather than entitlements. These "rights of citizenship" were received in exchange for sacrifices made in the fulfillment of "obligations of citizenship," although beginning with the Civil War pension system, sacrifice became less important as a criterion. The most important citizenship obligation was that of military service, and this factor was what was replaced in the American welfare system, first by the fulfillment of other obligations, then, more recently, by the concept of entitlements.

Social Security, the first major civilian program of the American welfare state that was not associated with military service, reflected the value of individualism in that it was to be a contributory system, providing benefits for those who fulfilled the obligation of being gainfully employed. Moreover, it was expected to be short-lived. The principle of benefits in exchange for military service to the state was manifested strongly in the first major federal educational-assistance program aimed at students—the post–World War II GI Bill of Rights. This program, as well as many subsequent elements of the American welfare state, incorporated the value of individualism. In the short run, it provided cash benefits in return for services rendered. In the longer run, however, it was aimed at helping veterans become competitive in the labor market.

There is no question but that in the post–World War II United States there have been major increases in the size and scope of federal welfare programs. What is more important than these changes in scale is that during this period, the assumption that citizenship rights were to be earned through the fulfillment of citizenship obligations was replaced—gradually and perhaps temporarily—by the assumption that entitlements—frequently in the form of cash grants—were due to people by virtue of their presence in society—an assumption that itself is rooted in post–Civil War developments that broadened the definition of sacrifice and extended benefits to the dependents of those who had made sacrifices. This has contributed to the system that the economist Kenneth E. Boulding has referred to as the "grant economy," in which economically unproductive members of society—such as children, the aged, and the ill—are supported by the transfer of goods and services to them.

The grant economy and the development of social-welfare institutions in general presume both that society has a sense of collective responsibility and that it will produce a sufficient economic surplus to allow resources to be transferred to economically unproductive segments of society. These conditions were clearly met in the post–Civil War period. With America in the throes of its industrial revolution, entitlements were affordable. As economic growth has slowed during the twentieth century and as federal deficits have been growing during the last quarter of the century, it is not surprising to find questions being raised about the magnitude of the entitlement system and about the appropriateness of entitlements that do not require some service. In short, the United States as a nation is rethinking the balance between exchange and grants in its welfare system, and military service has reemerged as an important arena of exchange.

Boulding has suggested that the grant economy increases social cohesion, in contrast to the individualizing effects of exchange economies.[3] Ironically, although the military has effectively used such programs to produce cohesion through "taking care of its own," Boulding does not regard such expenditures as a legitimate use of the grant economy, because he sees military expenditures as neither positive nor beneficial to society.[4] This ideological position appears frequently in analyses of the military in the welfare state. However, the American welfare state has never been a pure grant economy. In large measure, except in the cases of the unemployable and of dependents who have been deprived of breadwinners, it is aimed at providing jobs or job training, rather than long-term cash support. The military, as a major employer for less-advantaged segments of society and as a provider of training for civilian jobs, is an important part of the institutional structure of the social-welfare system.

Initially, in the United States, military benefits were available only to those who had made the greatest sacrifices such as disability benefits for those who had been injured and survivors' benefits for the dependents of those who had died. These benefits were then broadened to provide for those who had served but had not been injured and for their dependents and survivors. After World War II a much broader benefit program was made available to veterans under the first GI Bill of Rights. All of these programs were tied to military service and could thus be viewed as exchanges.

Subsequent welfare programs linked neither to disability nor to service have shifted the balance from an exchange economy toward a grant economy and have contributed to the aforementioned GI bill without the GI. In the all-volunteer-force era, with an increasing percentage of married military personnel and with indications that the happiness of service families affects both the retention and the performance of personnel, the defense establishment has attempted to increase family benefits in the interest of retaining personnel. There is a basis in equity for such programs: family members share with military personnel many of the disadvantages of service. Thus, benefits are exchanged for service. However, much less federal money is currently being allocated for welfare benefits for military personnel and their dependents than is allocated as entitlements for those who are not required to serve—that is, people who are neither in the armed forces nor dependent upon those who are.

The recipients of these entitlements, in turn, have come to be represented by interest groups—another derivative of the post–Civil War period. These groups are frequently based upon ascriptive characteristics, and their participation in the political process in pursuit of their members' entitlements has affected a wide range of policies. These include military manpower policy, as a guaranteed job has come to be viewed as an entitlement and as military service has come to be a major source of employment, particularly for socioeconomically disadvantaged groups. The participation of these interest groups in the political process, side by side with interest groups representing firms and industries that provide goods and services to the military establishment, may contribute to national fragmentation and to economic decline through the grant economy, rather than provide the national cohesion that Boulding envisaged.[5]

POST-CIVIL WAR: DISABILITY
AND SURVIVORS' BENEFITS

Historically the United States has granted pension benefits to soldiers who have been mobilized during times of conflict. Because the numbers of people involved in conflicts had been relatively small and because benefits had been legislatively restricted to those who had actually served in combat or had service-related disabilities, the benefit programs prior to the Civil War had been small. In 1840, less than 4 percent of Americans over the age of sixty were receiving federal military pensions.[6] The programs that had been established were firmly rooted in a principle of compensation for sacrifices made in defense of the state. The Civil War, which involved a massive mobilization and our first national draft, redefined the role of the state as a provider of benefits for veterans and their survivors.

The Civil War pension system, established in 1862, was initially consistent with the principle of benefits earned through sacrifice and was intended to provide compensation only to soldiers who had been permanently disabled as a direct consequence of service in the Union army, and to the widows and children of Union soldiers who had died as a result of injury or illness sustained during military service.

Initial disbursements under the program were modest and remained fairly stable during the decade of the 1870s. However, the size of the Civil War mobilization had produced a generation of veterans who were not entitled to pensions under the death or disability criterion but who constituted a significant proportion of the electorate. Both political parties in the North sought to woo voters with more readily available benefits, and in 1879, disbursements increased markedly when the Arrears of Pension Act authorized lump-sum payments of accumulated benefits to soldiers who had registered belatedly to receive pension benefits. A special-interest group, the Grand Army of the Republic (GAR), mobilized the veteran population and pressed for further liberalization; and the impact of the veterans' vote on the congressional and presidential elections of 1888 turned the tide.[7]

In 1890 a new Civil War pension law extended benefits to veterans who had served at least ninety days in the Union army or navy during the war, had been honorably discharged, and had subsequently become disabled. The disability did not have to be service-related, although disabilities due to a veteran's "own vicious habits" were disqualified; and in 1906, attainment of the age of sixty-two was legislatively defined as a disability within the intent of the pension law. The criteria for receipt of benefits were thus made less stringent, and disability entitlement became an old-age-insurance system for almost 760,000 former soldiers, as did a more broadly based survivors' benefit program, which expanded as the number of veterans was reduced by mortality. The cost of the precedent that was set by broadening the definition of disability will be felt most severely a century after the legislation, as more and more veterans of the massive mobilization for World War II and the smaller mobilization for the Korean War, who tend to live longer than did Civil War veterans, reach retirement age and its associated health problems.

Other benefits related to military service, such as the provision of housing, were later extended to the civilian dependents of military personnel. Most recently, Congress has debated but not approved the transfer to the civilian dependents of the service person of educational benefits earned through military service. This remains a live contemporary issue, as the primary function of military-related educational benefits has changed from a recognition of sacrifices made and costs incurred to a motivation for military enlistment and retention.

In 1890, when the provision that disability be service-related was deleted from the law, only about 10 percent of Union veterans had reached the age of sixty-five. Most were middle-aged. By 1891, however, the Bureau of Pensions had grown to become the largest executive agency in the world, with more than six thousand employees; and by 1893, pensions made up 42 percent of all federal expenditures. At the beginning of the twentieth century, most Union veterans were in their sixties or older, and there were nearly a million veterans and survivors on the pension lists. In 1913, although the number of veterans was declining because of deaths, pension outlays were still climbing, and about two-thirds of native white males aged sixty-five or over who lived outside of the South were drawing federal veterans' benefits.[8]

It is important to note that this early massive social-insurance program had relatively little impact on the most disadvantaged segments of the American population, thus reflecting the fact that the country was still in a transitional phase on its way to nationhood and the welfare state. Blacks, by virtue of their exclusion from military service for most of the war, were excluded from the pension system as well. The immigrants who provided America's growing industrial work force had arrived after the war for the most part. And southerners, who were coping with the postbellum economic stagnation of their region, had lost the war. The recipients of Civil War veterans' pensions were disproportionately either northern white rural landowners or members of the urban middle class.

The military-pension system has grown to be a major federal expenditure and has been subjected to frequent policy debate;[9] and it was changed in the mid-1980s as it applied to new military personnel. Currently, career military personnel are eligible to retire after twenty years of active duty and, with few exceptions, must retire with no more than thirty years of active duty. Because they tend to enter the military when they are between eighteen and twenty-two years of age, they retire at an age that would be mid-career in most civilian occupations—in their mid-forties. This system provides an incentive for people to leave active duty rather than remain, and it builds into the federal budget a large expenditure for "retired pay"— that is, compensation for not being on active military duty.

Expenditures for retired pay, which fluctuated between 1 and 2 percent of the defense budget between 1947 and 1962 (in current dollars) and which did not exceed 4 percent until 1971, reached almost 10 percent of defense expenditures in the early 1980s. They now constitute more than 6 percent of the defense budget; the percentage decline since early in the decade reflects not a decrease in absolute retirement costs, but an absolute increase in other military expenditures, primarily in budget elements other than personnel costs. During this period, costs for active-duty personnel declined from more than 40 percent of the defense budget to less than 20 percent, despite the maintenance of a large peacetime force-in-being, as expenditures were shifted away from people toward military hardware. This shift, of course, has implications for the institutional position of the military as an element of the welfare state.

Recent changes in the military-retirement system may in the long run help to bring its increasing costs under control. However, in the interest of honoring commitments to personnel who were on active duty before the change, the plan contained a "grandfather clause," which allows personnel who were already in the military to retire under the existing system. Major savings will not be realized for almost four decades, because military personnel who entered the service prior to the change and who remained for at least twenty years begin to draw benefits under it when they retire and will continue to draw such benefits until they die.[10]

In addition to debate about the cost of the military-retirement system, the 1980s saw the emergence as an interest group of divorced military spouses, who claim access to their former spouses' military retired pay as part of divorce settlements, because they have shared the hardships of military life that justified their spouses' retired pay. As the percentage of military personnel who are married increases and as divorce becomes more common, former spouses' access to military benefits will continue to be a legal and political issue and will highlight the general trend, without judging it, of extending benefits to those who have not served directly. Indeed, in 1982, the Uniformed Services Former Spouses Protection Act extended medical care, commissary privileges, and exchange privileges to unremarried former spouses who were divorced after February 1, 1983.

WORLD WAR I: HOUSING FOR DEPENDENTS

Prior to World War I, army and navy officers were either assigned to quarters or were given an allowance for quarters, but family size was not a determinant for the assignments of quarters or for allowances. Civilian dependents, of course, lived in officers' quarters, but there was no assumption that they were entitled to living space. They simply occupied a portion of the officers' quarters, as did his material possessions. Prior to the twentieth century, unlike officers, enlisted personnel were not married and therefore did not need family housing.

Formal legislation establishing the basis for quarters allowances for army officers was passed in 1878 and for navy officers, in 1899; but in neither case was family size considered a basis for the allowance. The benefit of housing for a military officer did not formally extend to his family. Neither was family size a criterion when the first legislation authorizing quarters allowances for enlisted personnel was passed in 1915. As had been the case with the pension system, women became the recipients of benefits only through their association with men who served in the military.

On April 16, 1918, a temporary World War I measure was the first to recognize family size as a basis for quarters allowances in determining the number of rooms for which an officer was authorized. This act recognized that dependents, as well as the military members of their families, had specific needs for space and shelter. The provisions of the 1918 act were extended by later legislation until the early 1940s.

In 1940, allowances recognizing family size and need were authorized for the top three enlisted grades. The Pay Readjustment Act of 1942 changed the basis for housing allowances from the number of rooms for which personnel were eligible to a combination of pay grade and family status. The current system of rental allowances was developed in 1949; it extended family housing allowances to all personnel at the rank of sergeant or above, with allowances for lower-ranking personnel being made at a "without dependent" level. That exemption was relaxed during the Korean conflict by the Dependents' Assistance Act of 1950. Several subsequent readjustments have been made over time in an attempt to assure that military personnel and their dependents will be provided with housing that is roughly equivalent to what they would have if they were all civilians. This has led to increased expenditures for family housing, although the defense establishment still falls far short of providing on-post housing for all military families, and the location of families off-post has implications for military cohesion.

Before World War II, enlisted personnel tended not to be married, but the proportion of married personnel increased steadily thereafter, with a brief decline during the Vietnam War. The percentage of enlisted personnel who were married was 33 in 1953, 48 in 1960, and approached 60 by the late 1970s. In the 1980s, military personnel have been marrying at a younger age than their civilian peers.[11] Expenditures for family housing were less than 0.1 percent of the defense budget during the 1950s, moved toward 1 percent in the 1960s, and have been slightly above 1 percent during the 1970s and the 1980s. Responsibility for the continued housing needs of service people was built into the first GI Bill of Rights, and the Veterans Administration's home-loan-guarantee program is the second most widely used benefit (after educational benefits) among American veterans, with about one-third of veterans participating.

The increase in military families produced requirements for family medical benefits as well. Historically, medical care was provided to military dependents on a space-available basis, and availability varied greatly according to time and place. The provision of medical care to dependents was officially authorized during World War II, but it was still on a space-available basis, and during the war, virtually all space was dedicated to the treatment of active-duty personnel.

It was not until 1956 that the Dependents' Medical Care Act provided the first statutory basis for the provision of medical care to military dependents, as well as retirees, retirees' dependents, and retirees' survivors. The act authorized the secretary of defense to contract with civilian sources for the provision of health and medical care to military dependents. Ten years later, the Military Medical Benefits Act established the CHAMPUS program, which was basically a medicare program for the civilian dependents of military personnel, and in 1971 the program was expanded to include certain surviving dependents of servicemen. It has been revised periodically since then, and the military has been experimenting with other ways of providing for the health-care needs of members of military families.

THE MILITARY AS A WELFARE SYSTEM

Although married military personnel and concomitant family benefits did not become widespread in the United States until the second half of the twentieth century, it is clear that programs aimed at the fulfillment of welfare functions—such as social insurance, housing, medical care, education, and so forth—have developed within the military system and have become increasingly important parts of that system. What is less obvious is that benefits tied to military service, which itself was seen as a manifestation of citizenship, played an important role in legitimizing the principle of welfare and in maintaining the citizenship rights of welfare recipients.

The problems that welfare institutions address are not new. Societies have historically had to find the means to provide for the ill, the infirm, the aged, orphaned children, and other categories of people who could not provide their own sustenance. In the civilian sector, prior to the advent of the welfare state, it was commonly felt that people were responsible for their lot in life, and if they became dependent upon others, it was due to laziness, stupidity, or sloth. Social institutions were established to deal with such people. They were institutions in the physical as well as sociological sense of that term—for example, poor houses; and their inhabitants forfeited many rights and perquisites of ordinary citizenship. They were constrained in where they could live and in the kinds of work they could do or were required to do; and they were limited in their legal recourse.[12]

The military traditionally functioned as a welfare institution to the extent that it provided a locus for segments of the population that were not easily assimilated into the structure of civilian society—for example, the unemployed. While as a nation the United States emphasizes and celebrates the "minuteman" image of the early militia, it is clear, as I noted in chapter 2, that this image is largely a myth. The militia system did not work. The early American military was manned largely by people who could not find employment in the civilian sector or who saw in military service a means of achieving geographic mobility from places where there were no jobs—primarily in the East—to areas where there were job opportunities—primarily on the western frontier—at governmental expense.[13] For these people, army service was not a bad job in comparison to available civilian employment opportunities.

Myths and legends are not simply lies. They fill social needs, and they legitimize social institutions and processes by reflecting social ideals and values. The myth of a citizenry's fulfilling an obligation of citizenship and defending the common security, rather than regarding the military as an employer of last resort, differentiated the army from other early institutions that fulfilled social-welfare functions. Whereas the clients of other welfare institutions were regarded as less than full citizens, military personnel were regarded as good citizens.

Clients of other institutions who were taken care of because they were outside the productive economy were looked down upon, whereas military personnel were cloaked in the social honor that derived from their association with the military institution and the myths that legitimized it.[14] Because benefits that were received—whether housing, medical care, education, or disability insurance—were regarded as earned entitlements in exchange for the fulfillment of a citizenship obligation, the soldier was not looked down upon for accepting them. And as the exchange nexus broadened, benefits were extended without stigma from those who had been disabled, to those who had served but had not been disabled, to the dependents and survivors of servicemen, to veterans, to the dependents and survivors of veterans, and most recently, to the former spouses of those who had served or were serving.

THE WELFARE STATE AND CITIZENSHIP RIGHTS

Prior to the Great Depression, recipients of public welfare—other than those whose benefits were based on military service—were stigmatized by the benefits and services that they received. They became less than full citizens. The growth of civilian welfare institutions during the 1930s and thereafter is not remarkable so much because new institutions were established as because the receipt of benefits came increasingly to be viewed as an entitlement due to a person by virtue of membership in a social group and not as dependent upon the fulfillment of citizenship obligations. Rather than receiving benefits simply because one was an individual citizen and rather than having one's citizenship challenged on the basis of receipt of those benefits, people received benefits because they were members of specific constituencies, for whose well-being specific governmental agencies were responsible: farmers, organized labor, small businessmen, and so forth.[15] The citizenship of recipients of such constituency-based benefits was not degraded by having received them,[16] although many people still view the receipt of welfare benefits based on individual citizenship rights, rather than interest-group membership, as being personally degrading.

In chapter 1, I noted the ongoing citizenship revolution which is extending the rights of citizenship to ever-expanding categories of people who had previously been excluded. I also noted that military service has been an obligation of citizenship and a way of achieving citizenship rights. One of the citizenship rights that has evolved is an expectation that the state will provide material protection (a) when risks are taken in the name of the state, as in the case of benefits earned through military service in wartime; (b) when actions of the state put individuals at risk beyond their means to avoid it or the capacity of private means of insurance to protect against it, as in the case of civilians in wartime; or (c) when their property is threatened by domestic events beyond their ability to avoid or insure against, as in economic depressions. The expansion of the welfare state is the twentieth-century response to these expectations.[17]

As I noted earlier, both the issue of states' rights and the value placed upon individualism hampered the advent of national social-welfare institutions in the United States prior to the Great Depression. Nonetheless, by 1935 the United States was allocating about 10 percent of its gross national product to welfare services—the level that has been used to identify welfare states elsewhere in the world.[18] This amounted to almost 50 percent of total governmental expenditures.

By 1933, the economic depression that had begun in 1929 had left 16 million people—about one-third of the total labor force—unemployed, and the gross national product had declined by 48 billion between 1929 and 1933. President Roosevelt's New Deal programs in response to the massive economic dislocation provided the infrastructure that extended federal welfare benefits to large numbers of people who were not military personnel, veterans, or military dependents. Jobs were provided under agencies that were established to help stabilize the economy, such as the Civilian Conservation Corps (CCC), in the administration of which the military played a major role; the Public Works Administration (PWA); and later, the Works Projects Administration (WPA).

In addition to providing employment and income, some of these agencies, such as the CCC, reinforced the principle of national service, and all suggested that during hard economic times, the federal government would become an employer of last resort. Moreover, the provision of jobs and income was complemented by New Deal social-insurance programs, such as the National Housing Act and the Social Security Act, which extended welfare-state benefits to those who were not employed under federal jobs programs. The economy was indeed stabilized, although complete business recovery was not achieved and massive unemployment was not ended until the 1940s, when large numbers of people were absorbed by the armed forces and when the federal government began to spend heavily on defense to meet the economic mobilization needs of World War II.

THE GI BILL AS SOCIAL WELFARE

Just as demobilization after the Civil War had produced a major broadening of the constituency for federal benefits, so was the Servicemen's Readjustment Act of 1944, a result of the post–World War II demobilization, to become the major basis of welfare expenditures for almost two decades. Faced with the demobilization of millions of young men who would flood the labor force of a recently repaired economy, who would be junior in terms of job seniority and educational attainment to their peers who had not served in the armed forces during the war and who might resent being economically disadvantaged because they had served their country, the United States established a massive program of education and training for veterans at governmental expense; government-guaranteed loans for homes, farms, and businesses; a system of job counseling and placement; and medical-care benefits that have served as the basis for the largest hospital system in the world.

As suggested above, the provision of medical services to military veterans will be a major political issue in the United States during the 1990s, as the aging of the veteran population from the mobilizations of World War II and the Korean War begin to overload the existing system and to increase the cost to the taxpayers of benefits provided. The number of veterans aged sixty-five and over was about 2.9 million in 1980 and about 5 million in 1985. It will reach about 7.2 million in 1990, when more than half of American men aged sixty-five and over will be veterans. The nation will have to determine the degree to which it will continue to provide medical care to veterans whose ailments may not be related to their military service, but it will have to do so in the face of an increasingly powerful veterans' lobby.

The educational benefit program did achieve its short-term objectives. Almost 8 million World War II veterans—more than half of the total eligible population—received training under the first GI bill. This reduced pressure on the employment system and improved the veterans' competitive position in the labor force. A second Veterans' Readjustment Assistance Act for Korean War veterans was passed in 1952, and more than 2 million veterans—or about 43 percent of the eligible population—participated in training programs under this support. In 1966 a third act was passed, to cover personnel who had served at least 180 days during the post-Korea cold-war period, and who had received honorable discharges.

This was the first GI bill that was explicitly intended primarily to provide benefits for veterans who had not served during wartime, although it ultimately covered veterans of the Vietnam War. More than a million veterans of the cold-war period—about 46 percent of the eligible population—were trained under the GI bill, as were almost 7 million Vietnam-era veterans—a record 72 percent of the eligible population. However, as we shall see below, the Vietnam-era veterans did not profit as much in comparison to their peers who did not serve as their predecessors had, in part because of changes in the availability of educational benefits that were not related to military service.

Research comparing veterans with their peers who did not serve in the military has demonstrated that prior to the Vietnam War period, veterans received higher levels of education than their nonveteran peers, and much of the difference could be credited to the educational benefits of the GI bills.[19] These differences, in turn, were reflected in differences in income in the civilian labor market.

Some economists have suggested that military service has a negative impact on subsequent earnings because military service delays or interupts a civilian career.[20] This is precisely the kind of effect that the framers of the first GI bill were seeking to avoid, and the evidence suggests that they were in the main successful during the pre-Vietnam period. A series of studies has shown that veterans from the World War II and Korean War periods earn more than their nonveteran counterparts, other things being equal, and that these positive effects are greatest for groups that have been disadvantaged in the civilan labor market: blacks, hispanics, and women.[21] Thus, military service can be thought of as contributing to the subsequent welfare of veterans in general and of veterans who are members of disadvantaged groups in particular.

The picture changes with regard to Vietnam veterans. Of all groups of veterans, Vietnam veterans have had the highest rate of utilization of the educational benefits of the GI bill. More than 72 percent of Vietnam-era veterans utilized their educational benefits, as compared to 50 percent or less of earlier veteran groups. Moreover, a far greater percentage of Vietnam veterans used their GI-bill benefits specifically for college educations, instead of other kinds of training, than did earlier veterans. More than 45 percent of Vietnam-era veterans used their benefits for college, as compared to 15 percent of World War II veterans, 22 percent of Korean War veterans, and 24 percent of post–Korean War veterans. Yet Vietnam era veterans, although they were better educated than the veterans of earlier wars, achieved less education than did their peers who did not serve and thus did not achieve an advantaged position in the civilian labor force. Their educational benefits did not offset the costs of their absence from civilian careers during military service.

The educational benefits of the GI bill were discontinued during the first decade of the all-volunteer force, because a volunteer force was presumed to impose a lesser degree of sacrifice on those who served than had conscription and because noncontributory educational benefits were not seen as a cost-effective incentive for recruitment. With the escalating cost of higher education, the widespread availability of educational-assistance programs that were not tied to service, the decrease in the size of the age group that was eligible for the military, and the desire of the services to recruit larger percentages of higher-mental-category personnel to man increasingly sophisticated weapons, a new GI bill was established in 1985, not to reward personnel who had served, but to induce civilian youths to serve. However, it was a contributory system.

THE 1960S AND THE EXPANSION
OF THE AMERICAN WELFARE STATE

Military veterans of World War II and the Korean War who returned to civilian society in the United States prior to the 1960s reentered a system in which welfare was a relatively small part of the budget, despite its short-term growth during the depression. Federal expenditures for welfare programs, including transfer payments to individuals as well as grants-in-aid to state and local governments, had fallen from about half the budget in 1935 to less than a third in 1955. In 1950, veterans programs still accounted for about 30 percent of public expenditures for social welfare. Higher education was still the exception rather than the rule in the young adult population, and benefits of the GI bill were the major source of grant support for higher education. Much of the welfare state still consisted of benefits that were received in exchange for military service.

During the early 1950s, between 14 and 15 percent of young adults were enrolling in institutions of higher education—a lower figure than the percentage of veterans who were using GI-bill benefits to go to colleges or universities. About 0.5 percent of the federal budget was devoted to educational programs that were not associated with military service. More than 7 percent was allocated to veterans' programs. The GI bill was the major element of the American welfare state during this period. Expenditures for veterans benefits exceeded nonveteran federal expenditures for health, education, housing, and community development into the 1960s.

The 1960s saw a change in this pattern. Spending priorities were shaped not only by the war in Vietnam but also by the War against Poverty and by President Lyndon Johnson's quest for a Great Society. Whereas President John F. Kennedy had asked Americans what they could do for society, groups within the citizenry asked Johnson what society could do for them. Previously neglected interests, some of which had been brought together by their common opposition to the Vietnam War, became mobilized as social movements seeking access to various citizenship rights and entitlements. Most notable were the civil-rights movement and the women's movement, which demanded and received increased educational and employment opportunities for their constituencies. Ironically, this expansion of welfare programs in response to domestic pressure from groups associated with the antiwar movement was supplemented by expansion in response to more bellicose international pressures as well. Advances by the Soviet Union in technologies with military applications led to domestic educational programs, such as the National Defense Education Act of 1954, which were intended to contribute to national security by upgrading the technological capabilities of the nation by providing support for civilian higher education in science and other defense-related fields.

From 1950 to 1960, public expenditures for social welfare hovered around 38 percent of the federal budget. By 1970, they were up to 48 percent. Between 1935 and 1973—the year of the advent of the all-volunteer military force—federal expenditures for educational assistance not tied to military service were increased twenty times. Unlike the period of industrial expansion following the Civil War or the economic revitalization of World War II, however, this growth in the welfare state occurred in the absence of more general economic expansion.

It is wise to remember that even during the Vietnam War, the military was used explicitly as a social-welfare institution, to provide job training, not grants. This was consistent with many other welfare programs of the 1960s, such as the Job Corps. In the summer of 1964, shortly after the Tonkin Gulf Resolution, the Defense Department announced plans to accept for service eleven thousand volunteers who would not qualify for military service under the then-current physical and mental standards and who presumably were not employable or were only marginally employable in the civilian labor force. Special resources would be invested in the training and rehabilitation of these men. However, Congress refused to authorize the $16 million that President Johnson requested for the training program for these men.

Undaunted, in 1966, Defense Secretary Robert McNamara had initiated Project 100,000. This program was designed to bring into the armed forces each year 100,000 underprivileged youths who previously would have been rejected for service on mental or physical grounds and who presumably would likewise be unemployable or marginally employable in the civilian labor force as well. The armed forces, according to the plan, would teach these youths skills, discipline, and self-confidence and would thus reduce unemployment, raise the earning potential of participants, and make them eligible for veterans' benefits—welfare programs that did not carry the stigma of benefits programs that did not involve service.[22]

About 240,000 men were brought into the military under Project 100,000. The social-welfare goals of the program were not achieved however. Again, Congress failed to provide special training funds, so volunteers for Project 100,000 received standard military training in which, in competition with higher-aptitude youths, many had failure experiences.

The armed forces were not about to provide expensive technical training to personnel with a low mental aptitude, so a disproportionate number ended up in the ground combat forces, where they were disproportionately exposed to the risks of war. Outside of combat, they were disproportionately used in unskilled jobs. In neither case did they receive training that would be applicable in the civilian labor force. Not surprisingly, they did appear disproportionately on the rolls of military delinquents, including deserters.[23] These were not consequences that had been discussed when Project 100,000 was initiated. Thus was the War on Poverty used to fight the war in Vietnam. While some of the alumni of Project 100,000 were successful, in the aggregate these volunteers contributed to the statistical disadvantage of Vietnam veterans by swelling the ranks of the veterans with people who were not likely to succeed educationally or to compete effectively in the civilian labor market.

Whereas in the early 1950s the veterans were entering a labor force in which fewer than 15 percent of young adults were getting college educations, by 1960 the figure was higher than 20 percent, and in 1973, when the draft was ended, it was one-third of the young-adult population, in large part because of expanded civilian educational benefit programs based on considerations of welfare or national security. And whereas veterans of the Vietnam War, despite Project 100,000, were making more use of the GI bill than had earlier veterans and were achieving higher levels of education than had earlier veterans, they were, for the first time in history, unable to keep pace educationally with their nonveteran peers, despite the formers' access to and utilization of GI bill benefits. This is not to say that veterans' benefits decreased. In fact, they grew in absolute terms as part of the general expansion of the American welfare state. However, they grew at a slower rate than did nonveterans' benefits. In 1950, veterans programs and educational programs that were not tied to military service each accounted for about 28 percent of public-welfare expenditures. By 1960, veterans programs had declined to 10 percent, and civilian educational programs had increased to 34 percent. In 1973, when conscription was ended, veterans programs were down to 6 percent, and civilian educational programs were 30 percent of public-welfare expenditures. Three years later, the post–Korean-War GI bill lapsed.

GUNS, BUTTER, AND POLITICAL
PRESSURE ON THE BUDGET

During the last decades of the twentieth century, the United States is facing a continued demand for high welfare expenditures both from groups who think that the past receipt of entitlements justifies the continuation of established patterns—such as farmers, unemployed industrial workers, and military veterans—and from groups who think that they are due entitlements because they have *not* received their fair share in the past, such as minority ethnic groups and military spouses. Given the nature of the American political system, the allocation of welfare benefits will in all likelihood be determined less by objective standards of need or contributions to planned economic expansion than by political and social definitions of welfare requirements.[24] Members of groups who demand welfare benefits, who exhibit the behavior that is sometimes disruptive of the social order but who can be appeased by benefit programs, will become beneficiaries of the grant economy, as will constituencies to which political authorities owe allegiance or to which they seek to appeal. In an era of slow economic expansion and budget deficits, when not all parties can receive what they desire, the grant economy is likely to produce fragmentation and one-issue constituencies, rather than the social cohesion that Boulding envisaged. In most cases the economy will provide benefits that are not tied to citizenship obligations.

These claims to welfare benefits will have to compete for budget dollars with programs for national defense. And defense funds must themselves be apportioned between personnel expenditures—many of which, such as medical, educational, and job training programs, as well as salary costs under some assumptions of the nature of military service, can be viewed as welfare spending—and military hardware, which is less easy to justify as welfare costs except to the extent that it creates jobs for the employees of defense contractors who otherwise, in a more rational system of selecting and pricing weapons, might be unemployed.

One could of course reasonably argue that national security is a public good and that necessary military expenditures in its pursuit are, *sui generis,* welfare expenditures. Indeed, analyses of military conflicts up through World War II have suggested that national mobilizations—particularly the one for World War II—have contributed to the development of the welfare state.[25] During the postwar period, however, there has not been consensus about what constitutes necessary military expenditures, and the maintenance of large standing forces in peacetime has been hypothesized to restrict welfare expenditures. Harold L. Wilensky, for example, has shown that for the period 1950 to 1966, great increases in military spending were associated with smaller increases in social-security spending and that those countries that spent the most on defense in the early 1950s showed almost no social-security increase during that period.[26] Of course, as I noted above, the greatest growth in United States expenditures for welfare occurred later. Albert Szymanski has calculated that the ratio of federal social expenditures to military expenditures was .48:1 in 1960, .89:1 in 1970, and 2.26:1 in 1979.[27]

The Vietnam War era produced a number of analyses suggesting that choices had to be made—and had been made—between guns and butter and that the United States had opted for weapons rather than welfare.[28] Assuming, for the moment, the validity of the distinction between defense and welfare, I suggest that these analyses are more ideological than economic; they reflect positions similar to Boulding's, noted above, with regard to military expenditures. They manifested opposition to the Vietnam War and opposition to conscription more than they reflect true economic trends.[29] They also expressed concerns about the military-industrial complex, and here there is some validity to their claims, not necessarily because the military-industrial complex is evil, as they are prone to assume, but because defense industries, which are beneficiaries of the grant economy, have contributed to economic inefficiency that has become increasingly difficult to tolerate in a limited-growth economy. Indeed, after extensive media coverage of overpricing and potential fraud by major contractors for defense hardware in 1985, Defense Secretary Caspar W. Weinberger appointed a subcabinet-level "procurement czar," who was responsible for correcting widespread abuses in that sphere.

The basic facts on guns-vs.-butter expenditures duing the post–World War II period seem to have been as follows:[30]

(a) The defense budget did increase during the Korean War and the Vietnam War. In terms of constant dollars, it dropped between the wars in Korea and Vietnam and during the post-Vietnam years, but it increased under the Reagan administration. In terms of absolute dollars, it increased massively, from $12 billion in 1950 to about $240 billion in 1984. This increase, however, is primarily a reflection of three and a half decades of inflation. In relative terms, defense expenditures declined from over one half of total federal expenditures during the 1950s to less than one-quarter during the late 1970s. Even with the recent increases, defense costs have remained at or below 30 percent of federal expenditures during the 1980s. Veterans' benefits have also declined as a proportion of the federal budget but have done so less precipitously.

(b) Welfare expenditures have increased steadily since the early 1950s, from less than $8 billion in 1950 to more than $350 billion in 1984. Again this growth has largely been the result of inflation, but it has clearly been greater than the growth in defense spending, which it has surpassed since the 1960s, and it has shown a marked increase as a proportion of the budget. Federal transfer payments have exceeded 40 percent of federal expenditures during the 1980s.

(c) There has been no clear-cut trade-off between guns and butter. Welfare expenditures have increased when defense expenditures have decreased, to be sure. However, they have also increased when defense expenditures have increased and when defense expenditures have remained constant. The greatest impact of defense expenditures on welfare is probably caused by changing allocations within the defense budget.

(d) There has been a clear trade-off between a balanced budget and deficit financing. Faced with a choice between guns and butter, Americans have elected to buy both and to go more and more deeply into debt. As welfare and defense spending have both increased, revenues have not been generated to pay the bills. The inflation that the United States has experienced during the post–Korean War years has not been accompanied by offsetting sustained economic growth. Consequently, the nation has faced a growing budget deficit.[31] Reductions in either welfare or military spending will have an effect on the deficit, other things being equal; but they will not necessarily have an effect on other spending.

If we admit that some expenditures within the defense budget fulfill welfare functions—even if welfare is not the primary justification for the expenditure—the trend is different, and there is a trade-off. Since the advent of the all-volunteer force, the nature of military service as a form of government employment has been stressed;[32] and particularly during the late 1970s, the military was viewed by many as the employer of last resort.

Research aimed at addressing the linkage between the military and the welfare state has found that during their preservice years, young people in the military were second only to the unemployed in their participation in civilian training and job programs that had been federally sponsored. That is, they had previously been participants in welfare programs. However, the military youth were the least in favor of accepting welfare-grant payments or food stamps. The data did not discount the view that the military is an extension of the welfare state; rather, they support the view that some people regard either benefits in exchange for service or the provision of jobs as a benefit to be preferable to cash grants as entitlements. From this perspective, personnel programs within the military, particularly job-training programs, can be viewed as fulfilling a welfare function. Then military service itself comes to be viewed, not as an obligation of citizenship, but as a right of citizenship—the right to a job. For its personnel, the military is an extension of the welfare state, not in the sense that it is a source of transfer payments, but in the sense that it contributes to the process of building the nation-state and of bringing socially and economically marginal groups into it.[33]

I have already suggested that the allocation of benefits is a political decision, and recent research has confirmed this in the case of military personnel costs. If the basic proposition is true, then personnel costs—which reflect the number of people employed in the military, levels of compensation, and related costs—should go up under political conditions favorable to the expansion of the welfare state. Alex Mintz and Alexander Hicks have shown that this was the case during the period 1949 to 1976, when the welfare state was expanding in the United States. They found that the component of the defense budget that was most affected by a range of civilian economic factors—including inflation, unemployment among union members, civilian expenditures, and federal revenues—was the personnel component.[34] The analysts saw this as a manifestation of elected officials who were seeking the support of military employees, both uniformed and civilian.

The picture has changed during the decade of the 1980s. Personnel costs, which comprised almost 23 percent of the defense budget in 1979, had fallen to 20 percent by 1982, and were below 19 percent in 1983, as military expenditures were shifted toward hardware items. Thus, military personnel were put in the double bind of (a) having welfare benefits more widely available to people who were not in the service than to those who were serving, and (b) having funds within the military shifted away from personnel programs. However, the former of these issues was offset to a degree by reductions in welfare entitlement programs outside the military, and the passage of a new GI bill in 1985 increased the importance of military service as a basis for the receipt of benefits.

CITIZEN RIGHTS AND OBLIGATIONS
DURING THE 1970S AND THE 1980S

The growth of a system of entitlements during the 1960s and the 1970s, in conjunction with the decline in citizenship education, which I described in the last chapter, could not help influencing the way in which young Americans view their relationship to the state. The way they view this relationship, in turn, provides a context for their views regarding military service. Americans who feel that citizenship carries important responsibilities may see service as one of those responsibilities; they may favor reward systems, such as the GI bill, that recognize the fulfillment of those responsibilities. Americans who see citizenship as being manifested most strongly in benefits and entitlements will object to having those benefits tied to the fulfillment of obligations such as serving in the military or even registering with the selective service. And Americans who view employment as an entitlement and view military service as a form of federal employment will be concerned about policies that might limit the access of disadvantaged groups to military service.

The generation that came of age during the 1960s and the 1970s has frequently been referred to as the "me generation," a reflection of presumed self-centeredness and a lack of concern for the general public good. Some of the more successful members of this generation presumably have become the "Yuppies" of the 1980s. To the extent that the presumption is correct, one would anticipate this generation's placing more emphasis on rights of citizenship that would benefit themselves than on their responsibilities of citizenship that would benefit the larger social order. One would also anticipate that those segments of society that were less affluent or successful and were the beneficiaries of the greatest expansion of the welfare state as a result of the turbulence of the 1960s would be most likely to see benefits as entitlements, rather than as part of an exchange process in the 1970s and the 1980s. It is well to remember, however, that American society is complex and pluralistic. While differences may exist between segments of society or from one generation to the next, there are also great variations within generations and social groups. Care must be taken to avoid overly simplistic characterizations.

In 1979, Morris Janowitz surveyed more than fifteen hundred college students in regard to their attitudes toward citizenship rights and obligations.[35] His results are telling. Among the students surveyed, the four citizenship rights that he identified as central—the rights of free speech, religion, franchise, and trial by jury—were regarded as far more important than any obligation, including the obligations associated with those rights. The students were more likely to claim their right to a jury trial than their obligation to serve on juries, and they were more likely to feel they had a right to vote than an obligation to vote. However, some students did feel obliged to fulfill citizenship responsibilities.

The primacy of rights over obligations or privileges that one must earn were reflected as well in a 1982 survey by the Roper Organization.[36] Respondents were asked whether four potential benefits were rights or privileges that a person should have to earn. The four benefits were (1) adequate provisions for retirement, (2) an adequate standard of living, (3) a college education, and (4) a raise in wages or salary each year. Again the results were telling.

Majorities of 60 percent and 52 percent responded that the first two of these—retirement provisions and standard of living—were rights, not privileges to be earned. This perception varied by income and by race. Among the poorest respondents—those with incomes under $10,000—70 percent thought that retirement provisions were a right, and 65 percent thought that an adequate standard of living was a right. And among black respondents, 83 percent thought that retirement provisions were a right, and 74 percent thought that an adequate standard of living was a right.

The remaining two benefits were seen as rights by significant minorities of the sample: 24 percent for college education, and 32 percent for annual wage increases. Again, there were differences by income and race, although with only one exception—57 percent of black respondents thought that annual wage increases were a right—only minorities of all strata that were analyzed claimed these benefits to be rights. Nonetheless, there clearly is a constituency for entitlement programs, and that constituency, not surprisingly, consists of people who are most disadvantaged in the economy.

Attitude data bearing on whether the ascending generation is truly a "me generation" were collected in several surveys conducted during the 1970s and the 1980s. The Gallup poll repeatedly asked, "Would you favor or oppose requiring all young men to give a year of service to the nation—either in the military forces or in nonmilitary work either here or abroad, such as Vista or the Peace Corps?" More than 60 percent of the respondents in each of these surveys favored such a program. The youngest respondents were about 13 percent less likely to favor such a program than were the total samples, and support for such a program increased linearly with age. But small majorities of young adults did favor such programs.

Note that the basic question did not require military service, and that it referred only to men. When young men in the samples were then asked, "In the event a program of national service were put into effect, would you prefer military service or nonmilitary service," majorities specified nonmilitary service.

Respondents were also asked whether they favored or opposed a program of national service for young women. More than 20 percent fewer respondents favored such a program for young women than favored it for young men. Again the youngest were the least favorable, but there was an obvious gender-based difference in perceptions of potential responsibilities of citizenship. When asked, "Suppose all young women were required to give one year of service, which would you prefer, military or nonmilitary service," the women, like the men, preferred nonmilitary service.

The pattern of youths' being somewhat more self-centered than their elders carried into the decade of the 1980s and extended beyond federal programs. A Gallup poll in early 1982 asked repondents, "Do you, yourself, happen to be involved in any charity or social service activities, such as helping the poor, the sick, or the elderly?" Of a national sample, 29 percent answered affirmatively, but the percentage was 12 percent less among the youngest adults, and it increased with age. A Gallup poll that was conducted later in 1982 asked respondents to rate the importance of a series of social values. Young adults were the least likely age group to attach high importance to "working to better America," and the percentage increased with age. However, while in each of these surveys, young adults were less likely than older adults to be committed to the collective good, sizable minorities of young adults did indicate concern with and responsibility for the collective well-being. There clearly is a tendency toward self-centeredness among younger adults, but there is also far too much variation to use this tendency to characterize an entire generation. And while the younger adults tend to be more self-centered than their elders, there is diversity in the older generation as well.

Perhaps the most dramatic demonstration of the diversity of views in regard to having benefits tied to the fulfillment of obligations was the debate on the Solomon amendment to the Selective Service Act in 1982. In the face of a large number (albeit a small proportion) of young men's failing to register with the Selective Service System, Congressman Solomon of New York submitted legislation requiring civilian recipients of governmental grants, guaranteed loans, benefits, or other assistance to certify that they had registered with selective service if required by law to do so. That is, the recipients of benefits of citizenship were asked to demonstrate the fulfillment of an obligation of citizenship.[37] The amendment was passed by a ratio of three to one, but it was opposed by organizations such as the American Civil Liberties Union, which felt that individuals should not, in order to receive benefits of citizenship, be required to assert that they had complied with the law, perjure themselves by having to lie about compliance, or incriminate themselves by admitting to noncompliance.

MILITARY SERVICE AS AN OBLIGATION AND A WELFARE BENEFIT

The orientations of American youth toward the military and toward its relationship to citizen obligations and welfare benefits are reflected in attitudes, expectations, and behaviors that are complex and ambivalent. This complexity and ambivalence reflects in part the difference between a large peacetime deterrent force, which is recognized as a provider of jobs but whose military function until recently was not well understood by those who served, and the larger force that we may have to mobilize very rapidly in the event of a war.

Trend data on the attitudes of male civilian high-school seniors showed a decline in expectations of serving in the military during the 1970s, when the armed forces were declining in attractiveness as an employer. The trend then changed direction, and expectations of serving began to increase during the 1980s.[38] By 1982, almost 25 percent of male high-school seniors expected to serve in the military, compared to less than 18 percent in 1979.

Equally interesting was the fact that most of those who expected to serve also wanted to serve, although a residual group of young men who didn't want to serve expected that they would anyway, probably because they expected to have difficulty in getting a civilian job or because they expected a renewal of conscription or because they expected a war. More than 40 percent of these young men thought that America would be involved in a major world upheaval during the next decade, and about 30 percent feared that nuclear or biological annihilation would be the fate of mankind within their lifetimes.

If the military could reasonably anticipate that the young who expected to serve in the armed forces would in fact enlist and would be of the quality that the services require, manpower problems would be minimized. However, a large proportion of high-school seniors who expect to enter the military subsequently change their minds.[39] More importantly, expectations and preferences for military service were in closer harmony among young men who did not aspire to college educations than among those who did. It is the college-bound, of course, whose representation in the ranks the services are most anxious to increase. Members of the high-school class of 1982 overwhelmingly endorsed the principle of receiving a paid college education in exchange for three years of military service, and the Youth Attitude Tracking Survey, which was sponsored by the Department of Defense, showed educational benefits to be a major factor in differentiating between people who had either a high or a low inclination to enlist in the military.[40]

While the availability of educational benefits is an important incentive to enlistment, which links the military more firmly to social welfare again, the primary incentive in the peacetime volunteer force is the provision of a job; and here the expansion of military employment among groups who are disadvantaged in the civilian labor force is noteworthy. The next chapter will discuss the processes and the implications of the expanded use of women and blacks in the United States military as part of the growth of citizenship rights and benefits.

The quest for federal employment and for educational benefits does not reflect a total absence of recognition of military service as a citizenship obligation. In chapter 3, I noted the persistence of patriotism as an incentive to enlistment, and indeed the Youth Attitude Tracking Study showed that a desire to do something for the country was the most powerful factor differentiating young men with high and low propensities to enlist in the military. However, it was mentioned relatively infrequently, even among those with high propensities to enlist. Consistent with that, but reflective of the upcoming generation's ambivalence as well, among the male high-school seniors who were surveyed during the 1970s and the 1980s, about an equal number indicated that they would volunteer as indicated that they would not if it were necessary for the United States to fight in some future war—about 40 percent in each case.[41] More important, even among young adults, a majority—more than 60 percent according to a Gallup poll in mid 1982—still favored the continued registration of young men so that in case of a national emergency, the time needed to call men up for a draft would be reduced.

The picture that emerges, then, is one of two different pools of military manpower. The peacetime deterrent force, while its primary function is the provision of national security, is articulated with the welfare system as well, providing job training, employment, income, and security to those who are disadvantaged in the civilian labor force and financial assistance to those who are seeking higher education in an era of rapidly escalating college costs. These welfare functions are received in exchange for service, not as entitlements.

Should the nation go to war and have time to mobilize, on the other hand, Americans will draw on a mobilization base that is rooted in a sense of citizen obligation which motivates volunteers and legitimizes conscription. This is similar to the pattern of past mobilizations except for the size of the force-in-being prior to hostilities, the speed that the mobilization will require, and the fact that the ethic of national service—the value that legitimizes conscription—has been structurally weakened. These factors dictate that a war will be fought, at least in its early days, disproportionately by people who have joined the military in order to receive jobs or educational benefits in exchange for service. In the next chapter, I will discuss the evolution of the military as an employer for two important economically disadvantaged groups. In chapter 6, I will describe the factors that should affect the articulation of this force-in-being with the mobilization base in the future. And in the last chapter, I will discuss the relegitimation of the ethic of national service.

5
Race, Gender, and the United States Military

The social processes that we have been dealing with have had a marked impact on the social composition of the United States armed forces. If carrying the processes of rationalization to extremes has weakened the American defense establishment by reducing the soldier to a cog in a machine, undercutting the interpersonal processes of leadership and cohesion necessary for military effectiveness, and weakening the patriotic justification for conscripted military service, as was suggested in chapter 3, it also brought about a change in living and working conditions in the military, making service more attractive as a form of employment. This became particularly important for people who were disadvantaged in the civilian labor force. The very impersonality that was demanded by organizational rationality required that the utilization of people in the military be increasingly based on their abilities, rather than on the ascriptive characteristics that have traditionally been associated with military service: most notably, being white and male. The current force is the first volunteer force we have had that did not have racial quotas.[1]

At the same time, the evolution of the welfare state in America, in the context of social values that emphasized individualism and of historical traditions that associated welfare benefits with service to the state, led disadvantaged groups to increasingly press for the right to serve in and work for the military on a basis equal to that of white males as a manifestation of equal citizenship obligations; as a means of receiving the benefits that have historically been associated with the fulfillment of those rights; as a source of equitable employment opportunity in the context of a discriminatory civilian labor market; and in the case of black males, I suspect, as an assertion of masculinity. Because of the declining size of the pool of white eighteen-year-old males, in turn, the services increasingly had to be receptive to the utilization of blacks and of women as sources of "manpower" in a peacetime force and to grant them (almost) equal access to the benefits associated with military service, rather than restricting them to periods of military emergency and granting them less access to benefits. Although there are clear differences between the racial integration of the armed forces, which began during the Korean War, and the ongoing gender integration of the United States military, which began in earnest with the conversion to an all-volunteer force in 1973, the parallels between the two processes are remarkable.

THE RACIAL INTEGRATION OF THE ARMED FORCES

Black soldiers have participated in every war in which the United States has been engaged, but in every one up until the Korean police action, they have been denied status equal to that of their white peers through segregation, subjection to quotas, and exclusion from combat specialties and officers' commissions. Some five thousand blacks fought on the side of the colonists in the Revolution and participated in the early battles, including Lexington, Concord, and Bunker Hill.[2] The use of blacks, however, was a source of controversy. Some colonial leaders believed it was morally wrong to ask slaves and former slaves to share in the burden of defense; and white supremacists thought that blacks were inferior and untrustworthy. In 1775, bowing to political pressure, George Washington prohibited any additional enlistment of black soldiers.[3] An estimated twenty thousand blacks, primarily slaves in the southern colonies, served with the British as scouts, soldiers, and supply handlers, in the hope of being emancipated. In an effort to reduce such "defections" and to help solve the problem of manpower shortages, the Continental Congress allowed free black soldiers to reenlist, and most states allowed the use of black substitutes to fill militia draft quotas. After the war, however, blacks were excluded by policy from the federal forces and the state militias.

Policies are one thing, manpower needs in wartime quite another. Benjamin Stoddert, the first secretary of the navy, had excluded blacks from the navy and the marines. Nonetheless, blacks served in the naval war against France from 1798 to 1800, and several thousand blacks served in the War of 1812, in which they constituted about a sixth of the navy's enlisted personnel and were integrated into all ratings.[4] They were effectively excluded from the ground forces, and at the end of the war, with manpower requirements reduced, the exclusionary policies were enforced in the navy as well.

At the onset of the Civil War, President Lincoln initially excluded blacks from service in the Union army, both to maintain the loyalty of the border states and to emphasize that the issue over which the war was being fought was the maintenance of the Union, not the abolition of slavery. Despite that policy, the navy, ever mindful of its manpower needs, authorized black enlistments in September 1861.[5] Similar pressures on manpower were felt by the ground forces, and by mid 1862, some Union generals were raising black regiments despite Lincoln's policy.

In 1863 the Emancipation Proclamation provided for the enlistment of blacks, and the states began to establish black units. More than 185,000 blacks were recruited and organized by the Bureau of Colored Troops. About one-tenth of the Union army and a quarter of the navy were composed of blacks. If one includes black volunteers who served in independent and state units, then almost 390,000 blacks served with the Union forces.[6] Almost 10 percent of the blacks who served—more than 38,000—were killed—a fatality rate almost one and a half times that of white troops. The largest number of fatalities in any unit of the Union army was suffered by the Fifth United States Heavy Artillery, which lost 829 soldiers.[7] Thus, a pattern of blacks being overrepresented among American combat casualties, which also occurred in Vietnam, was established in the Civil War.

The Confederacy, as might be expected, was slower than the Union to explore the use of black troops. It was not until early in 1865 that the Confederacy authorized the enlistment of "slave soldiers," and a few companies of black soldiers were organized. However, Gen. Robert E. Lee surrendered in early April of that year, and none of these units saw combat.[8]

One of the often-overlooked ironies of the Civil War was the antiblack sentiment that had been expressed in the North. Not only was Lincoln's initial resistance to using black troops a partial response to sentiment that expressed doubt as to whether black troops would be effective or loyal soldiers, but also the antiwar movement in the North and the Civil War draft riots, discussed earlier, had racist undercurrents.

The draft riots reflected the convoluted logic that the movement to abolish slavery had caused the war, that the war had caused the draft, that the draft discriminated against the [white] poor, and that this discrimination was therefore the fault of the slaves and other blacks. Several hundred blacks were killed during the New York draft riots. Martin Binkin has reported that "the streets were littered with the dead and dying, and the mutilated bodies of black victims hung from the trees and lampposts."[9] Thousands more blacks fled from the city.

After the Civil War, the United States Army established six black units, to consist of 12,500 soldiers: the 9th and 10th Cavalries, and the 38th, 39th, 40th, and 41st Infantries. However, because of a shortage of funds, the infantry units were reduced to two—the 24th and 25th Regiments.[10] These units accounted for about 10 percent of the army's personnel. The segregated structure guaranteed that except in an emergency, black soldiers and white soldiers would not serve together. The navy, by contrast, continued to allow blacks to serve on an integrated basis in the enlisted ranks, usually in the lowest of them.[11]

Civilian life offered few advantages to the average young black male during the late nineteenth century. The armed forces, by contrast, offered employment, education, food, clothing, shelter, and a measure of social status. Military service was a relatively good job. It was not difficult to fill the black military units.[12] During Reconstruction, the United States Military Academy at West Point was opened to blacks, but only on a token basis. During the half century after the Civil War, thirteen black cadets were admitted; but only three graduated. During this same period, the United States Naval Academy did not admit any black midshipmen.[13]

THE TWENTIETH CENTURY

Blacks fought in the Indian Wars. And in the Spanish-American War, the 9th and 10th Cavalries participated in the charge up San Juan Hill, and black sailors distinguished themselves in the battles of Manila and Santiago. The presence of black troops in predominantly white towns, particularly in the South, was not without tensions. Indeed, there had been a riot in Tampa, Florida, two days before black regiments were to sail for Cuba during the Spanish-American War. White units had clashed with black units over the former's use of a two-year-old black boy as a target for a marksmanship demonstration. The 2nd Georgia Volunteer Infantry had then restored order, leaving the streets "red with Negro blood" in the process.[14]

The tensions involving black soldiers peaked during the early twentieth century; they were reflected most dramatically by the so-called Brownsville Riot. Black soldiers arrived at Fort Brown, Texas, in July 1906. The bars in nearby Brownsville either were segregated or they excluded blacks completely. One night in mid-August, a group of men rioted in the streets of Brownsville, discharging firearms into buildings, killing a bartender, and wounding the chief of police. An investigation concluded that soldiers from Fort Brown had been involved, but it failed to identify any specific individuals. The investigating officer recommended, and the army's inspector general concurred, that unless the guilty parties came forward, all enlisted personnel in the black battalion should be dishonorably discharged. President Theodore Roosevelt, who had praised the performance of the black soldiers under his command in the Spanish-American War, ordered the dishonorable discharge—without benefit of court-martial—of 167 black soldiers, three full companies.

Some of these soldiers had had as many as twenty-six years of service, and six of them had been awarded the Medal of Honor. They were denied pay, allowances, pension, benefits, and access to civilian federal employment.[15] Although fourteen were readmitted to military service after a year, it was not until 1972 that the army ruled that the investigation had been biased; the army also changed the records of these soldiers to reflect honorable discharges but did not award any back pay or allowances. In 1973, Congress awarded the last survivor of the Brownsville group a pension of $25,000 and medical benefits.[16]

Both black participation in the United States military and racial tensions involving black soldiers continued in the pre–World War I period. During the Mexican Punitive Expedition of 1916–17, Gen. John J. Pershing used the 10th Cavalry as a major part of his operation in pursuit of Pancho Villa.[17] Also in 1917, however, after a fight in Houston, Texas, between white policemen and black soldiers of the 24th Infantry over the alleged abuse of a black woman, more than a hundred soldiers from the regiment mutinied against their officers, armed themselves, marched downtown, and continued the battle. Many policemen, citizens, and soldiers were killed or wounded. More than one hundred black soldiers were indicted and convicted; nineteen were hanged, sixteen were sentenced to life imprisonment, and the rest were dishonorably discharged and sentenced to prison terms ranging up to fifteen years.[18] This incident reflected the racial tensions that characterized America as World War I approached.

In the navy, official policy was still to allow blacks to enlist for all ratings and to serve with integrated crews. Informal practice, however, was to reflect the segregated nature of American society; and in 1919, the navy instituted a formal segregationist policy for the first time in its history. The ten thousand blacks who served in the navy during the war were almost all messmen, stewards, or coal handlers in the "black gangs" of the engine rooms.[19] The Marine Corps recruited no blacks.

The army continued its segregationist policies. Leaders in the black community had begun to suggest that blacks might earn their citizenship rights in American society by helping to defeat the kaiser,[20] and blacks were represented in the army roughly in proportion to the general population—about 10 percent. The great majority of them—more than 80 percent of the two hundred thousand black soldiers who served in France—were assigned to menial noncombat roles. Blacks constituted only one-thirtieth of the combat strength and one-third of the military labor force.[21]

Reports of the performance of the relatively few black combat units were mixed. The all-black 92d Division attracted a great deal of criticism when its 368th Regiment broke and ran during the Meuse-Argonne offensive in September 1918.[22] On the other hand, both the French and the president highly commended the 369th Regiment, which served directly under French command, for its performance in combat.

The black veterans of World War I returned, not to a newly recognized citizenship status, but to a society of continuing race riots, lynchings, and increasingly discriminatory practices within the armed services. The navy ceased to recruit blacks; instead, it filled the ranks of the messmen's and stewards' branch with Philippine nationals, a practice that persisted until 1932, after which blacks were again recruited as messmen. The army remained segregated, set an official quota that would keep the representation of blacks at no more than their representation in society (this quota was in fact never approached during the interwar years), kept the officers corps white, and excluded blacks from the air corps. At the beginning of the World War II era, as a result of these policies, blacks were serving in the navy only as stewards and messmen, were absent from the air corps, and were under a quota in the army, where they served in segregated units and in menial jobs but were virtually excluded from the officers corps. On the eve of Pearl Harbor they accounted for 5.6 percent of the army. There were five black officers, three of whom were chaplains.[23]

The Selective Service and Training Act of 1940 specified that the selection of draftees and volunteers for military service was not to be influenced by race or color. Also in 1940, the War Department adopted a policy to increase black accessions so that they would be roughly proportional to the general population, to establish black units in all branches of the army, and to admit blacks to officer-candidate schools so that they could serve as pilots in black aviation units. However, the services were given discretion in determining enlistment standards, and the War Department's policy insisted on racial segregation at the regimental level in order to maintain troop morale.[24] Because the navy had enough volunteers not to require draftees, it was able to continue its policy of enlisting blacks only as messmen.

In 1942 the navy liberalized its regulations and opened additional shore billets to blacks. Training continued to be racially segregated, however, and blacks went to sea only as messmen and stewards. No black officers were commissioned in the navy. The Marine Corps also began to recruit blacks for the first time in 1942, to serve in segregated battalions occupying islands in the Pacific that had been captured from the Japanese by white units, so that the whites could pursue the Japanese further.

The following year, under War Department pressure to meet the goal of proportionality, the navy recognized that it would have to open up sea billets to blacks. The navy experimented with ways of sending blacks to sea, including assigning all-black crews to two antisubmarine vessels.[25] Not until 1945 did the navy integrate basic training and allow blacks to serve as members of integrated crews on noncombat ships.

The army also resisted the principle of proportional representation. Segregation was presumed to be neccessary for the maintenance of cohesion, and segregation required separate training facilities, as well as care not to locate black units in places where their presence would offend a white host community. The black soldiers, in turn, resented the treatment they received from the army, and the early 1940s saw racial tensions manifested in myriad ways, ranging from insubordinate acts by black officers (e.g., refusing to sign documents in support of segregation) to actual race riots.[26] In short, blacks were considered as much an administrative problem as a manpower resource.

The racial problems notwithstanding, more than a million blacks, or almost 8 percent of the force, served in the armed forces during World War II. More of them served proportionately in the army than in the other branches, and most of them continued to serve in menial jobs. Of the blacks in the army, 78 percent were in the service branches—primarily quartermaster and transportation corps—compared to 40 percent of the whites. On the other hand, fewer than 10 percent of the blacks and more than 30 percent of the whites were in the combat arms.

In the fall of 1944, an army board (the Gillem Board) was established to determine how better use might be made of black soldiers within the army's segregated structure. That December, shortages of white infantrymen as replacements for line units forced the army to increase its utilization of blacks as combat soldiers.

A call for a limited number of black noncombat soldiers to volunteer for service as infantrymen to fight "shoulder to shoulder" with white soldiers and to share the privilege of defeating the enemy produced more than forty-five hundred volunteers in two months.[27] Of these, almost three thousand were retrained as infantrymen and were assigned, in all-black platoons, to serve in divisions that had previously been all white. The Gillem Board, which issued its report in 1945, thought that these black troops had performed well in the context of white divisional units. The board was critical, however, of the performance of the all-black 92d Division, which had been criticized during World War I as well. These performance problems were eventually attributed to poor planning and preparation on the part of the army and to the assignment to black units of inferior white officers, who themselves resented the assignment.[28] The Gillem Board recommended that opportunities for blacks in the military be increased; that racial segregation at the small-unit level be continued but that black platoons, companies, and battalions be incorporated into larger white units; and that a quota system be implemented, to keep the army at no more than 10 percent black.[29]

Racial tensions were still high in America. Blacks who left the service feeling that they had earned the rights of citizenship were subjected to snipings, house burnings, and the murder of members of their families, to remind them of their place.[30] And while the armed forces were recognized as discriminatory, civilian institutions were recognized as more so. Thus, after the war a larger proportion of black soldiers than of white soldiers sought to reenlist. The quota was used to hold down black reenlistments, producing additional resentment in the black community.

The World War II period had seen the political mobilization of black Americans—a surge in the citizenship revolution. In 1941, A. Philip Randolph, president of the Brotherhood of Sleeping Car Porters, threatened to organize a march on Washington; and this had helped President Roosevelt decide to establish the Fair Employment Practices Commission. In 1942, Randolph's movement organized several marches and demonstrations. Also in that year, the Congress of Racial Equality (CORE) was formed by whites in Chicago to support the black quest for equality. Race had become a salient political issue, and both major parties put antidiscrimination planks in their 1948 election-campaign platforms. In July 1948, three months before the election, President Harry S. Truman issued Executive Order Number 9981, which declared a policy of "equality of treatment and opportunity in the military." Executive Order 9981 did not end segregation in the military, however. It did state a policy, and it established the President's Committee on Equality of Treatment and Opportunity (the Fahey Board) to work with the secretaries of defense and the services to implement the policy. A review of service policies by the Fahey Board in 1949 found that the navy had been integrating crews since 1946 (although it placed a ceiling of 10 percent black representation on any one ship); that the Marine Corps, while it maintained segregated units, had integrated basic training; and that the new air force, which was not constrained by traditional notions of military manpower, was in favor of integration, had ended racial quotas, and was making personnel decisions on the basis of ability alone. Only the army remained in favor of segregation. At the time, 40 percent of the occupational specialties and 80 percent of the army's schools were still closed to black soldiers.

The army thought that the conclusions of the Gillem Board and of a subsequent study by the Board to Study the Utilization of Negro Manpower (the Chamberlin Board) had demanded segregation in the interest of cohesion and military effectiveness, since the army thought that most whites did not associate with blacks and that most blacks did not have the skills required for the army's more technical occupations. The Fahey Board believed that if skills, rather than race, were the issue, then the army should establish quotas on the basis of achievement instead of race.

The army agreed to experiment with an achievement-based system, thus becoming the last service to accept integration. It did so on the basis of an informal agreement with President Truman that if a system based on equality of treatment and opportunity produced a racially disproportionate force, racial quotas could be reestablished.[31] However, when the Korean War broke out in the summer of 1950, neither the army's training bases nor its operational units had been integrated. The 24th Infantry Regiment was committed to combat as an all-black unit.

The mobilization for the police action accomplished what the executive order had not. By 1951, one-quarter of the army's recruits were black, and the black training units could not absorb them. As black infantrymen completed their training, they were assigned where they were needed most—to fill vacancies in previously all-white line infantry units. Thus was the army integrated, but not without opposition from some senior commanders. The army's research on this process showed that racial integration enhanced combat effectiveness and that segregation limited combat effectiveness, so it recommended a policy of integration.[32] By the end of the war, more than 90 percent of the blacks in the army were in integrated units. The air force and the Marine Corps had also eliminated segregated units. In late 1954 the Defense Department officially announced that all-black units had been abolished in the armed forces.

Throughout the 1950s and the 1960s, the military was ahead of civilian institutions in American society with regard to racial integration. Whether this was because of the nature of military discipline, which allowed the president to impose policy on the institution, or whether it was influenced by the fact that all lower-ranking enlisted personnel—regardless of race—were treated, as one analyst suggested, "like Negroes" anyway, thus making integration a relatively smooth process, the military stood in stark contrast to the rest of society.[33] This contrast was not without problems for the military: black servicemen, who were effectively integrated into the armed forces, faced hostility and discrimination when they were off the base, and they had difficulty with segregated living accommodations, restaurants, and public facilities such as schools and transportation systems.[34]

Despite the integration of the forces, blacks continued to be underrepresented in the services in comparison to their proportion in the civilian population. In 1964 the President's Committee on Equal Opportunity in the Armed Forces (the Gesell Committee), on the basis of a two-year study, found that blacks were concentrated in the lower pay grades, that the reserves and the National Guard were still segregated or were only integrated to a token degree, and that discriminatory practices still existed on military installations and in their host civilian communities.[35] Military service might have provided good jobs and benefits to blacks in comparison to the alternatives that they had in the civilian economy, but there were still significant constraints on their opportunities in the military as well.

The underrepresentation of blacks in the military that the Gesell Committee had studied was dramatically reversed by the widening conflict and the expanded United States involvement in Vietnam. Here, for the first time in the twentieth century, rather than being underrepresented or excluded from combat, blacks were more likely than whites to be drafted, to be sent to Vietnam, to serve in high-risk combat units, and to be killed or wounded in action.[36] During the early 1960s, with blacks accounting for slightly more than 10 percent of the population aged nineteen to twenty-one, they accounted for a quarter of the casualties in Vietnam. Clearly their "right to fight" was no longer being constrained.

The discriminatory mechanisms that were responsible for a disproportionate number of black casualties were primarily socioeconomic rather than racial. However, the black population was relatively poor, and so it felt socioeconomic discrimination disproportionately. A disproportionate number of the soldiers in Project 100,000, which I discussed in the last chapter, were black.

Moreover, some of the dynamics were racial. The Marshall Commission found that the Selective Service System, which was supplying a disproportionate number of black cohorts of draftees to the ground combat forces in Vietnam, was operating through local boards, more than 98 percent of whose members were white.

Regardless of the degree to which the overrepresentation of blacks was the result of racial or socioeconomic biases, it contributed to a perception that the black community was being asked to carry too much of the burden of the war, which itself was increasingly being portrayed as a white man's war waged against people of color. Reflecting the increasingly active civil-rights movement in American society, racial tensions were growing within all the services. This was manifested most dramatically by race riots among soldiers in the United States and Germany during the late 1960s, among prisoners in a military stockade in Vietnam in 1968, among marines at Camp Lejeune and Kaneohe Naval Air Station during the summer of 1969, at Travis Air Force Base in the spring of 1971, and on the aircraft carriers *Kitty Hawk* and *Constellation* in October and November 1972.[37] Racial tension was clearly a problem for the military as it entered the era of the all-volunteer force.

The racial tensions experienced by the military services reflected major changes in United States race relations during the two decades that bracketed and included the Vietnam War. In 1954, largely through the efforts of the National Association for the Advancement of Colored People (NAACP), the Supreme Court had ruled against the legality of segregation in public schools. The NAACP had then sought to extend, through the courts, the principle of desegregation. The strategy of working through the judicial process was changed abruptly in late 1955, however, when Rosa Parks ignited a protest movement in Montgomery, Alabama. If blacks, despite the law, were going to be segregated on public transportation, blacks were not going to use—or support—the facility at all. The Montgomery bus boycott gave the movement for racial equality a new charismatic leader—Dr. Martin Luther King, Jr.—and took the most dramatic activity of the movement out of the courtroom with the strategy of nonviolent civil disobedience.

King's strategy of nonviolence was increasingly challenged by less moderate groups, and the mid-1960s were punctuated by urban riots that expressed the discontent of a black population that was becoming more and more urbanized. The rioting peaked in 1968, after the assassination of King in Memphis, Tennessee. In his final years, King had broadened his concerns from civil rights to the Vietnam War. The quest for social and economic equality that the civil-rights movement represented, as well as the association between civil rights and a concern about militarism that King had forged, provided part of the context within which the debate on the end of the draft was conducted, and the all-volunteer force was shaped.

The Gates Commission had projected that the racial composition of an all-volunteer force (AVF) would not be substantially different from that of the conscription-era army. However, in the early years of the AVF, more than one-quarter of the new recruits were black—double the fraction in 1970—and in some years, as many as one-third of the new recruits in the army have been black. Youth unemployment was high during the early years of the AVF, especially in the black community. The armed forces became the employer of last resort for many young blacks.

Black soldiers have also been more likely to seek reenlistment than have white soldiers, which has increased the overrepresentation of blacks further still. In December 1987, 30 percent of the enlisted soldiers in the army were black, as were 22 percent of enlisted personnel across all services. However, blacks were underrepresented in the officer ranks in all services (6.6 percent), with the army having the largest representation of black officers (around 10 percent) and the navy having the smallest (about 3.0 percent).

The overrepresentation of blacks in the enlisted ranks of the military can be seen as rational market behavior. Blacks in the military perceive that there is less discrimination there than in civilian employment.[38] Black adolescents regard the military as a channel for social mobility.[39] These perceptions seem to reflect an economic reality that carries over into civilian life. Before the Vietnam War, black veterans were economically advantaged relative to their nonveteran peers,[40] perhaps as a function of the benefits that they earned through their military service.

The response of the services to the racial discrimination that has persisted can likewise be seen as rational managerial behavior. In 1972, an army lieutenant colonel, D. R. Butler, who was assigned to the Military Personnel Center, compared Officer Efficiency Reports (OERs) for black and white officers over a fifteen-year period. He found that black officers had received lower efficiency ratings than white officers. His results were never published, but they were regarded by the army as indicative of discriminatory practices that undercut the efficient use of personnel resources. Several steps were taken to correct these practices:[41]

1. Mechanisms for comparing OER scores by race were incorporated into the army's affirmative action plan.
2. All officer-promotion and school-selection boards were informed of Colonel Butler's results.
3. All noncommissioned-officer-promotion boards were also informed of the results, on the assumption that the phenomenon of racial disparity might occur in Enlisted Efficiency Reports as well.
4. As a matter of policy, a minority representative was placed on all such boards.
5. The general conclusions of the analysis were reported to all major commands in the army.

6. In 1973, the army commissioned a large-scale research effort to identify patterns of institutional racial discrimination in a wide range of areas, as a result of which a new affirmative-action plan, based upon principles of management by objective, was issued. This plan identified areas of continued differential treatment by race, specified agencies that were responsible for reducing the differentials, and set timetables by which progress was to be achieved.

The response of the other services and of the Department of Defense was also a management response. In 1971, in the wake of the racial disturbances that I discussed earlier, the Defense Race Relations Institute was established at Patrick Air Force Base, Florida; its goal was to change behavior through educational programs.[42] As racial discrimination decreased in the armed forces and as problems of the integration of women into the military came to the fore, the mission of the institute was broadened, and it became the Defense Equal Opportunity Management Institute (DEOMI).

THE INTEGRATION OF WOMEN

Blacks are the overrepresented minority in the American armed forces, but women are the underrepresented majority. Constituting slightly over one-half of the civilian population that is age-eligible for the military, women constitute slightly more than one-tenth of United States armed forces personnel. The same barriers that have historically been raised against black participation in the military have been raised against female participation as well. At various times, women have been completely excluded, allowed to serve only in auxiliary units, administratively segregated in their own branches, restricted by quotas, allowed to serve only in limited occupational specialties, restricted from command positions and access to senior officer ranks, and excluded from combat specialties, although not necessarily from combat areas. Women have not been integrated to the extent that blacks have been. Women have served in all United States wars. Clearly, the parallel between the integration of blacks and women is not a perfect one.

There are physiological issues that affect gender integration—particularly the issue of pregnancy and differences between sexes in average upper body strength—that are irrelevant in discussions of racial integration. There are striking similarities, however, in the social dimensions of the two debates: for example, appropriate role definitions for blacks and for women, the extension of full citizenship participation to both groups, and the presumed effects of racial or gender integration on the cohesion that military units must have in order to operate effectively in a combat environment. And despite the historical fact that women have generally been excluded from central positions in the military, American society has been willing to draw upon both groups for military personnel when faced with shortages of either whites or men.

Women did not serve officially as members of the United States armed forces until the twentieth century. By posing as men, a small number of women did manage to serve as soldiers as early as the Revolution. Probably the most famous of these was Deborah Sampson, who served as Robert Shirtlife in the 4th Massachusetts Regiment for more than three years during the early 1780s. While she was being treated for a fever by a military surgeon, her sex was discovered, so she was discharged. The presence of a few such cases in George Washington's army has virtually been undisputed. Present-day feminist historians have argued that the numbers were considerably larger. Linda Grant De Pauw, for example, has claimed that "tens of thousands of women were involved in active combat."[43] Other contemporary historians have argued that the data do not support this assertion.[44] Many women, of course, fulfilled support functions, as nurses, cooks, laundresses, and the like. They did so as civilians, however. These functions had not been incorporated into the structure of the armed forces.

The pattern that had been established during the Revolution persisted throughout the nineteenth century. A small number of women disguised themselves as men in order to serve as soldiers, and several earned places in American military history. For example, under the name of George Baker, Lucy Brewer served as a marine on the USS *Constitution* during the War of 1812 and was later acknowledged to have been "the first girl marine."[45] And Sarah Borginis served with Zachary Taylor during the Mexican attack on Fort Brown in 1846; she achieved the rank of brevet colonel.

The participation of women in military operations increased dramatically during the Civil War but was usually still outside the structure of the regular force. They continued to serve in support roles as nurses, cooks, and laundresses. In addition, they played major roles in espionage and sabotage, reflecting a general tendency for women to be employed in unconventional warfare even when they are excluded from conventional military formations.[46]

Some women continued to disguise themselves as men and serve as regular soldiers. Loreta Velasquez, for example, whose husband was serving as a Confederate officer, glued on facial hair, purchased a Confederate uniform, recruited a troop of soldiers, and commanded them in a number of battles, including First Manassas, as Lt. Harry T. Buford.[47] She was found out when she was wounded, but she rejoined the army as an infantryman and secured a commission as a cavalry officer before she was again wounded and discovered, which ended her military career.

Almost in anticipation of the entry of women into the armed forces through the medical field early in the twentieth century, some of the most dramatic contributions made by women during the Civil War were concerned with health care. Clara Barton, who founded the American Red Cross and helped to establish the first National Cemetery at Arlington, Virginia, brought nursing services and supplies to troops on the battlefield. Dr. Mary E. Walker gave up a medical practice to serve as a nurse with the Union army. She was ultimately commissioned as a lieutenant in the Medical Corps, thus becoming the first woman doctor in the army. She was awarded a Congressional Medal of Honor, which was withdrawn in 1917 but was restored in 1976.[48] Dorothea Lynde Dix, who had played a major role in the reform of mental hospitals, was appointed superintendent of women nurses by the secretary of war in 1861, and she recruited and trained about six thousand nurses for the Union army. In accordance with the dominant pattern of the mobilization model, however, when the war ended in 1865, the female nurses were demobilized, and military-patient care was provided by enlisted men.

Faced with a typhoid epidemic during the Spanish-American War, the army recruited more than fifteen hundred female nurses. They served as civilians, employed under contract, not as military personnel. Female nurses who supported the army either as military personnel or as contract civilians during the nineteenth century proved their utility enough that Dr. Anita Newcomb McGee, who had supervised the nurses during the Spanish-American War, was asked to serve as acting assistant surgeon in charge of the Nurse Corps Division and to draft legislation to give nurses quasi-military status. In 1901, Congress established the Army Nurse Corps as an auxiliary unit. Nurses did not have military rank and pay, nor did they have retirement and veterans' benefits. Women, who did not yet have the right to vote, could not really serve as citizen-soldiers or earn the citizenship rights associated with military service. In 1908 the Navy Nurse Corps was established under the same conditions.

The navy had been the first service to integrate racially, and it led the way toward the incorporation of women as well, at least temporarily, during the pre–World War I years. Early in 1917, Secretary of the Navy Josephus Daniels, anticipating the nation's forthcoming involvement in the World War and recognizing a shortage of personnel in those administrative specialties into which women were beginning to move in the civilian labor force—for example, clerical workers, typists, stenographers, and telephone operators—authorized the enlisting of women in these specialities in the Naval Reserve as yeomen (F). Regulations had to be bent a bit, since yeomen were required to be assigned to a ship but women were prohibited from shipboard duty. The problem was solved by assigning all yeomen (F) to a navy tugboat that was buried in the mud in the Potomac River.[49]

A year after the establishment of yeomen (F), the Marine Corps authorized the recruitment of marines (F). During the course of the war, some thirteen thousand women served in these roles, and some eventually moved out of clerical duties and into more traditionally male domains, such as draftsmen, recruiters, and translators.[50] The War Department continued its prohibition against enlisted women in the army.

Women did of course continue to serve as nurses. Twenty thousand served in the Army Nurse Corps, half of them overseas. Another fourteen hundred served in the Navy Nurse Corps. Thus, some thirty-four thousand women served in uniform in World War I, and many of them were highly decorated. The War Department, which had been under increasing pressure, including requests from commanders in the field, to bring female enlisted personnel into the army, had capitulated to the point of allowing female civilian employees onto army posts, provided that they were of "mature age and high moral character." But with the end of the war, the pressure was dissipated. The female auxiliaries to the navy and the Marine Corps were demobilized, and the navy's statutory authority to recruit "citizens" was amended to restrict such recruitment to "male citizens."

The Nineteenth amendment to the United States Constitution, which extended the franchise to women and thereby gave them broader citizenship rights than they had previously held, was passed in 1920. During the period between the world wars, three plans were developed for the integration of women into the army. The first two envisaged a women's corps that would be part of the regular force structure, rather than an auxiliary. Both were rejected by the army staff.[51] The third was developed by the army staff in 1939 at the request of Gen. George C. Marshall, who, as chief of staff, anticipated manpower shortages if the United States were drawn into the war in Europe. Marshall's plan called only for a women's auxiliary and anticipated that only a small number of highly educated women would serve; it did not call for a large-scale female mobilization to free large numbers of men for combat. Despite the limitations on the nature of service and despite the strong interest of the chief of staff, the movement of the plan through the formulation process was almost imperceptible.

Late in 1940, conscription was reestablished, and women's patriotic organizations lobbied for the right to be part of the mobilization effort. Congresswoman Edith Nourse Rogers of Massachusetts, who had been concerned that the women who had served and suffered in World War I had not received veterans' benefits because they had not had regular military status, announced her intention to introduce legislation to gain regular military status for them. General Marshall resurrected his plan for a women's auxiliary, and he asked Congresswoman Rogers to introduce it in lieu of her proposal for full military status. She did so in May 1941. Later that year, the army asked the navy to support a proposal to establish women's auxiliaries for both services. The navy demurred and, in fact, tried to dissuade the army from supporting a women's corps for itself. Congresswoman Rogers's bill languished in congressional committees for a year.

Pearl Harbor was attacked in December 1941, and with the need for mobilization, Rogers's bill, which established the Women's Auxiliary Army Corps (WAAC), was reported out of committee and was passed in May 1942. The navy also found itself facing a manpower shortage, and two months later, Congress passed legislation establishing the Marine Corps Women's Reserve and the Navy Women's Reserve, whose members—called WAVES (Women Accepted for Volunteer Emergency Service)—would have full reserve military status rather than status as auxiliaries. That winter, the Coast Guard Women's Reserve was established. Despite its initial reluctance, the navy had once again moved ahead of the army in minimizing the importance of people's ascriptive characteristics when attempting to meet its manpower needs.

The auxiliary status of the WAAC was a problem from the outset. Its members were not part of the army, did not get the same pay as males doing the same job, and did not get military benefits, protection, or rank. The women's auxiliary of the army suffered in the recruiting market relative to the women's reserve branches of the other services. By February 1943, the WAAC was failing to reach its recruitment goals, and shortly after its first anniversary, it was converted by legislation to the Women's Army Corps (WAC), which had full military status.

After the establishment of these reserve branches, women were eligible for commissions. However, while they were not auxiliaries as they had been in World War I, neither were they equal to their male counterparts. They were in gender-segregated reserve branches, whose very existence was under statutory limitations. They were not trained for combat; rather, they were intended to free men for combat. There were statutory limitations on how high they could rise in the rank structure. And they were subject to numerical quotas, although these proved to be unrealistic—unrealistically low at the outset and unrealistically high later on. When the WAAC was founded, for example, it had been projected to peak at twenty-five thousand recruits in its second year. However, commanders in the field requested a total of eighty thousand WAACs, so strength projections were raised, first to sixty-three thousand and later to 1.5 million.[52]

Ultimately, about 350,000 women served in the armed forces during World War II, most of them in traditionally female fields such as administrative and clerical jobs, health care, and communications. As had been the case in World War I, however, some moved into more masculine domains, such as parachute riggers, aircraft mechanics, gunnery instructors, and so forth. Several hundred additional women, who did not get full military status and benefits during the war, served as Women's Airforce Service Pilots (WASPs) and ferried military aircraft to overseas theaters of operation. During the war, military women served in all combat theaters. There were more than eight thousand WACs in Europe on V-E Day, and more than five thousand served in the Pacific.

The army excluded women from jobs that involved great physical strength, long training, working in "improper" environments, the supervision of men, and combat, although in late 1942, the army experimented with gender-integrated crews for antiaircraft guns on the east coast of the continental United States.[53] The women proved effective, so the Anti-Aircraft Artillery requested increased assignment of WACs; but the threat of aerial attack on the East Coast decreased, and noncombat jobs were found for the women in the army. Despite the constraints, the army identified more than a million positions that could be occupied by women. The Navy opened all specialities to women. However, WAVEs could not initially be assigned outside the continental United States, and while they were later allowed to serve in U.S. territories, geographical constraints limited the utilization of them. The constraints did not apply to nurses, however. Thirty-seven military nurses became Japanese prisoners of war at Corregidor, and five others were captured on Guam.

Interestingly, the aviation components of the services were the most receptive to the increased utilization of women during World War II. Perhaps this was because, as a newly evolving technology, military aviation was less tied to traditional definitions of gender roles in military activity than were the ground or naval forces. Nearly half of the women in the army—some forty thousand female soldiers—served in the army air forces as Air-WACs. More than a quarter of the WAVES—some twenty-three thousand women—served in naval aviation as crew members and instructors. Almost a third of the women marines served in support of aviation activities, in specialties such as parachute riggers and air-traffic controllers.[54] None of these women in uniform served as military pilots. As noted above, the WASPs did fly military aircraft; but they had civil-service rather than military status and did not fly combat missions.

At the end of the war, the U.S. military demobilized, from a force of more than 12 million personnel in 1945 to about 1.5 million in 1948. The number of women in the service declined from 266,000 to about 14,000 during this period; to some extent, this decrease was caused by an awareness on the part of the women that the statutory authorization for the WAC was scheduled to expire in 1948.[55] However, conscription lapsed in 1947, and in the face of declining male enlistments, the recently unified Defense Department sought continued authorization to utilize women in the military in order to avoid manpower shortfalls.

The Women's Armed Services Integration Act, passed in 1948, provided regular status for women in the military. It established a ceiling for enlisted women of 2 percent of total enlisted strength and a ceiling for female officers of 10 percent of female enlisted strength. This latter ceiling did not include nurses, who, as noted above, were regarded differently from other women in the military. The act required women to be eighteen years of age to enlist (males could enlist at the age of seventeen), to have written parental consent up to the age of twenty-one (males needed such consent only if they were under eighteen), restricted the ranks to which female officers could rise, and restricted their dependents benefits unless they could demonstrate they were the primary breadwinners in their families. No similar demonstration was required of male personnel, whose role as breadwinner was assumed. The act assigned all army women who were not nurses or medical specialists to the Women's Army Corps. (Women were not organizationally segregated in the other services in the same way.) The act established a separate promotion system for women, and it explicitly excluded women from service aboard combat aircraft and aboard navy ships other than hospital ships or transports (it did not, however, exclude women by statute from participating in ground combat).

The Communist coup in Czechoslovakia and the Russian blockade of Berlin led to the passage of a new Selective Service Act shortly after the Women's Armed Services Integration Act was passed. With the reinstitution of conscription, the dependence of the services on female personnel decreased. In the civilian economy, women who had moved into the civilian labor force to staff America's offices, factories, and shops while millions of men had been fighting the war moved back into traditionally female roles. Military service was not one of these roles. During the two decades after the passage of the 1948 integration act, the representation of women in the military, including nurses, never exceeded 1.5 percent.

When the Korean War erupted in 1950, the primary military manpower pool was the small depression generation. The Defense Department sought to mobilize sources of personnel that were underutilized in peacetime—notably women. Within a year, Congress had (temporarily) lifted the 2 percent limit on female enlisted strength. There had been only 22,000 women in the services when the war broke out, including 7,000 nurses. The Defense Department sought to increase the number to 112,000, only 16,000 of whom would be nurses. For a variety of reasons, the recruitment campaign to meet this goal failed miserably.[56] The number of women in service did more than double, however, to a peak of almost 49,000 late in 1952, although it never even reached the 2 percent limit that had been suspended.

The turbulence of the 1960s in America, which manifested itself in opposition to the war in Vietnam and in pressures for equal treatment for racial and ethnic minorities and for women, led to policy changes regarding military manpower, as well as to the social programs that I discuss in chapter 7. In 1966 the Defense Department created a task force on the utilization of women in the services, and in 1967, acting partly on the recommendations of that task force, several provisions of the 1948 act were changed. For the first time, women were allowed to be promoted up to the permanent rank of colonel and to be appointed as flag-rank officers. The 2 percent limita-

tion on female enlisted strength was removed. Gender differences in retirement benefits were eliminated. The Defense Department announced an immediate increase of sixty-five hundred women in the armed forces.

Unlike the mobilization during the two world wars, that for the Vietnam
War itself did not lead to a major expansion of women in the military. Service
policy was to keep women—except nurses—out of combat zones. While between five thousand and six thousand nurses and female medical specialists
served in Vietnam, the total number of other military women in the theater
was less than fifteen hundred, including about five hundred WACs, about
six hundred WAF (more than half of whom were officers), and thirty-six
women marines.

The 1967 legislation did not create gender equality of service conditions
any more effectively than Executive Order 9981 had ended racial segregation. The law left intact separate promotion systems in all services except
the air force, which had only one system from the outset. It left women in
the army in a segregated corps. It did not redress the unequal treatment
of the dependents of male and of female military personnel. It continued
to exclude women from the service academies.

The debates on the draft during the late 1960s and the work of the Marshall Commission and the Gates Commission made it evident that a conversion to an all-volunteer force was likely, and the Defense Department
knew that larger sources of volunteer military personnel would have to be
found. Interestingly, the report of the Gates Commission, which served as
the blueprint for the establishment of the all-volunteer force, made no men-
tion of the increased use of female military personnel. Indeed, the Gates
Commission seems to have assumed that the all-volunteer force would not
need female personnel at all. However, by the time Congress passed the
Equal Rights Amendment in 1972, after rejecting an amendment to exclude
women from conscription, the military services were already planning major increases in their use of women.

During early years of the all-volunteer force, there was a quadrupling of
the use of women in the U.S. armed forces. At the end of fiscal year (FY)
1973—the year when the all-volunteer force was born—there were about
43,000 enlisted women on active duty, or about 2.2 percent of the total enlisted force. By the end of FY 1975, there were 95,000 enlisted women on
active duty, or about 5.3 percent of the force. At the end of FY 1978, 117,000
women constituted 6.6 percent of the enlisted force; and in December 1980,
151,000 women made up 8.8 percent of the enlisted force. During the Carter
administration, through the end of 1980, this expansion had been projected
to reach 12 percent in the mid 1980s, with 223,700 enlisted women and
30,600 female officers serving in the armed forces. At the beginning of 1981,
however, the newly elected Reagan administration announced that it would

reexamine those goals and that it would keep the number of women at the 1980 level during the period of reexamination.

This "pause" in the expanded utilization of women affected the services in different ways. The army stopped recruiting women in mid 1981 for the remainder of the fiscal year. The Marine Corps, which had expanded its programs for women during the 1970s, "refined" these programs as it entered the 1980s, closing some specialties and some units to women. The navy started to assign more women to sea duty, and it is still projecting slight increases in the use of females. As I noted previously, women were used early and often in military aviation. Reflecting this, the air force was already 11 percent female in 1981, with women serving in all officer career fields and all but four enlisted career fields and with 30 percent of the women serving in traditionally male specialties.[57] In December 1987, 10.3 percent of active-duty military personnel were women, with differences among the services ranging from 12.6 percent in the air force to 4.8 percent in the Marine Corps. Women constituted 10.5 percent of the officer corps and 10.2 percent of the enlisted force.

The expansion in the number of women in the services was accompanied by important organizational changes. The major source of officer accessions—the Reserve Officers' Training Corps (ROTC)—was opened to women in 1970 by the air force and in 1972 by the army and the navy. Under congressional mandate, women were admitted to the service academies in 1976, more than a century after they were opened to blacks. In 1978 the Women's Army Corps was abolished. By 1980, when the pause in the increased use of females was declared, there were twenty-two thousand female commissioned officers in the U.S. armed forces. In December 1987, there were more than thirty-one thousand.

There were concurrent increases in the occupational roles in which women were allowed to serve. Traditionally, women in uniform not only had been excluded from combat roles but also had been concentrated in jobs that, in the civilian labor force, were defined as appropriate for their gender: health-care, clerical, and communications fields. During World War II, women had served in—and had proven their ability to perform—tasks that had previously been defined as male. At the end of the war, however, the traditional restrictions on gender roles were once again enforced. In 1972, during the gestation period of the all-volunteer force, less than 10 percent of enlisted women were in jobs that were not traditionally female.

By 1976 the percentage of enlisted women in "nontraditional" jobs had quadrupled, to 40 percent. And by the time the 1980 "pause" in the expansion of the utilization of females was announced, 55 percent of all enlisted women were in jobs that had not traditionally been done by women.[58]

The exclusion of women from combat roles remains, although its definition and implementation vary from time to time and from service to service. The exclusion of navy women from warships, which was explicated in the 1948 integration act, was continued under 10 U.S. Code 6015 until, in 1978, Judge John J. Sirica ruled that the navy could not use this statute as the sole basis for excluding women from duty aboard ship, thereby constraining their career opportunities as naval personnel. The navy, which had been seeking greater flexibility in the assignment of women than the law allowed, did not appeal the ruling, and it has been assigning increased numbers of women to shipboard duty. Navy women still are not allowed to serve on combat vessels or on aircraft engaged in combat missions.

Women in the air force are similarly constrained by 10 U.S. Code 8549 from serving on aircraft engaged in combat missions. The army has no parallel statutory constraints on the potential utilization of women in ground combat operations. The army does maintain a combat exclusion policy for women, which is based in part on Congress' presumed intent in passing combat-exclusion legislation affecting the other services, on assumptions regarding the negative impact that gender integration would have on unit cohesion and on the subsequent ability of units to perform their missions (similar to the assumptions that were made prior to the Korean War about the effects of racial integration on cohesion and unit performance, on the difficulty of clearly differentiating between combat and noncombat in land warfare, on assumptions about the ability of women to do the job [also similar to assumptions made about blacks from the earliest days of the Republic], on assumptions about the logistical problems of providing for feminine hygiene and toilet facilities in the field, and primarily on the basis of traditional notions of military service and of appropriate roles for women.

All of these concerns have been subjected to empirical tests and found wanting, except for the issue of congressional intent. Here the army is probably correct. When Congress excluded women from warships and combat aircraft, it is likely that it failed at the same time to exclude them from infantry and armored warfare only because it presumed that nobody would propose that women be used in such roles in the first place. When the Equal Rights Amendment was debated in Congress during the fall of 1983, after it had failed to receive the necessary ratification by the states after it had first been passed by Congress, the issue of whether passage would require military personnel to be assigned to combat jobs regardless of gender was again a central concern.

From the perspective of the services, a major issue has been the effect of gender-integrated units on mission effectiveness—a concern parallel to the one that had been raised with regard to race prior to the Korean War. In 1975 the army conducted a series of field tests to determine the Maximum Women's Army Content (MAXWAC), on the assumption that if increasing numbers of women were added to units, a point would be reached at which the unit's effectiveness would be decreased. Noncombat units were to be filled with up to 35 percent female soldiers (the percentage actually went up to 37). The evaluation of three-day field exercises showed that gender composition had no impact on a unit's effectiveness. The army then expressed concern that the three-day exercise in the continental United States did not approximate sufficiently an actual deployment, so in 1977, women were deployed in NATO's annual REFORGER (Return of Forces to Germany) exercises, and the impact of their presence was studied. Again, in this thirty-day REFWAC experiment, their presence did not decrease the unit's performance. There were concerns in the army that even REFWAC did not closely enough resemble a tactical field situation to evaluate the effect of the women's presence, but the follow-up TACWAC study, which was proposed by some, was never carried out.

During the early 1980s, a Women in the Army Policy Review was conducted, the major focus of which was to evaluate the utilization of women in army jobs against criteria both of the physical requirements of those jobs and of the location of those jobs in relation to combat. The review recommended that gender-free strength tests, based upon validated job requirements, be used in the assignment of personnel. It also recommended that twenty-three military occupational specialties that had previously opened to women be closed on the basis of the proximity of those jobs to actual combat operations in the event of war. More than twelve hundred women were serving in those specialties at the time they were defined as being inappropriate for women. Thirteen of these specialties have subsequently been reopened to women.

Much of the resistance to women in combat seems to stem from assumptions that women in units will interfere with male bonding, and thus with a unit's cohesion.[59] Similar arguments about bonding, based on race rather than gender, have been raised previously in Amerian military history. The masculine subcultural norms that currently pervade the American military and that anchor the male-bonding arguments are unquestionable. The assumption of the intractability of these norms and their projection to future wars, however, seems no more defensible than were earlier assumptions regarding the importance of racial homogeneity in combat units. Indeed, the stress of military operations itself fosters cohesion, and observations of gender-integrated units on field training exercises suggest that it is the commonality of experience of the soldiers involved in such operations, rather than their gender, that produces cohesion.[60] Whatever the reasons for the exclusion of women from combat specialties, one consequence of it is clear: unequal access to benefits. In particular, some of the most attractive packages of educational benefits that are associated with military service in the 1980s are associated with service in specialties that are difficult to recruit personnel for. These are disproportionately combat specialties. The exclusion of women from these specialties restricts women's access to the benefits.

It is particularly interesting to note the manifestations of organizational rationality that the gender issue has produced. One characteristic of organizational rationality is the utilization of scientific research to inform organizational decisions. Samuel Stouffer, reflecting on his experience as a researcher for the War Department during World War II, has noted that while in the area of military hardware no decisions were made without a careful and expensive series of tests, when it came to personnel issues, ideas were either rejected out of hand or implemented across the board, without a research base.[61] The situation is clearly different today.

I suspect that no other single issue in the United States armed forces has been subjected to as many research studies and analyses over as long a period of time as has the integration of women into the services. Ironically, the subject of this research has been another characteristic of organizational rationalization—the elimination of ascriptive characteristics in the utilization of personnel. The major constraints of race as an ascriptive characteristic were overcome more than three decades ago, and constant gains have been made subsequently. Not long ago, I anticipated that the extension of similar treatment to women would lag by that three-decade period.[62] Movement toward equality of military employment and toward the manifestation of citizenship rights and obligations has clearly been made, but more years and probably more research will be required before women will be given an equal right to fight. In the interim, however, even under conditions of inequality, large numbers of women are finding employment in and earning citizens benefits by serving in the armed forces.

6
Arms and the Man
toward the Year 2000

Both the nature and the importance of manpower in America's national-security doctrine have changed drastically during the post–World War II period. The major changes have had the consequence of minimizing the importance of people in the military equation. Only recently has this trend been reversed to any appreciable extent.

In pre-Napoleonic Europe, wars were limited in size, scope, and objective, and they ended when they had served the political purposes of sovereign states.[1] Military technology was not sophisticated, and the major military resources were manpower and the ability to transport armies. Armies were limited in size by the proportion of the male population that could be spared from the productive domestic agricultural economy (women were culturally excluded from the role of soldier). And periods of war were followed by periods of peace.

From the era of the Napoleonic Wars and the French Revolution to World War II, however, the European states adopted the mobilization model that I discussed earlier. This change was reflected in nations' raising much larger armies (still of men) than previously through militia call-ups, conscription, and voluntarism when they were at war. They fought larger-scale wars with these larger forces, in order to achieve military as well as political objectives, and they largely demobilized the forces after peace had been restored.[2] Nations did maintain small cadre forces during peacetime to allow them the flexibility to respond to situations that called for military force but did not require full mobilization. These cadres came increasingly to be commanded by military professionals, trained in the art and science of war, who regarded war as inevitable and military victory as the ultimate tool to be used in the pursuit of political objectives in the international system.

As the United States, which traced its military traditions to European roots, evolved as a nation, it emulated this pattern. From the outset, a small standing federal force was frequently engaged in low-intensity military operations against hostile colonial powers or native tribes, but the major military manpower system was the locally based militia, which was theoretically available for mobilization. As the nation matured, the mobilization base became national rather than local. This pattern held throughout much of the World War II period. Armies were still mobilized for war. These armies were predominantly male, although as we noted in chapter 5, by World War II, women were being recognized as a source of "manpower" in times of military need. And manpower—the ability to field and reconstitute combat units—was the most important, although certainly not the sole, military resource.

CHANGES IN WORLD WAR II

World War II changed this pattern in four major ways that I have mentioned earlier. First, it produced strategic bombing as a policy of war. Second, it produced a bipolar international system. Third, the confluence of the first two produced a posture of deterrence as America's major policy vis-à-vis the Soviet Union. And four, it ultimately produced a recognition that a definition of the world as consisting of two hostile camps and of strategic deterrence as the major mission of modern military forces was too simplistic and that other potential military missions and other forms of conflict had to be taken into account. These four changes provide the context within which United States military manpower policy is formulated today.

Strategic Bombing Doctrine

During World War II, military doctrines that had previously focused on land warfare between opposing armed forces were encroached upon by doctrines of strategic bombing that called for aerial attacks on the enemy's centers of population and industrial production, thereby destroying both the enemy's will to continue and its ability to materially sustain its military forces by making noncombatants the targets. This was the "socialization of danger"—the disappearance of the distinction between civilians and military personnel as targets—that Harold D. Lasswell had referred to in his discussion of the "garrison state." Under the strategic warfare doctrine, Britain and the United States conducted massive bombing operations on Germany and Japan. Had the basic assumptions of the strategic-warfare doctrine been correct, labor-intensive land warfare would have become less important, and military manpower policy would be less of an issue today.

Strategic bombing did not, however, fulfill the promise of its theory in World War II. The enemies' will to continue and their ability to sustain their forces were not destroyed. Massive land operations had to be undertaken, and the enemies' homeland ultimately had to be occupied militarily. The United States was slow to learn this lesson, however—it had not been learned by the time of the Vietnam War two decades later—and airpower, committed primarily to the delivery of strategic weapons, rather than to the provision of close air support to ground-combat troops, held the central position in United States defense policy during the postwar years. Indeed, while the air force was evolving from the United States Army Air Corps as a separate service, the ground forces—both army and marine—had to develop their own aerial capabilities to support ground-combat operations. Military manpower did not disappear as a factor in the equation, but it became less important in the calculus of policy makers. And the distinction between military and civilian diminished in the shadow of a doctrine that focused on the latter rather than on the former as strategic targets.

The Bipolar World and the Worst-Case Scenario

The second major change at the end of World War II consisted of a split in the alliance that had defeated the Axis nations and of a continuing adversarial relationship between the Soviet Union and the Eastern European nations that had been drawn into its sphere of influence, on the one hand, and the Western European nations (including West Germany and Italy) and their allies in the Pacific (including Australia, New Zealand, Japan, China, and South Korea, which had been partitioned from North Korea at the 38th parallel at the end of World War II). Concerns about Soviet expansionism in Europe, which had been nourished in part by Soviet actions predicated on their own perceptions and fears of capitalist encirclement and placed in the context of two World Wars, led United States military doctrine to focus on preparation for a confrontation between the Soviet Union and its Warsaw Pact allies, on the one hand, and the NATO alliance, on the other, which would be fought on the European continent.

The Deterrence Posture

The policy of strategic bombing during wartime had been reinforced in the postwar bipolar world by the advent of nuclear weapons, over which the United States held a monopoly for four years after the war. Given its possession of the atomic bomb, the United States assumed a posture of unilateral deterrence: a nation that threatened the United States would have visited upon it—via an airborne delivery system—the most devastating weapon that had yet been devised. This recognition supposedly would dissuade potential adversaries. After 1949, when the Soviet Union emerged as the second nuclear power, unilateral deterrence evolved into bilateral deterrence, and the doctrine of mutually assured destruction (MAD), which, despite recent agreements on the reduction of intermediate-range weapons, is likely to persist into the foreseeable future as the major basis of calculations of the NATO–Warsaw Pact balance.[3]

The nuclear-deterrence posture basically asserts that each major power has enough nuclear military capability that even if it should be attacked and if a large portion of its military power and indeed its society should be destroyed, it will nonetheless be able to retaliate and impose a level of destruction on the attacking nation that the attacker would find unacceptable.[4] A society does not require weapons superiority to assume a deterrence posture. It merely needs enough retaliatory strength to impose destruction on an enemy after having suffered a massive attack, in addition to the will to use that strength. One of the more subtle components of this doctrine is a shift from the "absolutist" position that sees warfare as inevitable and military victory as the ultimate tool to be used in the pursuit of political objectives, on the one hand, to a more "pragmatic" orientation, which recognizes that some political ends cannot be achieved militarily and that there are situations in which military victory is not the ultimate objective of armed forces.[5]

The deterrence doctrine is a defensive one that requires high-technology offensive capability. It does not require large standing armies, although during the post–World War II era, the United States has stationed large numbers of troops abroad as a trip wire, to assure its allies that if they are attacked and if American troops are killed, America's military strength will be called into play. Most important, the doctrine calls for continued investment, during periods when we are not actively at war, in countermeasures to reduce the lethality of the enemy's weapons systems—for example, President Reagan's strategic defense initiative ("star wars"), which is the most recent iteration of this process—and for the development of weapons that the enemy in turn cannot counter. This basically is the genesis of the arms race. In this process, military hardware assumes even greater primacy over manpower. The ascendancy of air power and the doctrine of massive retaliation have made the role of a land army in actual combat ambiguous. Rather than preparing for flexible responses to a range of scenarios, the levels of intensity between deterrence and total war were largely disregarded from the late 1940s until the Vietnam era.

A disparity between the size of the Soviet armed forces and the United States armed forces, in terms of manpower, is frequently cited as a justification for America's continued investment in military technology as a "force multiplier." Interestingly, however, in the United States, far more attention is being paid to bilateral limitations or reductions in stockpiles of strategic weapons—the force multipliers—than to bilateral reductions in the size of the forces, whose imbalance was originally used as the justification for the technologies.

Tactical Operations

The fourth major change in the United States military—one that was hinted at in Korea in 1950 and then was not directly addressed again in military policy until the 1980s, although it emerged as a concern of the Carter White House and of social-science analysis in the intervening years—was a broadening of the military mission to include, as appropriate goals for armed forces, wars of lower intensity than strategic exchanges—that is, conventional wars, peacekeeping, and other low-intensity military operations—along with the achievement of military victory in strategic warfare. This reflects the shift from "absolutist" to "pragmatic" orientations. No longer was the primary goal of armed forces to use the maximum capability at their disposal to engage and defeat an enemy. Rather, their primary goal became preventing an enemy from using its maximum military capability. The Korean "police action" was the first such undertaking by the United States, and it demonstrated that different goals require different configurations of force.

Conventional warfare. Throughout the 1940s, the United States developed its atomic deterrent and strategic air power, focusing on the European continent. Despite increasing tensions between the two partitioned Koreas, the United States was caught unprepared for a labor-intensive land war, which did not involve atomic weapons, outside of Europe, when North Korean troops crossed the 38th parallel in June 1950. Within two weeks of the invasion, President Truman had authorized the use of United States military forces in Korea, and within another week, the United Nations had added forces from fifteen other nations to a United Nations command to engage in a "police action." Nonetheless, by early September, the South Korean army and its allies had been driven to the southeastern tip of Korea.

On September 15, UN troops, commanded by Gen. Douglas MacArthur, made a daring landing at Inchon, on the west coast. The North Korean forces fell back, and MacArthur pursued them into North Korea, almost to the Yalu River, the border between North Korea and the People's Republic of China. In late November, Chinese troops joined with North Korean troops and launched a counterattack that drove the United Nations troops south again. After months of heavy fighting, the center of the conflict returned to the 38th parallel, and in 1953 an armistice agreement was signed. Peace negotiations have never been concluded, and although the two Koreas are divided by a demilitarized zone, sporadic hostilities persist.

The Korean police action sensitized the United States to the need for maintaining forces-in-being during peacetime, given the speed with which war can unfold in the modern world. It set a precedent of defining as police or constabulary operations, rather than wars, military operations that were mounted by multinational forces and were waged without recourse to the nuclear weapons that were available. It also sensitized the United States to the likelihood that major wars might be waged in northern Asia, as well as in Europe, and might involve adversaries other than the Soviet Union; but Americans did not generalize further than that. The Soviet Union had emerged as a nuclear power, and United States military doctrine again came to focus primarily on war in the European theater, which was compounded by the threat of strategic exchanges between the United States and the

Soviet Union involving not only bombers but also increasingly powerful and accurate ballistic missiles, and by an expanding investment in nuclear sea power as well as air power. This technological trend made the ground forces the most labor-intensive component of the services, while the air and sea forces increasingly emphasized investment in high-technology big-ticket items.

The Vietnam War in the 1960s provided a dramatic example of the lessons that the United States had failed to learn. The nation was not prepared for the escalation of that war and for the manpower demands of a ground war—particularly a largely unconventional ground war—elsewhere than in Europe or northern Asia. The nation did not mobilize its reserve military units, and it produced widespread opposition to an inequitable conscription system that eventually led to the demise of that system. The United States failed to recognize the close relationship between the political and military dimensions of the war. The United States tried to substitute strategic bombing for effective political warfare, and it lost the war.

Constabulary operations. In 1960, recognizing the limitation of the deterrence strategy to the upper end of the conflict-intensity spectrum and recognizing the likelihood that, United States military doctrine notwithstanding, there would be hostile confrontations involving conventional forces in places other than Europe, Morris Janowitz proposed the constabulary concept of military force:

> The use of force in international relations has been so altered that it seems appropriate to speak of constabulary forces, rather than of military forces. . . . The military establishment becomes a constabulary force when it is continuously prepared to act, *committed to the minimum use of force, and seeks viable international relations rather than victory.* . . . The constabulary force concept encompasses the entire range of military power and organization.[6]

In his original formulation of the constabulary concept, Janowitz had anticipated that armed forces would look upon such operations as less prestigious than traditional military operations, in part because any involvement in domestic police activities is seen as detracting from the national-security mission. He emphasized that the constabulary concept did not refer to domestic police operations and, indeed, that the "extensive involvement of the military as an internal police force . . . would hinder the development of the constabulary concept in international relations."[7] Because in the modern world the dividing line between war and peace is space rather than time, "it is no longer feasible . . . to operate on a double standard of peacetime and wartime premises. Since the constabulary force concept eliminates the distinction between peacetime and wartime military establishment, it draws on the police concept."[8]

The term *constabulary* was perhaps an unfortunate choice. It carries the image of the unarmed British constable, keeping peace through civility, morality, and his whistle. Janowitz assumed that the military shared this popular conception because peacekeeping is viewed as being restricted to the low end of the combat-intensity spectrum:

The military technologists tend to thwart the constabulary concept because of their essential preoccupation with the upper end of the destructive continuum and their pressure to perfect weapons without regard to international politics. The heroic leaders, in turn, tend to thwart the constabulary concept because of their desire to maintain conventional military doctrine and their resistance to assessing the political consequences of limited military actions which do not produce "victory."[9]

In the event that peace keeping should fail, units that are involved in peace-keeping operations must be prepared to fight. Therefore, constabulary units cannot be organizationally differentiated from regular military formations. Indeed, to make this transition successfully, they must be ground-combat formations, military units whose role under a strategic-bombing doctrine was ambiguous. The constabulary posture gives labor-intensive ground-combat forces a raison d'être.

However, a large force-in-being during peacetime, which is constantly prepared to act, is committed to the minimum use of force, but is capable of engaging in large-scale ground-combat operations if necessary, might have difficulty in maintaining its essential combat readiness.[10] This in itself would generate resistance among military professionals, and recently, Janowitz has affirmed that "the military have rejected, or at least resist, the concept of a constabulary because to them it sounds too much like police work."[11]

Although the concepts of deterrence and of constabulary operations have been used interchangeably in some of the literature, they are not equivalent. The differences are consequential for manpower policy. The two concepts refer to different ends of the combat-intensity spectrum. Deterrence is capital intensive and, to the extent that conflicts erupt, is oriented to military victory. While nonnuclear forces that fulfill a deterrence function were in part a trip wire during the 1950s and the early 1960s, they were expected to meet, with their own force, a first-echelon assault by opposing forces. Constabulary troops, by contrast, are expected to use minimal force and to minimize the force used by others.

Deterrence is concerned primarily with relations between the superpowers, where high-intensity warfare would be most devastating. The consequence of the process, to the extent that it is successful, is, not the achievement of worldwide peace, but the potential substitution of conflict between surrogates for conflicts between superpowers. Deterrence may prevent the superpowers from going to war against each other, but it does not preclude a major power from going to war against a nonnuclear power: for example, the Soviet Union in Afghanistan, Great Britain in the Falkland Islands, or the United States in Grenada or Libya. Nor does deterrence preclude nations that are not members of the nuclear club from going to war against one another, even if they have alliances with one of the nuclear powers. Thus it is possible that the success of high-technology capital-intensive nuclear technology in deterring war between the superpowers will increase the likelihood of more labor-intensive nonnuclear forms of conflict, thereby increasing the importance of manpower in a nation's total military posture. By decreasing conventional forces because of the existence of nuclear capabilities, a nation is left in the position of potentially having to respond to a nonnuclear threat with nuclear weapons, because the alternative nonnuclear response has been dismantled.

The fact that Americans' preoccupation with the European scenario and their dependence on deterrence and on air power had limited the nation's conventional response capability became obvious in the wake of the Vietnam War. So, during the late 1970s, the mission of the United States Army was broadened from a focus on high-intensity conflict in Europe and northern Asia. The revelation in September 1979 that the Soviet Union had more than two thousand heavily armed combat troops in Cuba and that the United States was not able to do anything about them; the seizure of the United States Embassy in Teheran two months later and the subsequent unsuccessful attempt by American armed forces to rescue the hostages; and the invasion of Afghanistan by eighty-five thousand conventionally armed Soviet troops in December 1979—the first time that Soviet troops had been used in combat outside of Eastern Europe since World War II—all dramatically demonstrated the salience of low-intensity-conflict scenarios in other parts of the globe and the inability of the United States to respond to them.[12]

President Jimmy Carter had in fact recognized this shortcoming in America's military capability. Presidential Review Memorandum 10 (PRM-10), issued in the early months of his administration, had noted the potential for conflict in the Persian Gulf region, and subsequently the Special Coordination Committee of the National Security Council had recommended the establishment of a rapid deployment force (RDF), a recommendation that President Carter approved in Presidential Directive 18 (PD-18), issued in August, 1977.

Neither the State Department nor any of the military services had been enthusiastic about the RDF concept, and the administration, concentrating on Europe again, had been preoccupied with the SALT II negotiations and with relations between the NATO allies. It took the discovery that Soviet troops were in Cuba, the capture of embassy personnel in Iran, and the Soviet invasion of Afghanistan to turn a portion of the administration's attention back toward the implementation of PD-18. The first official announcement of the RDF was on December 5, 1979. The RDF was to authorized to call upon units from each of the four armed services. These units included the army's 82d and 101st Airborne divisions, the two existing Ranger battalions, Special Forces units, and fifty thousand men from the Marine Corps, as well as other units. It was not long before some of these units were deployed on missions that have not been customary for United States armed forces.

AMERICA AS A PARTICIPANT
IN PEACE-KEEPING OPERATIONS

The constabulary concept was not without precedent in military experience. The League of Nations had fielded an international peace-keeping force in the Saar in 1934–35, and the United Nations had mounted twelve peace-keeping missions between 1945 and 1970.[13] Larry L. Fabian's analysis of these missions, which was intended to provide insights into how to use military forces successfully as peace keepers, suggested that consensus between the superpowers on basic peace-keeping principles was needed but that once this consensus had been achieved, these nations should maintain "distance and detachment" from the peace-keeping system.[14]

Along similar lines, Charles Moskos has hypothesized that "soldiers from neutral middle powers are more likely to subscribe to the constabulary ethic than are soldiers from major powers."[15] His observations of the UN Force in Cyprus did not support the hypothesis, but he recognized that the realities of international politics nonetheless made the neutral middle powers the primary and appropriate sources for international peace-keeping forces. This principle has become an accepted part of peace-keeping doctrine. Thus, not only United States strategic doctrine, which has focused on high-intensity warfare in Europe, but also commonly accepted international perspectives on peace-keeping operations have mitigated against having the United States seriously consider the peace-keeping role of ground-combat troops prior to the 1980s.

The willingness of American citizens to serve in the military as peace keepers rather than war fighters when the security of their own nation was not being dramatically threatened; the tolerance of professional combat soldiers to operate as peace keepers; and the tolerance of American taxpayers to support peace-keeping operations in which American troops are more likely to sustain than to inflict casualties and fatalities would not have been tested had the United States been able to maintain the distance and the detachment from such operations for which conventional peace-keeping doctrine calls. However, the doctrine was challenged twice in the early 1980s.

In accordance with the principle of the noninvolvement of major powers in UN peace-keeping forces, the Egyptian-Israeli Peace Treaty of March 26, 1979 (the Camp David Accords), specified, in article 6, section 8: "the Parties shall agree on the nations from which the United Nations Force and Observers will be drawn. *They will be drawn from nations other than those which are permanent members of the United Nations Security Council"* (emphasis added). However, on May 18, 1981, the president of the Security Council indicated that the council had not been able to reach an agreement on the proposal to establish the UN force and observers that the treaty called for, and the parties to the treaty agreed to the substitution of a multinational force and observers (MFO). At that point, Israel insisted that the United States participate in the force.[16] In a letter to the ministers of foreign affairs of Israel and of Egypt, Secretary of State Alexander Haig committed the United States to contributing to the MFO an infantry battalion, a logistical support unit, and a group of civilian observers.

Between the spring of 1982 and the autumn of 1985, battalions of the army's 82d Airborne Division alternated with battalions from the 101st Airborne Division for six-months tours in the Sinai, supported by additional U.S. troops. Subsequently, other elements of the army have been involved. Moreover, after the Israeli invasion of Lebanon in June 1982, United States Marines were sent to participate in a multinational peace-keeping force in Beirut, initially to cover the withdrawal of the Palestine Liberation Organization and subsequently, after massacres at two Palestinian refugee camps, to maintain a "presence."

While the importance of the Sinai MFO must not be minimized, the Beirut mission provided earlier and more dramatic demonstrations of the dangers of peace-keeping operations. Shortly after the marines landed at the Beirut International Airport in September 1982, one was killed and three were wounded when undetected explosives detonated. In February 1983, a marine captain made headlines by challenging the advance of three Israeli tanks with a loaded pistol at a marine checkpoint. The following month, at least five marines were wounded in Beirut during exchanges of fire. Most dramatically and tragically, on the morning of October 23, 1983, a large truck, filled with explosives, smashed into the marines' headquarters building at the Beirut airport and exploded with a force equal to 12,000 pounds of high explosives. More than 240 marines who were billeted in the building were killed. A simultaneous attack on the counterpart French peace-keeping contingent killed 56 French paratroopers. These attacks highlighted the growth of another form of low-intensity armed conflict—widespread terrorism, aimed at military personnel and frequently sponsored by unfriendly states—which had not figured in the post–World War II military calculations.

A tragedy of equal magnitude befell the Sinai peace-keeping force two years later. In December 1985, a chartered airplane—which was carrying soldiers of the 101st Airborne Division from the Sinai, where they had been attached to the MFO, back to Fort Campbell to rejoin their families and friends for Christmas—crashed at Gander, Newfoundland, killing all aboard the plane. These deaths were attributable, not to hostile fire or to terrorist activities, but to lowest-bidder contracting and poor aircraft maintenance.

The utilization of paratroopers and marines as peace keepers—units that had several other missions in America's matrix of global military commitments—highlighted the fact that Americans had little depth in their ability to mount such missions. Subsequently a move has been made to redesign much of the nation's ground-combat force from "heavy" configurations—which are equipped with armor, tracked vehicles, and heavy artillery and are oriented toward a European war but are slow to deploy— to "light" configurations—which are smaller and more rapidly deployable and are oriented toward lower intensity conflict elsewhere than in Europe. Battalions from two of these divisions have served with the Sinai MFO. Indeed, the pendulum has swung far in the direction of preparation for low-intensity operations; this raises the questions of how easily a nation that has been fed for decades on reports of the Soviet menace will adapt to supporting a large peacetime military force that is oriented toward other, less clearly specified threats and of how readily an armed force, which likewise has been trained and indoctrinated to prepare for a European confrontation, will adapt to lower-intensity scenarios without losing the capability to deal with a European war should the need arise.

Perceptions of Conflict Intensity

Perceptions of Civilians. The willingness of Americans to serve in and support a military establishment with the labor-intensive missions of constabulary operations and low-intensity warfare will be constrained by perceptions of the likelihood and the importance of such operations, as against the likelihood and the importance of conflict with the Soviet Union. At the height of the Cold War during the 1950s, Americans harbored extremely unfavorable feelings toward the Soviet Union.[17] In 1950, large percentages of those Americans who had heard of atomic weapons (and most had) felt that Russia would use them against the United States (80 percent in March, 91 percent in August).[18] During the period of détente, up until 1973, attitudes became more favorable, but throughout the 1960s, more than 60 percent of Americans continued to feel that in the event of another world war, atomic weapons would be used against them. After 1973, attitudes turned more negative again and reached a low point immediately after the Soviet invasion of Afghanistan. During this entire period, the American public favored the development of ballistic-missile defenses against an attack from the Soviet Union.[19] With the withdrawal of Soviet troops from Afghanistan and with the success of negotiations to reduce intermediate-range nuclear forces in Europe, Americans should expect perceptions of tensions to decrease.

Events such as the invasion of Afghanistan, however, along with other regional tensions in the world, seem to have sensitized Americans to the greater likelihood of lower-intensity conflict than of total war between NATO and the Warsaw Pact. In 1984 the National Opinion Research Center at the University of Chicago asked a representative sample of Americans for their evaluations of the likelihood of a series of military events during the next decade. Three of these were scenarios of conflicts of varying intensities. Rating these on a scale from 1 ("won't happen") to 7 ("certain to happen"), Americans saw the likelihood of conflict as varying inversely with the intensity of combat.[20] On this seven-point scale, the most intense combat scenario—total atomic war—had the lowest mean rating of likelihood (3.2). The least intense—repeated guerrilla wars against left-wing rebels—had the highest mean rating (5.4). The likelihood of a large-scale conventional war received an intermediate rating (4.5). In the views of American citizens, then, the kinds of wars in which they are likely to find themselves are those that are most dependent on manpower rather than technology. There should be, in the public mind, a justification for a large standing force oriented toward low-intensity ground-combat and peace-keeping operations; and any reductions in tensions between the United States and the Soviet Union should increase that justification.

Attitudes of military personnel. The expectations of the military personnel who will fight America's wars are no less important than those of the civilians who will support or oppose these military encounters, and the views of American soldiers regarding a wide range of conflict scenarios have been monitored in this regard for more than a decade. The inverse relationship between conflict intensity and estimated likelihood, which was reflected in the civilian data, appears here as well. For example, in a 1978 army survey of personnel in the chains of command of forty-five brigade-sized units, who ranged from sergeants to brigade commanders, the highest estimates of likelihood were assigned to peace-keeping duties, even though the United States was not yet involved in the Sinai MFO or in Beirut, and the lowest were assigned to nuclear war.

In another survey, which involved soldiers from the first battalion to participate in the Sinai MFO, the same inverse relationship between likelihood and combat intensity was expressed by a sample of paratroopers.[21] In each case, more than 80 percent of the respondents thought it likely that

Americans would become involved in a peace-keeping operation, while roughly half as many expected very high-intensity conflict. A third survey, of an airborne infantry company that went to the Sinai a year later as part of the MFO, gave low estimates of the likelihood of nuclear war (both tactical and strategic), high estimates of the likelihood of participating in a peace-keeping force (more than 80 percent), and graduated estimates of the likelihood of other scenarios (tactical biological warfare, tactical chemical warfare, large conventional wars, limited conventional wars, and guerrilla wars) as an inverse function of combat intensity.[22] Interestingly, this gradation of intensities among intermediate-range conflicts had not been as differentiated in earlier surveys. An analysis of these data suggests that direct participation in low-intensity combat missions, in which armed forces are used as instruments of policy, sensitizes soldiers to the sometimes subtle differences between and implications of these missions in ways that simply training for the missions does not do.[23] Participation becomes a mode of broader political education.

The Impact of Deterrence and Constabulary Missions

The expectation among soldiers that they are more likely to participate in low-intensity than in high intensity conflicts in areas other than Europe, the army's ground-warfare doctrine notwithstanding, reflects the lessons of experience. The question remains of whether this has implications for America's military-manpower posture. One issue, of course, is whether the ability of a volunteer military force to attract and retain personnel is affected by the degree to which the image of that force is one of fighting wars or of keeping the peace. Military recruiting advertisements do not depict armed-forces personnel in a peace-keeping posture. The second issue is the degree to which a military force that is doctrinally committed to fighting wars can adapt to a peace-keeping mission, what the implications of such adaptation are, and whether a combat unit that has been on constabulary duty can readapt to a deterrence or war-fighting posture.

The first of these issues is probably not important. With the exception of bursts of patriotic fervor that produce lines at recruiting stations immediately after gestures of hostility toward the United States in the international system, there is little evidence that a belligerent image has a long-term effect on the accession or retention of manpower. Indeed, recent data suggest that patriotism ranks relatively low as a motivater for military service, although as I noted earlier, patriotism does have considerable power to discriminate between young Americans who expect to serve in the armed forces and those who do not.[24]

The second issue, however, reflects concerns that Janowitz raised when he formulated the constabulary model. He has suggested that during peacetime, a large force-in-being that is constantly prepared to act, is committed to the minimum use of force, but is capable of engaging in large-scale combat operations if necessary might have difficulty in maintaining its essential combat readiness.[25] This theme was subsequently echoed by Jonathan Alford, who has noted the "insolubility" of maintaining the combat effectiveness of a voluntary military force—particularly a ground combat force—that is indefinitely placed in a deterrence posture.[26] Similarly, Gregory D. Foster has suggested that deterrence has an effect on "the fighting ethic" and that in the case of the United States, the fighting ethic has suffered.[27] The fighting ethic can be regarded as part of the attitudinal/motivational component of combat readiness.

Most of the data that exist on the combat ethic fail to support the concerns of Janowitz, Alford, and Foster. David Gottlieb's interviews with junior enlisted personnel at Fort Sill, Oklahoma, suggested that even those in combat specialties did not really think about going to war as part of the job of a peacetime army.[28] However, many of his respondents had been interviewed relatively early in their military training and had not been fully socialized to the soldier's role. By contrast, studies of personnel in combat units, who have undergone more complete organizational socialization, have shown that they regard going to war as part of the job and that they are prepared to do that job.[29] The combat ethic in general does not seem to be problematic among American combat troops. The effect of constabulary duty on this ethic, however, has not been as thoroughly analyzed.

Before the first United States infantry unit was deployed for duty with the Sinai MFO, the Israeli Defense Force warned the United States Army about a phenomenon that it called "creeping Bedouinism"—that is, adaptation to the slow pace of desert life, which might dull the sharp cutting edge of a combat force. This syndrome can be regarded as a special case of the problem of maintaining combat readiness during a period that, in the past, would have been regarded as peacetime. Janowitz has hypothesized that this problem would be least severe in the air force, where "the routines of flying aircraft create units in being"; in navy units, which "have traditionally represented a force in being and maintained a group solidarity derived from the vitality of seamanship"; and in radar and missile crews, which "because of the deadly character of the weapons they handle, feel a sense of urgency which helps them to overcome boredom."[30] He expected the problem to be most severe in ground combat units, which are the most likely elements of military organization to be called upon to participate in actual constabulary operations. Interestingly, among ground forces, Janowitz has seen the problem of combat readiness as being least severe among elite combat units, because of the risk and danger of their training. These have been the very units that have been assigned most frequently as the American contingents in recent multinational peace-keeping operations.

American soldiers in the Sinai did in fact adapt. They also got bored—an almost universal characteristic of soldiers on peace-keeping duty.[31] And it may be that the boredom of constabulary operations and the adaptation to the slow pace of a mission in which one's duty is to be "a presence" contributed to the laxity of marine security in Beirut that allowed the marines' headquarters to be bombed by terrorists.[32] Nonetheless it seems to be the case that although American soldiers regard future peace-keeping missions as highly likely, these soldiers consider such missions to be deviations from their primary mission: to be prepared to go to war.

Low-Intensity Warfare

In an unrelated event two days after the bombing of the marine barracks in Beirut, the United States launched a two-pronged airborne and helicopter-borne assault on the Caribbean island of Grenada. Involved in the operation was much of the rapid deployment force: both of the army's Ranger battalions; a marine amphibious assault unit, which had been en route to Beirut to relieve the unit that had been bombed on constabulary duty; most of the units of the 82d Airborne Division, including elements that had recently returned from peace-keeping duty in the Sinai; and other American units. It was the largest United States ground-combat operation since the Vietnam War.

The fact that recent veterans of the Sinai MFO were included in this mission provided some insights into the ability of soldiers who had recently experienced the boredom of peacekeeping to adapt to the high-activity levels of actual combat. The operation had been a military victory, and while there had clearly been problems in intelligence gathering, in command and control, in medical support, and in interservice cooperation—problems that would probably have led to disaster in a larger military operation—individual military personnel performed well. And when paratroopers who had participated in both the Sinai MFO and in Urgent Fury (the invasion of Grenada) were asked for their evaluations of the two missions, more than 40 percent of them reported that the MFO was inappropriate for their unit—a response that was given by fewer than 2 percent with regard to the Grenada invasion.[33] There was significant persistent resistance to the peace-keeping role.

Conventional Warfare in the South Atlantic

The fact that there has not been a major military confrontation between the United States and the Soviet Union since World War II might be taken as an indication of the success of the doctrine of deterrence. Most recent wars have been internal or regional and have involved third-world nations rather than major powers. It is important to recognize, however, that the Soviet invasion of Afghanistan, the U.S. invasion of Grenada, and the spring 1986 U.S. bombing of targets in Libya as a response to terrorism allegedly supported by that state, are not the only examples in recent times of major powers' being engaged in combat operations. The 1982 war between Britain and Argentina in the South Atlantic is worthy of our consideration: it exemplifies the fact that wars involving major powers have not been made obsolete; it gives us additional insights into the ability of troops to shift from a deterrence posture (e.g., service with the British Army of the Rhine) or constabulary duty (e.g., in Northern Ireland) to an active combat mode; and at the time it was fought, it was purported to have had implications for the evaluation of conscript, in comparison to volunteer, armed forces.

On April 2, 1982, Argentine troops invaded and took control of the islands that they call the Malvinas and that the British call the Falklands.[34] The British had been aware of a large Argentine naval force in the vicinity of the Falklands since March 31 but were otherwise caught unaware. The British mobilization was nonetheless impressive. Much of the British fleet had recently returned to port and was on Easter leave, including special marine forces who had just completed three months of NATO arctic exercises. The recall of personnel by telephone and radio appeals was accomplished within forty-eight hours of the fall of Stanley, capital of the Falklands.

On May 21, some five thousand British troops established a beachhead at Port San Carlos, about 50 miles west of Stanley. On May 26/27 they broke out from the beachhead and advanced successfully on Stanley, winning important battles and ultimately capturing strategic high ground outside of Stanley. Argentine forces became demoralized, collapsed organizationally, discarded their weapons, and abandoned their positions. On the night of June 14, Argentina formally surrendered.

The war in the South Atlantic was the largest and most protracted armed engagement involving large military formations that a major Western power has staged in recent years. It yields lessons regarding the relative importance of technology versus manpower, methods of manpower accession, and the quality and organization of personnel—lessons that I believe are relevant to the United States military as it embraces low-intensity conflict as an element of its mission.

The technological lessons of the South Atlantic war, which paralleled similar lessons learned in the smaller-scale Grenada campaign, were that the most lethal weapons available to modern armed forces—the nuclear arsenal—will not be used in low-intensity operations and that in the absence of a willingness to use such weapons, the military outcome of such warfare will be based on the ability of ground-combat forces to close with, engage, and defeat the enemy. Technology plays an important defensive role, and it helps to shape the context within which such ground engagements take place, but it does not determine the outcome.

With regard to the accession of the manpower involved in the war, as the conflict evolved, it quickly became defined in terms of a volunteer military force (the British) confronting a conscripted force (the Argentines). Some analysts have considered the outcome a victory of military voluntarism over conscription. Thus, for example, Lawrence Freedman has suggested that "the key difference between the two sides was the organization of their military forces and their professionalism. . . . Argentine forces were riven by conflicts between . . . regulars and conscripts, which impaired their performance."[35] In the same time frame, the Israeli Defense Force was "proving" the opposite in Lebanon: the effectiveness of conscripted soldiers over volunteers in combat operations, the political dimensions of that conflict aside.

To say that the British ground troops waged a low-technology campaign is an understatement. Weather conditions that grounded aircraft, as well as the loss of helicopters aboard the *Atlantic Conveyor*, which had been attacked by air on May 25, limited the availability of air transport. The only good road into Stanley was well defended, and other "roads" were merely tracks, rendering virtually useless the wheeled vehicles and even the heavy-tracked vehicles that modern armies depend upon for mobility. The assault on Stanley was accomplished by a long overland march, on which the troops carried their own supplies. The major British tactical advantage lay, not in high-technology physical warfare, but in psychological warfare, including widespread publicity given to Argentine defeats; the tactic of isolating Argentine units; the encouraging of frightening rumors about the fighting capabilities of the Ghurka Rifles and the way in which they treated prisoners; and an airdrop of British pamphlets encouraging the Argentine soldiers to surrender.

The British were sensitive to the political and human dimensions of warfare. These dimensions included factors that I discussed earlier. The British population and the troops who served as their agents sensed a threat to sovereignty, which they felt was worth going to war over. The Argentines, in contrast, seem to have engaged in the initial occupation of the Malvinas under the influence largely of the belief that it would not lead to war, and they lacked the commitment to pursue the war to its successful conclusion if shots were indeed fired in anger. As the distinction between what is military and what is political becomes increasingly vague and as military forces are increasingly used as instruments of policy in operations that may or may not lead to war, political awareness becomes an increasingly important component of military life.

The British campaign in the South Atlantic also pointed to the importance of intangibles such as cohesion and leadership, which tend not to enter the cost-benefit analyses of military budgeteers, which at times seem to run counter to the American value placed on individualism, but which are crucial for military victory. In wartime, while soldiers may be led to their deaths (albeit not gladly) by a leader to whom they have affective ties, while they may receive psychological support against the stress of combat from the proximity of a buddy, and while they might willingly give up their lives so that a comrade in arms might live, they are considerably less anxious to be managed to their deaths or to die for strangers, and they are less capable of standing up to the psychological stress of combat as isolated individuals.

The British have maintained cohesive units by means of their regimental system. They have been less concerned about force levels than has the United States, and they have let the size of the force be determined by the recruit market. Victories in battle in the South Atlantic were won by units that were proud of their traditions. The Argentines, on the other hand, maintained a castelike distinction between officers and enlisted ranks that mitigated against cohesive ties between leaders and subordinates. This failure was compounded when the Argentines, in the defense of the Malvinas, dispersed personnel from their elite formations among other units, thereby losing the benefits of cohesion. The only real resistance to the British advance came from elite Argentine formations that had remained intact. On both sides, cohesion, where it existed, contributed to effective performance in land warfare.

THE BATTLEFIELD OF THE FUTURE

The ongoing race in military technology between the United States and the Soviet Union, in the historical context of low intensity conflicts in Afghanistan, Lebanon, Grenada, and the Falkland Islands, has led the United States in the late 1980s to prepare doctrinally for a wider range of combat scenarios than it has heretofore. The major doctrinal and organizational thrust has still been to upgrade the preparations for the European conflict that Americans have been anticipating since World War II. In this regard, the basic organization of armored, infantry, and mechanized divisions has until recently been the same: they have been configured to fight a high-intensity, high-technology battle on the ground and in the air on the European continent. These units have been armor-heavy, producing costs in strategic mobility in exchange for the benefits of increased fire power and increased protection from enemy fire. The United States has not had the airlift capacity to move heavy divisions, with their personnel and equipment, from North America to Europe rapidly. It would take almost thirteen hundred sorties by long-range transport aircraft to move a standard infantry division of more than eighteen thousand men overseas. If all of our existing C-5 and C-141 aircraft were operational and available for such a mission, they would have to make an average of more than four round trips each, and they could not accomplish the deployment of one such division in less than a week and a half under the most ideal conditions.

To offset this constraint, we have pre-positioned military supplies in Europe, where we hope that they will still be intact should American troops have to draw them from storage to use in a war, and we have garrisoned a large United States army in Europe. Given airlift limitations and the speed with which a war in Europe might be fought, it is this army, along with the troops of America's NATO allies, that might have to fight what one senior commander has referred to as a "come as you are war." The European scenario, which is clearly the most costly, is also seen by most analysts to be the least likely. However, it is not impossible; for just as the resistance of the major belligerents in this theater to the use of nuclear weapons increases the need for constabulary troops, it also may increase the importance of heavy conventional forces, both for deterrence and for fighting wars, should deterrence fail, although some factions within the German Social Democratic Party (SPD) have argued that a lighter and larger militia force in Europe, without offensive capabilities, might reduce tensions without sacrificing deterrence.

At the other extreme, the recognition of potential American involvement in other parts of the world, which are less dependent on heavy armor but which require more rapid mobility, has recently led the United States Army to deviate from a fifty-year trend toward heavier and larger divisions in the mid-1980s and to develop light infantry divisions, the basic organization of which is different from the armored and mechanized divisions that have been used to defend Europe. Interestingly, these lighter units might be more compatible with the SPD's emerging view of "defensive defense."

Given the ascendancy of new bomber and fighter technologies for the air force and given the trend toward a larger and more nuclear-powered navy, as against manpower needs in the competition for defense resources, the army has had to design these divisions within the existing size of the force. Thus there is a trade-off between heavy divisions that are oriented toward a European or north-Asian conflict and these new lighter and smaller units, which would require only 478 air-transport sorties to deploy and which optimally could be moved in four days. The certification exercise of the organization, equipment, and doctrine of the first of these light divisions took place in August 1986. In addition, all of the services have paid increased attention to smaller special-warfare units, and both the Defense Department and Congress have been developing means of coordinating joint service operations that involve such units in the hope of avoiding the kinds of problems that the United States encountered in the Iran rescue mission and in Grenada.

If perceptions of the differential likelihood of various combat scenarios reflect the reality of the world situation, soldiers in "light" divisions are more likely than is the United States Army in Europe to be deployed for peace-keeping operations or to go to war. However, the ability of these divisions to move relatively rapidly, unencumbered by heavy systems, would leave them highly vulnerable to armor-heavy mechanized forces of the Warsaw Pact were they called upon to participate in a European engagement—the least likely scenario by consensus, but the one that would involve the greatest down-side risk in terms of the costs of defeat, should it come to pass, and one for which the light divisions have an explicit mission. Because the differential configurations of units that are suited for operations at the extremes of the combat-intensity spectrum have implications for the use of manpower and personnel and because they constrain the interchangeability of units, consideration of these extremes is in order.

The High-Intensity Battlefield of the Future

The core of United States ground-combat doctrine deals with the major conflict for which Americans have been preparing since World War II and which has not come to pass—an invasion of the NATO nations by the Soviet Union and its Warsaw Pact allies.[36] Doctrine for this war assumes an "integrated battlefield," on which conventional, electronic, chemical, and nuclear weapons are apt to be used; an "extended battlefield," which would be characterized by deep thrusts to attack the second and deeper echelons of the attacking forces in order to offset their numerical advantage even as they attempt to strike deep into our rear areas; and an "airland battlefield," in which ground and air operations would be coordinated as they never have been before.[37] Thus the general doctrine is highly dependent on technology.

Opposing forces, for their part, are also likely to launch strikes deep into the rear areas of NATO forces, increasing the likelihood that personnel in support roles will become combatants. This is nothing new in military organization: rear-area personnel have frequently served as the reserves to fill vacancies created by casualties and fatalities in line units. What has changed are the probabilities of deep insertion by the opposing forces, because of advances in transportation technology, and the likelihood that the personnel who will be playing support roles at the division's rear boundary will be women. Thus it is likely that the rear area's commander will suddenly have thrust upon him/her the role of combat commander, in a defensive posture, commanding troops who, as I noted in chapter 5, are not supposed to be in combat given current statutes and regulations.[38] And while air-defense technologies will be crucial in this arena, it is also where close combat is likely to take place.

Our own deep thrusts into the enemies' rear echelons are apt to involve large combat units, including battlefield air interdiction and armor-heavy ground forces. The targets will be massed enemy personnel and equipment and will require attacks by large heavy operational units in order to inflict substantial damage.

Assuming that the attacking forces will be unlikely to use chemical, nuclear, or biological weapons in their own rear area and that our forces are unlikely to initiate the use of such weapons, our deep-thrust forces will probably be operating in an uncontaminated environment, so that vulnerability is likely to decrease with troop concentration. While the configuration of these maneuver units will probably be different from their current configuration, the elements of battle will probably be maneuver units, and soldiers on the deep battlefield will be in the company of their peers. The cohesion of units in Europe is itself being increased as our personnel-rotation system increasingly involves the deployment and assignment of intact units rather than individual soldiers, under the new manning system described in chapter 3.

The "traditional" battlefield—on which the first advancing echelon of hostile troops and tanks is confronted, which insulates the NATO rear area from massive deep intrusion, from which our offensive units will launch their deep thrusts into the enemy rear area, and through which our deep-thrusting units will withdraw after battle—is in many ways more sociologically and psychologically problematic. This is the high-intensity, high-technology battlefield, but it is one to which heavy combat units may be maladapted. As protection against the massive conventional fire power that will be directed at them, personnel on this battlefield will have to disperse themselves widely, in order to confuse the enemy regarding target priorities and reduce the vulnerability to the nuclear, chemical, or biological weapons that might be used against them. Thus, small mobile units may be the order of the day—the kind of units we are developing for peace-keeping and low-intensity warfare. Hence the ability of soldiers to make the psychological transition from peace-keeping to combat becomes paramount.

The United States' own technological developments presage greater dispersion on the battlefield, as the amount of territory that a traditional maneuver unit such as a battalion can control increases logarithmically over time as a function of increased fire power. The action of battle will be continuous—more like soccer than like football—and will take place around the clock, over periods of days rather than hours. The stress under which personnel operate will be much greater than what we have known in past wars. Danger will be ever-present, and fatigue will take its toll. The cognitive abilities of commanders are likely to decay faster than the physical abilities of their subordinates. Assuming that the opposing force has contaminated this battle area with chemical, nuclear, or biological weapons, U.S. forces will also have to anticipate that those of their units that remain operational will do so under the cover of protective gear that, while it insulates the wearers from contaminants, also effectively insulates them from effective communication with their leaders and peers.

The Rediscovery of Light Infantry

High-technology systems, to the extent that they work under wartime conditions, are an ever-present component of the European battlefield scenario, although the relative importance of personnel and technology will vary greatly across individual engagements. The cost of having this technology available is rapid deployability. The events of the late 1970s and the early 1980s have pointed to the importance of such deployability.

Before World War II, what are now regarded as "light divisions," in which people, rather than armor or ordnance, were the primary military resource, were America's standard maneuver elements. Unlike modern armor-heavy divisions, they were well suited to fighting in forested, mountainous, or even urbanized areas. Even in World War II, light units were important; this is reflected dramatically in the key role played by the highly maneuverable and low-profile U.S. 505th Parachute Infantry, as compared to the highly visible and vulnerable tanks of the British Grenadier Guards, in the battle for the bridge over the Rhine River at Nijmegen in the Netherlands.[39] The Germans also used light infantry effectively in defensive operations. This is the kind of unit that, save for U.S. airborne divisions, has become a rarity in the postwar United States Army.

Light divisions reappeared in the 1985 army budget as a means of creating forces to meet contingencies outside of central Europe and northern Asia; they are being configured to respond rapidly to low-intensity conflict situations that do not require full mobilization, much as U.S. cadre forces did under the mobilization model. They are limited in their organic airlift capability, vehicular mobility, and protection against armor and nuclear weapons. They will go to war as the British soldiers did in the Falklands, carrying weapons, ammunition, and life-support equipment with them.

The 7th Infantry Division at Fort Ord, California, was designated as the first new light division, and one of its first missions after certification was to provide a battalion task force for the Sinai MFO. The 25th Infantry Division in Hawaii has been transformed to the light-infantry configuration, and two new light divisions, the 10th Infantry Division (Mountain) and the 6th Infantry Divison, are being activated. The 9th Infantry Division, at Fort Lewis, Washington, which has served as the army's test bed for high-technology equipment, has shifted from its testing role to a hybrid "high technology light division," with more men and equipment than the other light divisions but with greater tactical mobility than conventional divisions have.

Thus, an increasing proportion of the U.S. active-duty army is being devoted to potential conflicts outside of Europe. These troops are more likely to have to go to war than are our deterrence forces. Hovering in the shadows, however, is the recognition that should war break out in Europe, U.S. light divisions, precisely because of their rapid deployability, will be among the first to arrive in that theater. Only one new light division is being activated in the National Guard: this is a reflection of the importance of speed of deployability in low-intensity operations and of the continuing debate over state versus federal control over the guard; but "round out" reserve brigades are included in the organization charts of active light divisions, which reflects the army's dependence on its mobilization potential.

MISSIONS AND MANPOWER
POLICY FOR THE FUTURE

The explicit broadening of the mission of United States military forces has implications for the allocation of defense resources, the structure of the force, and policies of acquiring military manpower. The acceptance of low-intensity and constabulary operations, which are labor intensive, suggests that the long-term trend in resource allocation away from manpower and personnel and toward weapons systems and weapons platforms will have to be reversed, and the deviation from the trend toward heavier ground combat units that Americans are seeing in the late 1980s may have to become a true reversal in the trend as well.

The wider range of missions requires that three specific military manpower needs be addressed. First, the strategy of deterrence, which continues to serve as the basis of relations between NATO and the Warsaw Pact nations, currently requires that an armor-heavy force-in-being remain committed to the mission of European defense; and to be credible in the deterrence role, these forces should be in place in Europe or, as a weaker alternative, have their equipment in place and protected in Europe so that only personnel have to be transported to this theater of operations. To fail to maintain this conventional deterrent places NATO in the unenviable position of having either to resort to nuclear weapons as a defense against conventional attack or to risk conventional defeat. Thus, we need conventional units. The American public continues to view the Soviet Union as a threat, and support for a European defensive force is likely to persist. There is likely to be debate, however, on how heavy these units need to be.

Second, the United States will have to maintain a force-in-being for low-intensity and constabulary operations. Its heavy forces in Europe, traveling without much of their equipment, could be diverted to this function, but only at the cost of weakening our heavy deterrence posture. The awareness among the American public and military personnel of the likelihood of low-intensity operations has been increased, and to the extent that they are seen as being in the national interest, they are likely to be supported. Most important, young Americans who join the armed services in the late 1980s recognize that they may be called upon to go to war. This is a dramatic change from a decade ago.

Public support is likely to be particularly high for constabulary operations, which are seen as contributing to peace. While the potential for the failure of peace-keeping operations requires that constabulary units be configured to wage war as well as keep peace, the utilization of light rather than heavy combat forces for such missions is appropriate. The lessons of recent history suggest that troops can shift from constabulary to low-intensity combat operations. The success of the Sinai MFO will probably require a revision in peace-keeping doctrine: the United States is not likely to be able to avoid participation in multinational peace-keeping forces in the future. However, it will have to ensure that units designated for constabulary operations will be able to operate in a high-intensity combat environment as well.

The third and most problematic component of the military-manpower picture is the mobilization base, particularly for high-intensity warfare. At the low-intensity end of the spectrum, if peace-keeping operations should fail, units on constabulary duty should be able to undertake the necessary combat operations. The situation is very different at the high-intensity end of the spectrum, should deterrence fail.

Troops who fulfill a deterrence function in Europe should be able to meet a first-thrust attack by Warsaw Pact forces. The success of those troops will be enhanced to the extent that early warning allows additional active-duty units—both light and heavy—to be transported to Europe, where the latter can draw equipment that has been pre-positioned, protected, and kept operational. Even under this optimistic scenario, however, there will not be enough troops to confront the Soviet numerical advantage on a high-intensity conventional battlefield.

Should Europe be the only arena of conflict, America's newer light units will certainly be used as European reinforcements. Highly vulnerable to armor when fighting unprotected on open plains, they nonetheless will probably be useful in urban or mountainous areas, and they can be integrated with heavy units in other terrain. However, American military doctrine assigns very low probability to there being only a single European arena of conflict. If America's heavy forces are engaged in Europe, its light forces are likely to be deployed to Latin America, the Persian Gulf, Africa, or elsewhere. Americans are thus likely to need a mobilization base for a European war. The nature of this mobilization base, as well as the related issue of the balance between heavy and light forces, will be addressed in the next chapter.

7
Missions and Options
for the 1990s

The United States has entered a fourth era of military manpower policy. The four eras have differed in the degree of evolution of nationhood in America, the postures that America has assumed in the international system, the missions that have been assigned to United States armed forces as a consequence of these postures, and the ways in which military manpower has been raised to fulfill these missions. Each of the first three periods has left a legacy that has influenced and constrained the current era and that has provided Americans with lessons regarding manpower policies that might help to fill their current and future needs. The historical trend has been toward increasing the range of America's military commitments to the point where there is now a serious question regarding its ability to honor them if necessary.

Part of this increase is due to the fact that the international system has been made more complex by the addition of participants in the processes of international affairs that are not nation-states: for example, supranational organizations, such as regional associations of states; and traditional tribal, ethnic, or religious societies, which are not states but have nonetheless increased their activity in the international system. Both kinds of actor have assumed increased military importance.

The United States has attempted to meet its increased commitments during the current period by adopting a "total force" posture that depends on National Guard and reserve units to augment active U.S. forces in fulfillment of the nation's military obligations. Because authority over the National Guard, as we have seen, is constitutionally divided between the federal government and state governments—a factor that continues to raise mobilization problems—and because the reserves during the Vietnam era became a way of avoiding active military service, the mobilization capability of the American armed forces remains problematic in the all-volunteer era. Moreover, since the total manpower pool is diminishing because of America's demographic history and because the active forces are responding to this increase by keeping a larger proportion of the force on active duty for longer periods of time, the manpower pool for the reserves is being constricted both by a total reduction in manpower and by a reduction in trained manpower coming out of the active forces.

In this chapter, I will provide estimates of the military manpower resources that the United States will require in order to face the missions and chal-

lenges of this fourth era. These estimates will assume peacetime conditions, but I will consider as well how these requirements will change should
the nation go to war. These estimates will also assume that the country will
continue to maintain a rotation base in the continental United States for
forces stationed overseas, rather than adopt a "foreign legion" model that
would require military personnel to spend virtually all of their time in
service outside the country. I will focus primarily on the army, which is the
largest and most manpower-intensive of the armed services, and the one
that is most likely to experience manpower shortfalls; but I will also pay
attention to the manpower needs of the air and naval forces. I will focus
primarily on the active-duty forces, because I assume that "total force"
policies notwithstanding, both the credibility of American armed forces as
a deterrent to war and the short-term ability to wage a conventional war
should deterrence fail are vested in the nation's active-duty forces. I
recognize, however, that should the United States face a major war, its most
serious manpower problems will be in the mobilization base. Finally, I will
discuss the alternative ways of meeting America's future military manpower
needs.

THE MILITIA ERA

The first era, which lasted from the birth of the Republic to the early part
of the twentieth century, was the militia era, during which the United States
was evolving from a federation of states to a unified nation. Its major military
mission was the hemispheric defense of the Americas under the Monroe Doctrine, during a period when transportation and weapons technologies allowed
the country the leisure to mobilize for war, when its posture with regard
to Europe was one of isolation, and when control of the manpower-
mobilization base was vested in the states. The strength of this model was
the normative definition of participation in national defense as a citizenship responsibility, which helped the nation elicit widespread participation
in the military in times of national emergency, although not necessarily
through the mechanisms specified by the model. Indeed, the major lesson
of the militia era was the inefficiency of this model in providing for national-
security needs. The responsibilities of citizenship during this era were defined more in local than in national terms.

While the United States has moved far from the basic militia model, the
country's current dependence on a "total force"—made up of both active-duty
and reserve components, with a portion of the reserve strength of both the
land and the air forces organized in National Guard units, the direct descen-
dants of the state militias—has left it with some of the advantages of this
model, such as a conception of weekend warriors as citizen-soldiers and of

military reserve units that experience relatively little personnel turnover and that therefore tend to be cohesive, as well as some of the disadvantages, including a degree of decentralized control of the armed forces.

THE FEDERALIZATION ERA

The second era extended from World War I to World War II. During this period the United States continued to subscribe to the mobilization principles of the militia model, and its major posture in the international system was still one of isolation from Europe and defense of the Americas. However, Americans acknowledged the problems of mobilizing for major wars a militia that was organized by the governments of the states, and Americans increasingly centralized the control of the military mobilization system in the federal government. They also used conscription to raise federal forces during the two world wars, although a relatively small all-volunteer force was maintained for more than twenty years during the interwar period, when the mobilization model did not require a large force-in-being. The nation maintained an isolationist stance, but its involvement in the world wars and its willingness to use military conscription in support of that involvement were manifest acknowledgments of its basic political, cultural, and economic links to the European nations that were its progenitors.

THE DETERRENCE ERA

These links were what defined United States military manpower policy (or lack of it) during the third era—the quarter of a century following World War II. During this period, Americans saw their national destiny inextricably connected with that of Western Europe. In the bipolar world that World War II produced, Americans saw the Soviet Union and its Warsaw Pact allies as the major threat to this North Atlantic community. The U.S. alliance with the other North Atlantic nations was also a reflection of a broader change in the international system—the rise of a network of regional organizations of nation-states, which became participants in international affairs and to which, by virtue of membership, the United States made military commitments.

Americans saw nuclear deterrence as the most effective way of dealing with their commitments to their NATO allies, and their alliance partners were generally happy with this posture. The country's national-security investments were in capital-intensive delivery systems for nuclear warheads: the intercontinental ballistic missiles, strategic bombers, and nuclear submarines, which today form our triad of strategic nuclear deterrence. These investments took precedence over expenditures for military manpower, which, under a conscription system, was a relatively inexpensive resource, and for conventional forces in general. Americans assumed that deterrence would work and that if it should fail, a strategic exchange would be over very quickly.

Beyond the forces needed to man and protect the nation's nuclear-weapons platforms—and to fight unanticipated wars in northern and southeastern Asia during the 1950s and the 1960s—the major functions of military manpower during this period were initially to be occupation troops and later to be a presence in Western Europe and northern Asia, assuring the nation's allies of U.S. commitment to them, and to serve as a trip wire, guaranteeing that in the event of another European or north Asian conflict, American troops would be involved and that follow-on American forces would have to be committed.

As Soviet nuclear capabilities began to achieve parity with those of the United States and as it became clear that there would be no winners in a strategic exchange, the United States began to admit the importance of conventional or theater nuclear deterrence and to recognize that the same forces that in the 1950s had been regarded as a trip wire for massive nuclear retaliation might in the 1980s have to fight and win a conventional war in continental Europe. The United States began to attend more to the status of its ground forces and to the possibility of geographically limited nuclear wars. Our Western European allies began to worry that a confrontation between the United States and the Soviet Union might be fought wholly on Western European soil. During this period, the United States did not articulate its strategic posture well with its military manpower policies. Rather, its manpower posture was constrained by domestic economic and ideological considerations.[1]

THE ERA OF MULTIPLE MISSIONS

The current era represents the aggregation of the perceived dangers that shaped U.S. policies and postures during the previous periods. It also reflects the increased role that supranational organizations and military forces that do not represent nation-states are playing in the international system. Most important, it is the first time we have attempted to maintain a large standing peacetime force over a long period of time on the basis of voluntary military enlistments—and at a point in the history of military technology when demands for military personnel who have higher average mental aptitudes are increasing and when the manpower supply is decreasing.

The standing peacetime force, large though it is, cannot meet the range of U.S. military obligations without being augmented by deployment-ready reserve forces. Half of the total strength of the army is in reserve components. Much of it is in the National Guard, which in 1985 constituted, for example, almost three-quarters of the army's infantry battalions, all of the infantry scout troops, all of the heavy helicopter companies, and all of the TOW anti-tank infantry battalions.[2] The Air National Guard, for its part, provides more than 70 percent of the strategic interceptor force for the continental United States. Thus, the force-in-being notwithstanding, the United States has returned to a dependence on a mobilization model of military manpower but has done so under all-volunteer conditions. The implications of this model and the magnitude of our manpower needs vary according to the region of the world but overall leave us in a precarious position if we must fight a major war.

The Americas

On our own continent, while Americans remain concerned with defending against strategic nuclear attack by the Soviet Union (this in fact was the justification for President Reagan's strategic defense initiative), the more recently identified threat is that of terrorist attacks on Americans—including American military personnel—in their own homeland.[3] America, which was once protected from attack by geographical isolation and slow transportation technologies, has become extremely vulnerable as a hub of international travel. Not only has the incidence of international terrorism increased, but so, too, has the nature of terrorism, as it has been transformed from a tactic used primarily by fringe political opposition groups to an instrument of the foreign policy of nations and of societies that are not nations.

Only in the 1980s has the United States begun to recognize that such terrorism is not simply criminality, to be dealt with by police agencies and the judicial system, and that the use of force and violence by terrorists in the pursuit of state or societal objectives is a form of military action. And it is only in the 1980s that preparation for dealing with such terrorism has become a routine mission for United States military forces. Of course, as we have learned, terrorist threats to United States military personnel are not restricted to the continental United States. They exist wherever such personnel are stationed, and the range of contemporary U.S. military missions requires the presence of U.S. armed-forces personnel all over the globe. What is crucial, however, is the recognition that state-supported terrorism is warfare, not simply crime; that Americans have become vulnerable to it everywhere, including their homeland; and that combatting terrorism, which is generally of low intensity on the combat spectrum, even though it could conceivably involve nuclear weapons,[4] requires a broader military orientation than the deterrence stance that dominated American thinking during the post–World War II years.

Beyond the direct defense of the United States, the United States military has also actively participated in the assertion of the nation's intolerance of the spread of perceived Soviet political and ideological influence in the Western Hemisphere. This modern-day incarnation of the Monroe Doctrine is not concerned with Western European recolonization of the Americas—the original basis of the doctrine—as our low-profile support of Great Britain in its South Atlantic war against Argentina over the Falkland/Malvinas Islands demonstrated. Rather, it is oriented toward containing and, if possible, reducing Soviet presence and influence in the hemisphere. This presence was nonexistent prior to the 1960s. Today, where Cuban military personnel or Soviet ideology are found, United States military personnel are not likely to be far away.

Latin America is regarded as too important strategically—because of its proximity to the United States, as a source of raw materials, and as a transportation hub—to be allowed to move into the opposition camp. Thus the posture of the United States will be oriented toward preventing the establishment of hostile military bases, as well as securing access to regional resources. Throughout the 1970s, most United States military personnel were trained for and committed to NATO or Asian scenarios. The move toward light divisions, prepared for low-intensity warfare, is an acknowledgment that deployments to developing areas such as Latin America have been added to the set of missions defined for our armed forces. However, the European mission persists, while the size of the force is not increasing.

There is no doubt that the public justification for the United States invasion of Grenada in 1983 was the rescue of American medical students from a new and hostile regime after the overthrow and execution of Prime Minister Maurice Bishop; but the fact that there were Cubans on the island, helping to construct a new airstrip large enough to accommodate Soviet military aircraft, was no less important a motivation for the operation. Characteristic of modern military operations, the political component of the invasion was justified by an invitation from a regional association of Caribbean states, and at the conclusion of the mission, the United States military personnel were replaced by a regional constabulary force.

No less important as a reflection of the military role of the United States in Latin America is the Reagan administration's opposition to the Sandinista government in Nicaragua, which has been manifested not only by its support of the insurgent contras, but also by the increasingly regular presence of U.S. military personnel in neighboring Honduras. The invasion of Grenada was a low-intensity conventional war, and should the United States become directly involved militarily in Nicaragua, it is likely to find itself in an unconventional conflict. In the 1980s the Central American theater has already served as a stage upon which the traditionally problematic interface between a national foreign policy and a military mobilization base, controlled partly by the states, has been played out. The Defense Department has been encouraging the increased training of United States military personnel—including those in the reserve components—for warfare in Latin America. More than five thousand National Guard troops from twenty-three states trained in Honduras in 1986.

The governors of several states, including Massachusetts, Ohio, Vermont, and Washington, objected to having National Guard units from their states sent for such training; so the governors refused to allow the units to participate. Such a veto of training missions for the guard was the governors' statutory right until 1986. In that year, in an amendment to the FY 1987 defense-authorization act, Congress stripped the governors of their right to refuse to send their National Guard troops for training on the grounds of location, purpose, or schedule of duty, although a governor could still refuse to send his troops for training if they were needed for state emergencies. This legislation continues the trend toward the federalization of control of the National Guard. In January 1987, Minnesota's Governor Rudy Perpich filed suit to overturn the law, and a bill was introduced in the Senate early in the One-Hundredth Congress to give governors the legal right to block deployments of the guard and to make the president the only person who could override a governor on this. During the 1988 presidential primary campaigns, the courts told Massachusetts' Governor Michael S. Dukakis that he could not prevent elements of his National Guard from being deployed to Latin America for training. Obviously, the debate about the mobilization of the National Guard is not over, and ambiguities remain with regard to the role of the guard in the total force.

Military manpower requirements for the Latin American theater are not great. Even with mutual defense commitments made through the Organization of American States, it is difficult to envision a scenario, short of direct Soviet intervention, that would require more than the equivalent of a division-sized active-duty unit, and the United States already has battalion- and brigade-sized active units based in the Panama area, a region that has become increasingly unstable during the late 1980s because of drug traffic, rather than political ideology.

In the event of conflict, these active units would have to be supported by reserve units, which would probably be from the Army Reserve, rather than from the National Guard, until matters regarding the control of the guard have been resolved. Both the active and the reserve units committed to this region would have to be configured and trained differently from those units intended for deployment to Europe or to northern Asia. A light division, trained in small unit operations and jungle warfare, with considerable representation of Spanish-speaking personnel, stationed for ease of deployment to Latin America, is likely to fill U.S. active-duty military-manpower needs in this area. The adaptation of an active division and of back-up reserve units to this mission, however, reduces their utility outside the Americas. While we can estimate United States needs in this hemisphere at between only 1 and 5 percent of the army's strength, units so designated should realistically be regarded as unavailable for deployment to Europe or Asia.

The United States currently has adequate airlift and sealift capability to deploy a division to this region. However, if such a deployment had to take place while hostilities were being addressed elsewhere in the world, the United States would probably face shortages of the necessary military carriers and personnel for troop movement.

Europe

In contrast to U.S. manpower needs in the Americas and the limited demands that U.S. obligations to the Organization of American States are apt to make on U.S. armed forces, the Western European theater remains a major responsibility. The NATO alliance does not now have enough forces in Europe to ward off a conventional attack by numerically superior Warsaw Pact forces. The U.S. deterrence posture in Europe is strengthened by the presence of increasingly effective nonnuclear combat systems, such as the Abrams main battle tank and other current-generation fighting vehicles and by the presence of tactical nuclear weapons, both of which can increase the damage that the United States can inflict upon an advancing enemy, hopefully to a level that will make an advance not worthwhile in the calculus of the Warsaw Pact. Both of these technologies bring with them their own problems.

More sophisticated weapons systems, in general, require smarter personnel to operate and maintain them. The correlation between the sophistication and the complexity of a system is of course not perfect. Some forms of weapons sophistication can compensate for lower-aptitude personnel to operate them, and some forms of sophistication can make the maintenance of weapons simpler, rather than more complex. With regard to operation, research conducted by the army has demonstrated that personnel with lower mental aptitudes perform better in current-generation main battle tanks than in earlier machines. Some critics of the expensive recruiting programs which are needed in order to bring personnel with higher mental aptitudes into the army, point to these figures as a way of saving costs: substitute better tanks for smarter people. However, the effects of machine quality and personnel quality are additive. While personnel with lower mental aptitudes perform better in new than in old tanks, persons with higher mental aptitudes perform better in new tanks than do persons with lower mental aptitudes. Because the total performance of the man-machine system is crucial in a situation in which NATO forces are outnumbered, the optimal combination is a new tank and smart soldiers.

With regard to the maintenance of modern combat systems, the ability to use personnel with lower mental aptitudes increases when components that are not working can be removed, replaced, and sent to rear-area depots for repair. The degree to which a high-intensity European battlefield will permit the army this maintenance luxury, even where it is technologically possible, however, remains problematic. The most reasonable assumption is that the heavy divisions that have been organized for European combat will require increasing numbers of smart soldiers, who are the most expensive to recruit and retain in a volunteer force. And if changes in combat doctrine for the European theater were to call for the decreased use of armor—the defensive defense posture—the demand for smart soldiers will still increase. Smart soldiers survive longer on the battlefield.

The presence of tactical or theater nuclear weapons raises another problem: the posture and resolve of the European parties in the North Atlantic alliance. To the extent that the doctrine of nuclear deterrence had assumed that the failure of deterrence would result in strategic warfare—an intercontinental exchange between the United States and the Soviet Union—allies of the United States agreed that deterrence would work and that warfare was not likely, because the costs of war to the superpowers would be too high. The presence of theater nuclear weapons in Europe, however, raised the specter that a conventional war might escalate to nuclear war in Western Europe, with a tacit understanding between the superpowers that at least at the outset, their own national heartlands would not be targets. With the direct costs of nuclear war to the superpowers thus reduced, deterrence was perceived to have become less effective. Europeans are likely to feel that the reduction of intermediate nuclear forces, which was negotiated at the Moscow summit in 1988, will increase their security, both by removing nuclear weapons from their soil and by increasing the credibility of the strategic deterrent.

In chapter 6, I noted that Americans—civilians and military personnel alike—regard nuclear war as the least likely scenario for future wars. This continues to be the case. Nonetheless, Americans' perceptions of the likelihood of nuclear war went up markedly in the mid-1980s, as a new generation of theater nuclear weapons were deployed and as citizens of the nation's Western European allies demonstrated against them.[5]

Surveys that asked Americans to identify the most important problem facing the nation showed that the percentage who feared nuclear war as the most pressing problem varied between 6 and 8 percent in a series of polls between April 1982, and July 1983, but had jumped to almost 24 percent in December 1983.[6] And as estimates of the likelihood of nuclear war increased, the desire of Europeans to be defended by the United States began to lag behind America's desire to defend them. This is true not only of the current generation of adults but of the ascending generation of college students as well. A 1985 cross-national survey of students showed that 66 percent of the Americans felt that the United States should defend its European allies if they are attacked by the Soviet Union, whereas only 36 percent of the West German respondents felt this way.[7]

It is not easy to detect a policy consensus among the members of NATO, but the widest gap seems to be that between the United States and the European members of the alliance. The United States' emphasis has been to improve conventional forces, perhaps on the assumption that recent changes in Soviet doctrine suggest a greater desire to avoid nuclear confrontation than seemed to be the case heretofore. If the Soviets prefer a conventional war and if the defensive capabilities of NATO's ground forces raise the costs to the Warsaw Pact of such a conflict, then the overall probability of war might be lowered. In short, the American posture seems to assume a more manpower-dependent conventional deterrent.

The avoidance of nuclear escalation is not guaranteed by this posture, however, and the step from conventional to theater nuclear war is an understandably unpleasant one for America's European allies to think about. These nations have preferred strategic nuclear deterrence and retaliatory capability over conventional deterrence,[8] presumably on the assumption that a direct threat to the Soviet and American heartlands would be a more effective deterrence posture than is a threat of war—either conventional or battlefield nuclear—that would be restricted to Western and Central Europe.

The difference between the Europeans and the Americans in deterrence posture, while more one of degree than of kind, has important implications for manpower. The Europeans have resisted American pressures to increase their contributions to the conventional defense of Western Europe, to the point that American critics have urged the withdrawal of U.S. troops in order to force the Europeans to take up the slack.[9] At the same time, some of the nation's major European allies have been quick to point to their maintenance of systems of military conscription as evidence of their commitment to the defense of Europe, a commitment that they claim is less evident in America's all-volunteer force. The European nations are in fact facing the same declining pool of young men that the United States is facing, and West Germany has already increased its period of conscripted service so as to maintain its force levels.

Given the European preference for strategic nuclear retaliation as a deterrence strategy, it is not clear that a withdrawal of American conventional forces from Europe would result in an expansion of conventional European forces. Given a Warsaw Pact advantage of greater than 2:1 over NATO in conventional forces, it is difficult to imagine that a U.S. force of less than two hundred thousand to three hundred thousand soldiers in Europe would be credible. This is what the United States currently has there: the equivalent of five active-duty heavy divisions—roughly 30 to 40 percent of the army's strength.

Indeed, to reduce this number would send confusing signals to America's allies and adversaries. The United States was not receptive to suggestions for reductions in forces which the Soviets made at the 1988 summit.

Both for rotation purposes and for rapid reinforcement in the event of a conflict, roughly equal strength should exist in the continental United States for deployment in Europe. These units need not be designated solely for European operations, but they should be structured for the armor-heavy operations of a European battlefield, and they should be prepared for deployment wherever such heavy operations are appropriate. Although ideally they would all be active units, pragmatically they need not be. As I noted earlier, strategic bombing has been the favorite child of the air force, and airlift capability has been a stepchild. Thus, even assuming that the equipment for additional heavy divisions has been pre-positioned in Europe so that only manpower need be moved, the speed of a large-scale deployment from the United States to Europe would allow the equivalent of at least two follow-on divisions to be reserve units capable of rapid mobilization.

In short, the United States appears to have enough strength to fulfill the deterrence function in Europe, although the deterrence effects of conventional and nuclear forces cannot be independently assessed. The nation also probably has sufficient strength in the active army and in the reserves to provide short-term reinforcements for a European conflict, those who could be deployed within the first two weeks.

The United States does not have enough strength in either the active army or the reserves to sustain and win a conventional war in Europe. The army's projected force structure of twenty-eight divisions by the early 1990s—eighteen active and ten reserve—falls short of what the United States would need for a major conventional war in Europe, particularly if we take into account that the light divisions have primary commitments elsewhere and that they are not well suited to the NATO mission, although it is assumed that if there were a European war, they would be deployed there. And the reserves would have to be rapidly mobilizable as units, rather than as individuals, because the army is adding active combat divisions within a constant strength ceiling by moving more support functions into the reserves. Not only is much of America's ground-combat strength in the reserve components, but so, too, are nine-tenths of fuel-supply units, three-quarters of ammunition-handling units, and almost two-thirds of all medical support.

These reserve units are, on average, less likely to be at or near full strength than are active units; they are less likely to have the most modern equipment; and they are less likely to be well trained. Moreover, the army is not likely to get the funding necessary to achieve the projected structure of forces.[10] The United States has therefore moved to a conventional ground-warfare posture based upon a mobilization that the nation cannot achieve. Nor would the United States have the military airlift to get that strength there rapidly if the manpower did exist. As is the case in the active air force, the Air National Guard and the Air Force Reserve have little strategic airlift capability.

There is little justification for expanding active U.S. forces to face a European contingency to which Americans attribute a low probability, because the nation's current force structure seems to be fulfilling the deterrence function well. It seems folly, however, to leave the United States short of a mobilization base that can sustain a conventional European campaign and that would require the country to consider the use of nuclear weapons well before our adversaries would have to. If the United States is to emphasize alternatives other than nuclear warfare in the current European environment, it needs greater depth in its landpower mobilization base and in its reserve airlift capability than it currently has.

Northeastern Asia and the Western Pacific

The United States does not have the same cultural and historical ties to the Orient that it does to Europe. However, America's economic ties to the Orient are increasing, and the strategic importance of the area is unquestionable. It dominates the western approach to the United States and the eastern approach to the Indian Ocean, and it contains the area of greatest physical proximity between U.S. and Soviet territory, at the Bering Strait. The Soviet Union has two close military allies in the region: North Korea and Vietnam. And the last two U.S. wars, Korea and Vietnam, were fought there. Theoretically, a state of war still exists under the 1953 Korean armistice.

Unlike the case in Europe, military alliances in northeastern Asia are bilateral rather than regional. The United States has significant obligations both to Japan—which maintains minimal military capability under its post–World War II constitution but which faces threats from Vietnam, to its ties to suppliers and customers in Southeast Asia, and from Soviet expansion in the western Pacific[11]—and to South Korea, which occupies a key strategic position, surrounded by the Soviet Union, China, and Japan.

To the south, ANZUS (Australia, New Zealand, United States), the only viable multilateral military-assistance pact in the region, has fallen victim to the Reagan administration's intolerance of New Zealand's attempt to keep the South Pacific free from nuclear confrontation for as long as possible.[12] The Association of South East Asian Nations (ASEAN) does not involve mutual military interdependence.

The U.S. military presence in the region is primarily navy and air force, which will provide the kind of military assistance that most of our allies in this area are likely to need. Of some 125,000 U.S. military personnel, only about 30,000 are soldiers. This does not mean that there is not a need for ground forces in the event of a conflict. Rather, it is a reflection of the fact that as in Europe, the major function of the American presence is to serve as a deterrent. Indeed, the structure of U.S. ground forces in South Korea, with a single infantry division but with corps and army headquarters, reflects a recognition that in the absence of forward-based soldiers, rapid reinforcement will have to take place should deterrence fail.

The major need for ground forces is likely to be in Korea, where the army of South Korea is at a disadvantage in terms of conventional weapons relative to the army of North Korea. As noted, the North Koreans are now supported by the modern military technology of the Soviet Union, so they pose a different kind of threat from what they did during the Korean War, when their support from China was primarily in terms of manpower.

There are two infantry divisions on the West Coast of the United States and one in Hawaii that can provide support in Northern Asia. One of the West Coast divisions is a prototype "light" formation, in terms of both manpower and equipment. The other has a unique configuration: it has rapidly deployable light vehicles. The infantry division in Hawaii is also being organized as a light division. These units are better suited for operations in the Middle East or in the South Pacific than in northeastern Asia. There are also two National Guard armored-cavalry regiments and a mechanized infantry division on the West Coast, and they are more appropriately equipped to confront a Soviet supported attack from North Korea.

The utilization of National Guard regiments in Asia, however, is no less politically problematic than is their deployment to Latin America. Indeed, according to the survey that I cited earlier, 66 percent of American respondents thought that the United States should defend European allies against attack, but only 38 percent thought that the United States should defend Japan against attack.[13] While animosity toward Japan may be heightened both by economic competition and by the role the Japanese played in World War II, it is doubtful that popular support for the protection of South Korea would be much higher. In the absence of popular support for a military engagement, national political leaders are likely to resist mobilizing and deploying National Guard units.

Heavy divisions elsewhere in the continental United States could be deployed to Korea, but that would weaken America's conventional deterrence posture in Europe. And where deployment to Europe assumes the utilization of heavy equipment that has been pre-positioned in that theater, the deployment of these same units to Korea would involve moving their equipment as well with the limited airlift capability of the United States. Equally important, much of this equipment is old. The program of modernization of conventional forces that the Reagan administration has begun is several years behind schedule, and many active and reserve units that were supposed to receive new tanks and fighting vehicles are still operating with older, less effective machines. This hardware factor constrains this country's deterrence posture in both Europe and Asia.

If the United States could assume that there would be relative tranquility in Europe while it was supporting South Korea in defending against an invasion from the north, it would probably have enough depth and airlift capability to meet the requirement. If, on the other hand, a Soviet-supported invasion by North Korea were to be accompanied by large-scale troop movements in Eastern Europe that would trigger a NATO build-up, the United States would rapidly find that its airlift capabilities were inadequate, its active forces were overextended, its dependence on old equipment was embarrassing, and its reserve units were depleted. The manpower-mobilization base of the United States does not have enough depth to confront concurrent Soviet-supported threats in Europe and in northern Asia, even if no shots were actually fired in Europe.

The Middle East

America's needs in this volatile region are the most difficult parameters to estimate in our military manpower equation. The Middle East is strategically important to the United States because it is located on the southern flank of the Soviet Union and therefore acts as a buffer on NATO's southern flank. The Middle East provides one-third of the world's oil, although it is more important as a supplier to America's NATO allies than it is to the United States. American support for the state of Israel is also a major factor in domestic U.S. politics.

The Middle East is a region of tremendous political complexity: it involves ancient nations, such as Egypt; new states that have been established since World War II, such as Israel, Iran, and Iraq; stateless societies, such as the Palestinians; and nations that have had difficulty in asserting their sovereignty even over their own people, such as Lebanon, with its seventeen different sectarian communities, several of which have their own militia forces. It is a region of conflict: this has included persistent Arab-Israeli tensions manifested in periodic wars and continuing terrorist and counterterrorist activities; a radical Islamic revolution in Iran, which was followed by a protracted war between Iran and Iraq that has led to a large U.S. naval presence to keep sea lanes open for shipping petroleum; a 1979 Soviet incursion in Afghanistan, which persisted for a decade until the Soviets began to withdraw in 1988; and continuing hostilities among rival religious groups and their militias in Lebanon, punctuated by periodic attempts on the part of Syrian military units to pacify the country and by the 1982 Israeli military incursion.

The instability of the region is what provides the basis for the threat and what defines America's military mission there as one of deterrence. The

Soviet Union has friends in the region, most notably Syria and Iraq, although the latter's need for arms to continue its war with Iran has caused it to widen its circle of friends and has been a moderating influence. The United States likewise has friends, including Saudi Arabia and Israel. An uneasy balance is maintained.

There is little evidence that either the United States or the Soviet Union is seeking active military involvement in international hostilities in the region. The United States has been content to allow Israel to serve as its military surrogate in most instances: an exception was the 1986 bombing of Libyan targets in retaliation for that country's alleged support of terrorist activities. And the Soviet Union seems to have learned a lesson in the geopolitical use of military force from its attempt to suppress opposition to the Kabul regime.

Nonetheless, were Iran to be further destabilized and were it to seem that a pro-Western government might be reestablished on the Soviet border, the Soviet Union might be tempted to intervene in that country. Having the Soviets in Iran would shift the balance of power in the region, would increase the vulnerability of NATO's flank, and would require that significant U.S. military strength, equipped for land-combat operations, be deployed to the region, to be stationed in such potential locations as Egypt, Saudi Arabia, Jordan, and Israel. Such an alignment of forces would extend the current bipolar division of Europe throughout the Middle East. It is probably to the interest of both superpowers to keep this from happening.

Instability in Iran must be taken for granted. The major constraint on Soviet action is probably the deterrent posture of the United States, and this is a difficult region in which to maintain a credible deterrent. The Soviet threat to Iran is large and proximate, with twenty-five divisions north of the country. The United States, on the other hand, is seven thousand air miles away. And while the initial elements of a rapidly deployable division could arrive in a matter of days, it would probably take a week, with current airlift capability, to deploy a full light division and probably two weeks to deploy the 82d Airborne Division, which is heavier and has armored vehicles and artillery.

The light divisions that the army is developing in the late 1980s are well suited for the deterrence mission in the Middle East, both because they are rapidly deployable and because they are designed to be effective in the kind of mountain warfare that a confrontation in Iran is likely to involve. They are also better suited than are heavy units for most other Middle Eastern missions. The major presence of United States ground forces in this region has been as peace keepers in the Sinai and in Lebanon. This sort of mission is likely to continue in the region, and while not all units assigned to these missions were officially designated as "light infantry," none were conventional heavy units. U.S. forces may also be called upon to provide protection to friendly regimes in the region, such as Saudi Arabia or Jordan, from external threats. Here, too, the rapid deployability of light divisions is an asset, even though a threat from an armor-heavy Soviet surrogate such as Syria would more effectively be countered by heavier forces. In the latter instance, our shortages in airlift capability for heavy forces, as well as the delays that have been experienced in force modernization, would again hamper effectiveness.

The Middle East clearly provides a justification for maintaining light divisions in the U.S. standing force, but Americans must recognize that these units should not count heavily in calculations about forces that the United States could deploy to Europe or northern Asia. Moreover, Americans must recognize that should a conflict in Iran extend beyond the mountains to open terrain, where Soviet armor will become more effective, or should a friendly regime face a threat from an armor-heavy Soviet surrogate, the highest-mobility light U.S. forces will not be sufficient for the mission. At a minimum, helicopters and light tanks, to serve as antiarmor weapons platforms, would be needed. And as the need grew in this area for heavier equipment that is now committed primarily to the European and northern-Asia theaters, both the deterrence posture in these regions and the air-lift capability of the United States would be stretched.

In short, the Middle East represents a wide range of potential conflicts that would require a variety of forces. Although American military engagement in this region would in most circumstances involve light rather than heavy forces and would require conventional rather than nuclear weapons, it has implications for our posture in other parts of the globe where higher-intensity and heavier warfare is regarded as being more likely. The dedication of army divisions to the light configuration that is needed for deployment to and operations in this area reduces the forces that should be included in the calculation of conventional deterrent forces that need to be oriented toward western Europe and northern Asia. While light divisions will undoubtedly be deployed to and used in these regions in the event of hostilities, their contribution to combat success will be much less than that of a heavy division. Moreover, to the extent that light forces have to be supplemented in the Middle East by heavier armor, artillery, or aviation units, the deterrence posture of the United States elsewhere will be further weakened.

THE CONSEQUENCES FOR MANPOWER POLICY

I have not reviewed the entire globe, but I have considered the four areas that represent the most important contemporary military missions of the United States. This overview is sufficient for identifying the nation's strengths and needs.

If we accept the principle that U.S. forces should be judged on the degree to which they are organized for deployment and victory in the most likely low-intensity combat situations, for providing a credible deterrent against higher intensity conflicts, and for successfully prosecuting a high intensity war without early dependence on nuclear weapons should deterrence fail, the report card is mixed.

At the low-intensity end of the spectrum, the United States has not yet developed an appropriate military response to state-supported terrorism. While some special units are likely to be developed in each of the services for such operations, counterterrorist missions are not likely to be manpower intensive. Rather, military reactions to states that use terrorism as instruments of foreign policy are likely to follow the precedent of the 1986 air raid on Libya but with doctrine and weapons developed specifically for that function.

Recent changes in the structure of U.S. active forces do put us in a better position to deal with low-intensity military engagements and unconventional operations in regions such as the Caribbean basin, the Middle East, and the South Pacific than was the case during the 1960s and 1970s. The movement away from heavy units, organized for the least-likely scenarios, will provide the United States with enough rapid-deployment forces to deal with most contingencies in these areas, although experience has shown that Americans may have much to learn about the coordination and management of such forces. More important, the United States has a persistent problem of getting its personnel to where it needs them, and this is a question of priorities.

Both the air force and the navy have emphasized strategic warfare over transportation roles; both are still orienting themselves to the least-likely scenario. Investment in missiles, in strategic bombers, and in aircraft-carrier and battleship battle groups has provided the United States with few ships in which to move troops. There are plans to mobilize much of the nation's commercial-aviation capability for military transportation in the event of a major war, but the most dramatic and common characteristic of U.S. mobilization plans has been their failure, and most realistic conflict scenarios involve engagements of a magnitude that the nation is not going to see as sufficient justification for the disruption of commercial aviation but that nonetheless outstrips our military airlift capabilities. Because there are no indications that either the air force or the navy is going to change its mission priorities for its active forces, the nation needs to devise an effective large-scale mobilization base for military transportation.

With regard to heavier forces oriented toward deterrence in Europe and Asia, doctrine and force structure seem to be effective. Major military confrontations in these theaters have been avoided. However, the conventional deterrence posture of the United States is in the process of transition. As a larger proportion of the nation's active-duty combat strength is shifted into light units to deal with the more likely contingencies elsewhere in the world than Europe and northern Asia, the deterrence mission in these core areas has increasingly become a responsibility of the reserve components. This is explicit in the posture of the total U.S. force. As more support functions are shifted into the reserves to increase the combat strength of the active forces, while their size is being kept relatively constant, it becomes increasingly unlikely that any active forces can go to war without reserve units to support them.

Much of U.S. combat strength, particularly that which is organized for heavy operations, is also in the reserves. Increasing commitments of modern military hardware are being made to the reserve components to enable them to help fulfill America's military obligations; but in the face of a declining manpower pool, with the services increasing their retention rates and thereby decreasing the flow of personnel that have had military training back into the civilian citizen-soldier labor force, in the absence of a draft that in the past has served as a motivation to join the reserves, and with political considerations constraining the utilization of the National Guard, the mobilization base is not as healthy as is the active force. The last factor is particularly important, because while the reserve components began to rebound during the 1980s after a major decline during the previous decade (the reserve shortage was estimated to be as high as 270,000 in 1979), much, if not most, of the rebound in selected reserve strength—that is personnel assigned to and serving in reserve units—was in the National Guard.[14] Additional gains in reserves will be realized during the 1990s as the result of a two-year increase in total service obligation for personnel who entered the armed forces after June 1, 1984. However, this gain will be in the Individual Ready Reserve—people who would be available as replacements or as fillers for existing units as needed—not in selected reserve rapidly mobilizable units.

In sum, with regard to manpower in the active forces, the all-volunteer force can be judged a success in the 1980s. Many of the problems of the 1970s have been addressed, and sufficient numbers of high-quality personnel are being recruited and retained, even in the face of a declining manpower pool. It is important to note that this success has not been achieved solely through the economic market dynamics that the Gates Commission recommended. Explicit attempts to link service to citizenship have ranged from the establishment of a "new GI bill" to recruiting campaigns that have supplemented labor-market appeals ("It's a great place to start") with reminders of civic responsibility ("We're not a company; we're your country").[15] Nevertheless, the overall evaluation of the active-duty volunteer force is that it is working and that it is doing so on the same terms as the nation's active-duty forces have historically been maintained in peacetime, albeit on a larger scale—a combination of economic incentives and civic virtues.[16]

What has changed is our dependence on a very large force of reserve units that can be mobilized very quickly. With the shifting of support functions to the reserves, the United States cannot wage much of a low-intensity war without calling up reserve units to support its active combat troops. Because of the shift toward light divisions within the active forces, the United States probably cannot maintain a credible conventional deterrence posture without increasing the level of equipment modernity, manning, and training of heavy combat units in the reserve components and without developing a rapidly mobilizable airlift capability in the reserve forces. If Americans assume that the worst-case scenario in terms of military manpower is not a strategic nuclear war but a conventional confrontation between the Warsaw Pact nations and NATO in Western Europe—which would probably be accompanied by Soviet troop movements near Iran; by increased military activity in Cuba, which would require the deployment of light U.S. combat units; and by saber rattling on the part of North Korea, which would require the dispersion of heavy active and reserve units of the United States— then the United States would need far more reserve-unit capability than it now has. The question is how to get it.

OPTIONS FOR OUR RESERVE FORCES

The central problem of military manpower has not really changed since the birth of the Republic. Americans have demonstrated historically that they can maintain an active federal military force on the basis of a combination of economic incentives and appeals to patriotism, with the major constraints being their willingness, as a nation, to accept the economic costs and their ability to instill a sense of civic obligation in the ascending generation. The United States can get high-quality recruits if Americans are willing to pay for them and have in fact learned that because of differentials in performance and attrition, high-quality recruits, although they are initially more expensive than low-quality recruits, may be more cost effective.[17] Americans have learned during the current era that they can maintain a moderately large active-duty force in peacetime on the basis of such dynamics. They have learned that the market model can incorporate factors that will increase the sociodemographic representativeness of the force. And they have also learned that processes of military socialization and the development of effective leadership and unit cohesion can build an effective active military force out of personnel who have been recruited primarily through labor market appeals.

However, in the event of war, this active force is not sufficient. The United States needs a large mobilization base, and unlike during earlier historical periods, a draft—even a standby draft that does not require new legislation—will not provide for our short-term needs. Much of the mobilization base has to be pretrained, organized in units to fulfill necessary functions, and rapidly deployable. The credibility of the nation's deterrence posture and its ability to wage a conventional war if deterrence should fail are dependent on this. Because the likelihood of a major war is low, it does not make sense to expand active-duty U.S. forces to prepare for one. Rather, the nation needs a mobilization base of citizen-soldiers who are organized in combat-support, heavy-combat, and airlift units in the American population.

The Market Model

One obvious alternative solution to the problem of how to recruit such a reserve force is to use the same dynamics that work for the active forces—that is, the labor market. Either pay a high-enough wage or offer attractive-enough benefits, and enough high-quality people will be attracted to the reserves. This, in fact, was the strategy that the Gates Commission recommended and that the Defense Department used during the early years of the all-volunteer force. Between 1973 and 1978, manpower in the selected reserves fell from 919,000 to 718,000 under the market model. It has improved since then, but reserve strength is still not sufficient to meet the worldwide commitments of the United States.

Some reasons for the decline are obvious. During the Vietnam War, joining the reserves was one way of avoiding being conscripted for the war. In quantitative terms, the reserves benefited from draft-motivated volunteers. But one must worry about the military contribution that would be made by a reserve force composed largely of people who joined it in order to avoid going to war.

With the end of conscription, the draft motivation to join the reserves disappeared. Also, as I noted above, the trend toward longer average service under volunteer than under conscript conditions meant that a smaller proportion of the force was being released into the civilan labor force and into the reserve manpower pool than had been the case under the draft. Most important, however, Americans have learned during the era of the all-volunteer force that economic incentives do not work as effectively for the reserves as they do for the active forces.

While active military service and its benefits may be attractive in comparison to available alternatives in the civilian labor market or to unemployment, reserve military service, which in labor-market terms is essentially a form of moonlighting, is less attractive than its civilian moonlighting alternatives. Moreover, high-quality civilian employees, who are likely to be in good jobs, are not likely to be motivated by economic considerations to moonlight.

For people who moonlight because they need the extra money, the number of hours they can work is a crucial determinant of the attractiveness of a position. Reserve service requires far fewer compensated hours of work than do most civilian second jobs, on the average. Reservists, unlike civilians in second jobs, must commit themselves for several years of service. Reservists can be mobilized in the event of an emergency. And their normal military training activities may occur at times when their primary civilian employers would like them to be at work.[18] Whatever the benefits of reserve service, the labor-market model does not highlight them. The wage elasticities for reserve military service have been shown to be considerably lower than both the elasticities for active military service and for civilian moonlighting jobs.[19] More people cannot be brought in as easily by raising pay, and reserve pay cannot be raised easily in any case, because it is tied to active-duty pay. An alternative model is needed for the reserves.

A Reserve Draft

One frequently suggested alternative to the problem of mobilization base is to draft people for the reserve components. This suggestion is consistent with America's early military history, when young men could, in principle, be drafted for service in the militia. In fact, as I noted earlier, even the militia was manned primarily by volunteers, not conscripts. The reserve-draft alternative also stands recent American military manpower policy on its head, by assuming a universal service obligation that, as I noted earlier, decayed with the militia.

In fact, the United States has had little trouble in manning its reserve forces under a federal conscription system, both because people have been motivated to volunteer for reserve service to avoid being conscripted for active service and because conscription has produced a constant flow through the military of people who usually have completed their active duty with a reserve obligation. A volunteer active force with longer periods of service reduces the motivation and constrains the flow. Ironically, it is possible that a draft for the reserves would produce draft-motivated volunteers for active duty, since the active-duty tour would, under the terms of most proposals, involve fewer years of commitment and would introduce less uncertainty into one's life.

Whereas using conscription to raise military manpower wherever it is needed in the force—including the reserves—might be justifiable in terms of the history of the militia in the United States, the consensus is that a reserve draft is not needed and would not work.[20] As we have seen, while federal conscription has never met with universal acceptance in the United

States, it has been tolerated for relatively brief periods during wartime, when the need for military forces has been obvious. The need for additional reserve units is current and persistent, and there is not a war to justify a draft.

I have also noted that conscription has been most acceptable when a sufficiently large proportion of the population at risk has been drafted in order to avoid raising major questions of equity. While the difference between what the nation has now in the reserves and what it would need in order to mobilize quickly in the event of a major war is substantial, only a minority of the potential pool would be needed, and the political liabilities of establishing a system that would be guaranteed to produce perceptions of inequity far outweigh the potential gains.

Most important, reserve units are different from active-duty units, and accession processes that were designed to raise active forces should not be assumed to be adaptable to the reserves. All active-duty conscription systems involve an element of coercion. They feed into structured military units that can keep track of who has reported for duty and who is participating, and they can enforce sanctions against those who refuse to participate. If a conscript fails to report or if a soldier on active duty absents himself, it will be noticed quickly.

Reserve service, on the other hand, is an intermittent event. The reservist is first and foremost a civilian, and his or her unit, commanders, and peers are not a constant presence to reinforce his or her sense of military roles and obligations. Records are decentralized; accountability is minimal; sanctions are generally ineffective. The performance of reserve military units in the United States, even when they have contained personnel who had reserve obligations after conscripted active service, has been determined by the voluntary participation of their members. Such participation has been influenced more strongly by normative than by legal considerations. This is not likely to change. How, then, might the United States structure a normative system that will provide the reserve forces that the nation needs?

Universal Military Service and Universal Military Training

The idea of holding all citizens responsible for participating in the defense of the Republic has been with us since the American Revolution. Recall that George Washington wanted a federal militia. The concept of such a militia was, of course, better suited to a time when the basic military weapon was the rifle, which most young men learned to use in their youth, than it is in today's more technologically complex military environment.

Recognizing that contemporary military technology requires a familiarity with systems that most civilians do not possess, the more recent counterpart to the federal militia as a way of enriching the mobilization base is universal military training—a concept that has been part of our national dialogue on military manpower policy since the Truman era. Universal service and training are alternatives that we have elected not to adopt.

The modern world is replete with examples of nations that tie citizenship to the fulfillment of military obligations more explicitly and universally than the United States does. The nation's major perceived adversary—the Soviet Union—exacts either active conscripted service or at least military reserve service from the great majority of its male population.[21] This is the basis of the perceived threat to our interests in Europe that requires us to expand our own mobilization base: those Western European allies who themselves maintain systems of almost universal male conscription, such as West Germany, are quick to remind the United States of this fact.

Whereas some nations, such as the Soviet Union and West Germany, depend on conscription primarily to staff their active-duty forces even in peacetime, other nations emphasize the importance of universal service in maintaining their mobilization base, which is the most pressing manpower problem in the United States. Israel, for example, conscripts virtually all Jewish males for a three-year period, after which they have a long-term obligation to serve in reserve units that train together regularly.[22] The great majority of Israel's active force is made up of conscripts, with a relatively small professional military cadre. The overwhelming majority of its armed forces, however, are in rapidly mobilizable and deployable reserve units. Switzerland similarly trains and arms its male citizens and requires that they undertake a long-term reserve obligation with annual training musters.

Why has the United States eschewed this mode of meeting the dilemma of a military mobilization base when it is clear that no other system is more likely to tie the principle of obligation to the concept of citizenship and when allies, adversaries, and neutral parties have all provided the United States with examples that work? The major reasons are to be found in the differences between these nations and the United States and in the latter's military needs.

The nations that most successfully maintain the most universal bases of mobilization—Israel and Switzerland—are small nations that have geographically proximate potential aggressors and histories of military conflict. Israel is a relatively young state, but it was born in war, and it has been involved in major military conflicts each decade since its birth. Switzerland, although it is a neutral nation, was a European battleground for much of its history, was a military power in the fifteenth century, and thereafter was a provider of mercenary troops, who were not volunteers but were provided by the state, in exchange for monetary payment, to other nations.

The larger nations that maintain the principle of universal service, such as the Soviet Union and West Germany, likewise have potential adversaries at their borders, which have frequently been threatened. Universal service is justified on the basis of territorial defense, not military expansion. The United States, by contrast, has a larger manpower base than do nations such as Israel and Switzerland and does not have enemies at its borders.

A system of universal military service or training in the United States might do much to inculcate a notion of citizenship obligation to the state. And I believe that such a notion is crucial to the establishment and maintenance of the kind of military-mobilization base that the nation needs, given its current military commitments. To establish this value through purely military means, however, would give the nation a larger force than it needs for most contingencies. Such a force would be expensive, it would disrupt many domestic social institutions and processes, it would assign to the military an educational task that Americans have been loath to let it assume in the past, and most important, it would probably be a destabilizing force in the international system.

With regard to universal military service, if the United States were to conscript only males, which flies in the face of the ongoing citizenship revolution and which I think is politically untenable in the long run, and if it were to require only two years of service, which is probably the minimum that it makes sense to consider, given the time that it takes to train personnel for the modern military, then even in the current era of declining cohorts of eighteen year olds, the active military force would be increased by a factor of two to three. If the United States were to include women as well, it would go from an active force of 2 million, which seems to be serving our needs, to an active force of as much as 12 million. This would clearly disturb the nation's potential adversaries.

This would also disrupt domestic social institutions: for example, the system of higher education, which is accustomed to receiving students out of high school; economic enterprises that are dependent on turnover among young entry-level personnel; and processes of having families. The nation would not be able to justify the disruption. It would not be able to justify, in the current budget climate, the tens of billions of dollars in defense costs that such a system would require. And it would not know what to do with that many military personnel.

Because the problem for the United States is not the active forces but the mobilization base, a system of universal military training, rather than service, may be more tenable. However, here too, even with a declining manpower pool, such a system provides greater numbers than are needed and, therefore, greater expense than is justified. The size of our active force would have to increase markedly in order simply to provide the training base to accommodate more than a million additional people each year, double that if women were to be included. Thus, cost would go up without necessarily increasing active-duty combat strength.

Given a choice between two years of service in selected reserve units and longer periods as replacement or reinforcement personnel in the individual ready reserve, sufficient personnel would probably elect the selected reserve to give the United States the rapid mobilization base that it needs. However, such short-term personnel would not furnish the level of stability and cohesion that characterizes this nation's National Guard or Israel's reserve units, which I believe contributes to combat effectiveness. Also, Americans would be putting between 0.5 million and 2 million (if women were included) new conscripts into the individual ready reserve each year. If the reserve obligation in these roles were four years, there would be an expansion of 8 million people in these reserve positions. A large individual reserve pool makes little logistical sense. In a major war, the United States would run out of ammunition and supplies long before a significant proportion of its individual reserves could be mobilized.

The disruption in people's lives and in social processes is less under universal military training than it is under universal military service. The former model does assert the principle of obligation, and it does provide a basis for enriching the most important component of the mobilization base. But it does so at a cost of imposing a reserve obligation on a much larger proportion of the population than can be justified by our current military missions, and at a cost that would be in the billions of dollars.

National Service

While compulsory military service and training systems establish the principle of service obligation and provide the needed enhancement of the mobilization base, they produce far more people than are needed by the military if applied universally, and the military oppose them for that reason. If applied selectively, they raise questions of equity, and they have little long-term political viability. More broadly based national service systems have been suggested as a means of gaining the advantages of the assertion of citizenship obligations and of the enhancement of military capability without overloading the military with excess personnel.

The problem of the overproduction of military personnel or reservists through universal-military-service programs (although it does at the same time reinforce the principle of citizenship obligation) has been addressed by more broadly based notions of national service that embed active and reserve military service in a wider range of alternative services to the state. William James proposed such a system early in the century in his classic essay "The Moral Equivalent of War."[23] However, the United States has never approached the mobilization of "the whole youthful population" that James proposed, and the weakness of most contemporary proposals for national service is probably that they strive for such universality on a compulsory basis.

Limited civilian national service was used during the depression—for example, in the Civilian Conservation Corps; and civilian alternative service was allowed in lieu of military service for conscientious objectors from World War II to Vietnam. The former system was unpopular, however, because it was regarded primarily as a form of welfare for the individual participants, rather than as a service to the nation; and the latter was clearly focused on a principle of wartime military obligation, rather than on a general citizenship obligation. However, about three dozen states and localities continue to operate youth conservation or community-service programs, so the idea of civilian service has persisted.

President John F. Kennedy built a foundation for a broader national service system with his establishment of the Peace Corps and the domestic Volunteers in Service to America (VISTA), and debate was accelerated during the Vietnam War as efforts were made to find alternatives to military conscription. As I noted in chapter 2, national service was suggested by several participants in the University of Chicago's conference on the draft, and the Marshall Commission was mandated to examine this alternative. It did so, and it rejected the suggestion.

The military manpower problems of the early years of the all-volunteer force, in combination with a growing awareness that the ascending generation of Americans seemed not to be imbued with a sense of national purpose or goals, produced a renewed interest in national service, which was motivated by both concerns. The beginning of the 1980s saw the principle endorsed by a number of conferences, reports, and groups, ranging from the Carnegie Council on Policy Studies in Higher Education and the Ford Foundation to the Committee for the Study of National Security.[24] Three national-service bills were introduced into the Ninty-sixth Congress and were widely debated. The principle of national service received widespread support. No system was established, however, because of a lack of consensus on what the principle should mean in practice.

Much of the political support for national service came from a perception that such a system would cure the ills of the all-volunteer force. The most popular and widely discussed plans gave young Americans the options of choosing between active military service, reserve military service, civilian service, or liability for a military draft. However, this residual conscription was the least popularly supported of the options, since a major motivation of the debate was to find an alternative to conscription.

Without this possibility of conscription, there was no guarantee that national service would solve the military's manpower problems. Most important, manpower and personnel policy initiatives during the early 1980s resolved most of the manpower problems in the active military forces, and much of the political motivation for considering national service was dissipated, even though interest in the principle remained.

During the late 1980s, even as members of Congress were discussing the reinstitution of conscription in anticipation of the continuing decline of manpower into the 1990s, the tide seemed to be turning once more against a system of national service. In order to guarantee military manpower, it would have to involve compulsion. If compulsion were to be used, simply instituting a draft would produce the manpower at much less cost. A universal system might reduce inequity to a degree, but major problems would remain in establishing the equivalence of various forms of civilian and military service. In the absence of such equivalence, inequities would remain. And compulsory service systems would be liable to constitutional challenge under Thirteenth Amendment protections against involuntary servitude.

While the courts have upheld Congress' right to raise armies through conscription and to require alternative service from conscientious objectors, there seems to be a very low likelihood that the courts would find that a compulsory system in which most people perform civilian rather than military service was justified by Congress' right to raise an army. And in the absence of manpower shortfalls, the justification for compulsion is lacking. The passage of a universal national service system seems unlikely.

The principle of national service remains attractive, but such a system must recognize a set of important pragmatic constraints. The most important of these is the recognition that the goal should be to establish normative expectations of fulfillment of citizenship obligations, not simply to provide manpower for the armed forces. If the more general goal is met, the specific needs of the military will also be fulfilled.

The nation currently has the luxury of being able to shape a system of national service through institution building precisely because the economic model has been effective in providing manpower for the active-duty armed forces. Universality and compulsion are legal and political liabilities that can and should be avoided. The system need not involve everyone. The active-duty military forces should not, in fact, be included in a system of national service, any more than other public-service occupations, such as teachers, librarians, and professional fire fighters, should be included. There is, however, a national need for a mobilization base in many of these public-service areas: armed forces reserves, volunteer firefighters, and so forth. It should be possible to structure an incentive system that would encourage voluntary participation in such a mobilization base, stimulate the provision of necessary services to the nation, and establish a service ethic.

In a recent study, Richard Danzig and Peter Szanton have noted: "Military veterans, Peace Corps alumni, and ironically, immigrants, are now virtually the only Americans who experience a sense of citizenship earned rather than simply received. Forms of national service that required sacrifice, intensive effort, or some risk might offer that sense to all."[25] I am less convinced of the importance of the level of the sacrifice, the intensity of the effort, or the risk in producing a sense of citizenship earned than I am about the importance of communicating to the ascending generation that service to the nation is expected, is valued, and is rewarded. Inculcating such a belief will aid in military mobilization if required, and it will contribute to a sense of nationhood in the more desirable case that military mobilization is not required. It will remove Americans from the Orwellian world in which unity is derived only from external enemies.

A program of national service along these lines would exclude positions that are filled as full-time jobs for market wages, such as professional firefighters, teachers, police, librarians, and military personnel. It would not deny the altruism involved on the part of some of these practitioners, but it would assert a difference between a job and a service. It would also exclude people who have only a nominal service role. Thus, individuals who leave the military with a service obligation but who do not train, have a mobilization assignment, or report to periodic musters, would not be regarded as having fulfilled a national service function. Those who train or who are periodically mobilized for specific assignments would of course be regarded as part of the national service.

The program would include people who have received training and have made themselves available for full-time volunteer positions for short terms—for example, in the Peace Corps, VISTA, or state and local conservation or community-service corps—and people who have volunteered for part-time service over longer periods of time—for example, volunteer firefighters and military personnel in reserve units who mustered and trained periodically.

The program would not have to include everyone. Indeed, it would be overloaded if it did. However, it should publicly celebrate the participation of those who elect to serve. It should also provide sufficient tangible rewards for participation to make it apparent that national service has long-term benefits to the individual as well as to the nation. Such rewards might include educational benefits, such as reduced tuition at public institutions of higher education or the forgiving of educational loans, tax benefits during or after service, and differential access to public employment, or incentives to private employers to reward such service. I believe that the combination of a service ethic and the fact of rewards for such service would enrich the commitment of America's youth to the nation and would provide the matrix within which an effective mobilization base of reserve military units could be developed.

At the same time, it is important to emphasize that manpower is only one element in the mobilization equation. I take it as a sign of improved national health that Americans have begun to pay attention to the human components of combat operations, rather than leaving high-lethality technology as their major military option. Having a United States military that is dependent on American citizens constrains policy makers to keep military operations consistent with national goals. This is an important part of civil-military relations in the United States.

As the nation shifts from preparation for more capital-intensive to more labor-intensive military operations, Americans must also assure that the pendulum will swing back from a posture of manning the equipment to one of equipping the man. U.S. soldiers, sailors, and airmen, whether serving in the active forces because it is a good job or in the reserve forces out of a sense of national service, are fulfilling a national-security function and are entitled to know that their equipment needs are of the highest priority. Such troops and units must have the materials that they will need in order to fight and survive in a war, should they be called to combat on the nation's behalf, and they should have the vehicles to get to the war. Having recognized the roles that people play in national defense, the United States must provide for them in those roles.

Notes

CHAPTER 1. SOCIAL TRENDS AND THE CITIZEN-SOLDIER

1. Philip Gold, *Evasions: The American Way of Military Service* (New York: Paragon, 1985), p. 57.

2. See Morris Janowitz, *Military Conflict* (Beverly Hills, Calif.: Sage Publications, 1975), pp. 70–88; and Jacques Van Doorn, "The Decline of the Mass Army in the West," *Armed Forces and Society* 1, no. 2 (Winter 1975): 147–57.

3. Jacques Van Doorn, *The Soldier and Social Change* (Beverly Hills, Calif.: Sage Publications, 1975), pp. 53–56.

4. Harold D. Lasswell, "The Garrison State," *American Journal of Sociology* 46 (1941): 455–68, and "Sino-Japanese Crisis: The Garrison State versus the Civilian State," *China Quarterly* 11 (1937): 643–49.

5. Harold D. Lasswell, "Garrison State Hypothesis Today," in *Changing Patterns of Military Politics*, ed. Samuel P. Huntington (New York: Free Press, 1962), pp. 51–70.

6. See, e.g., Samuel P. Huntington, *The Soldier and the State* (Cambridge, Mass.: Harvard University Press, 1957), pp. 346–50.

7. Harold Wool, *The Military Specialist* (Baltimore, Md.: Johns Hopkins University Press, 1968), p. 42.

8. Martin Binkin, *Military Technology and Defense Manpower* (Washington, D.C.: Brookings Institution, 1986), p. 6.

9. See Vincent Davis, "Levée en Masse, C'est Fini," in *New Civil-Military Relations*, ed. John P. Lovell and Philip S. Kronenberg (New Brunswick, N.J.: Transaction Books, 1974), pp. 89–108.

10. Carl von Clausewitz, *On War,* ed. and with an introduction by Anatol Rapoport (Baltimore, Md.: Penguin Books, 1968), pp. 19–20.

11. Morris Janowitz, *The Professional Soldier* (Glencoe, Ill.: Free Press, 1960), p. 418.

12. Larry L. Fabian, *Soldiers without Enemies* (Washington, D.C.: Brookings Institution, 1971).

13. Charles C. Moskos, "UN Peacekeepers," *Armed Forces and Society* 1 (1975): 388–401; see also his *Peace Soldiers: The Sociology of a Unified United Nations Military Force* (Chicago: University of Chicago Press, 1976).

14. See Harold L. Wilensky, *The Welfare State and Equality* (Berkeley: University of California Press, 1975).

15. J. F. Sleeman, *The Welfare State* (London: Allen & Unwin, 1973), p. 1.

16. Glen H. Beyer, *Housing and Society* (New York: Macmillan, 1965).

17. Theodore J. Lowi, *The End of Liberalism: The Second Republic of the United States,* 2d ed. (New York: Norton, 1979).

18. Gaston V. Rimlinger, "Social Security, Incentives, and Controls in the U.S. and U.S.S.R.," *Comparative Studies in Society and History* 4 (1961): 104–24.

19. See Kathi V. Friedman, *Legitimation of Social Rights and the Western Welfare State* (Chapel Hill: University of North Carolina Press, 1981), p. 73.

20. Kirsten A. Grφnbjerg, *Mass Society and the Extension of Welfare, 1960–1970* (Chicago: University of Chicago Press, 1977).

21. Friedman, *Legitimation.*

22. Reinhard Bendix, *Nation-Building and Citizenship* (New York: Wiley, 1964), p. 3.

23. See, e.g., Robert A. Dahl, *Who Governs?* (New Haven, Conn.: Yale University Press, 1961).

24. T. H. Marshall, *Citizenship and Social Class* (Cambridge, Eng.: Cambridge University Press, 1950).

25. Harvey C. Greisman and Kurt Finsterbusch, "Modernization of Warfare," *Society* 12 (1975): 53–57.

26. Morris Janowitz, "The All-Volunteer Military as a 'Sociopolitical' Problem," *Social Problems* 22 (Feb. 1975): 435.

27. Janowitz, *Military Conflict,* pp. 77–78.

28. See James B. Jacobs and Leslie Anne Hayes, "Aliens in the U.S. Armed Forces," *Armed Forces and Society* 7 (1981): 187–208.

29. David R. Segal, Nora Scott Kinzer, and John C. Woelfel, "The Concept of Citizenship and Attitudes toward Women in Combat," *Sex Roles* 3, no. 5 (1977): 469–77.

30. See Mady Wechsler Segal and David R. Segal, "Social Change and the Participation of Women in the American Military" in *Research in Social Movements, Conflicts and Change,* vol. 5, ed. Louis Kriesberg (Greenwich, Conn.: JAI Press, 1983), pp. 235–58.

31. See Morris Janowitz, "Observations on the Sociology of Citizenship." *Social Forces* 59 (Sept. 1980): 1–24.

32. Marshall, *Citizenship and Social Class.*

33. See David R. Segal, "From Political to Industrial Citizenship," in *The Political Education of Soldiers,* ed. Morris Janowitz and Stephen D. Wesbrook (Beverly Hills, Calif.: Sage Publications, 1983), pp. 285–306.

34. See Ezra S. Krendel and Bernard L. Samoff, eds., *Unionizing the Armed Forces* (Philadelphia: University of Pennsylvania Press, 1977); Alan Ned Sabrosky et al., eds., *Blue-Collar Soldiers? Unionization and the U.S. Military* (Philadelphia: Foreign Policy Research Institute, 1977); William J. Taylor, Roger J. Arango, and Robert S. Lockwood, eds., *Military Unions* (Beverly Hills, Calif.: Sage Publications, 1977).

35. Friedman, *Legitimation,* pp. 125ff.

36. See David R. Segal et al., "Trends in the Structure of Army Families," *Journal of Political and Military Sociology* 4 (Spring, 1976): 135–38.

37. Dennis H. Wrong, *Population and Society* (New York: Random House, 1977), p. 70.

38. See, e.g., Morris Janowitz and Charles C. Moskos, "Five Years of the All-Volunteer Force," *Armed Forces and Society* 5 (Winter, 1979): 171–218.

39. See, e.g., Martin Anderson, ed., *Registration and the Draft* (Stanford, Calif.: Hoover Institution Press, 1982); Andrew J. Goodpaster, Lloyd H. Elliot, and J. Alan Hovey, Jr., *Toward a Consensus on Military Service* (New York: Pergamon, 1982); Brent Scowcroft, ed., *Military Service in the United States* (Englewood Cliffs, N.J.: Prentice-Hall, 1982).

40. See David R. Segal, "Military Organization and Personnel Accession," in *Conscripts and Volunteers,* ed. Robert K. Fullinwider (Totowa, N.J.: Rowman & Allanheld, 1983), pp. 7–22.

41. This issue is discussed by David R. Segal and Katherine Swift Gravino in "The Empire Strikes Back: Military Professionalism in the South Atlantic War," in *The*

Regionalization of Warfare, ed. James Brown and William P. Snyder (New Brunswick, N.J.: Transaction Books, 1985), pp. 17–36.

42. Edmund D. Pellegrino et al., *The Successor Generation* (Washington, D.C.: Atlantic Council, 1981), p. 11.

43. See Gwyn Harries-Jenkins, "Armed Forces and the Welfare State," in *Civil-Military Relations*, ed. Morris Janowitz (Beverly Hills, Calif.: Sage Publications, 1981), pp. 231–57.

44. David R. Segal, "Military Service in the Nineteen-Seventies: Attitudes of Soldiers and Civilians" in *Manning the American Armed Forces*, ed. Allan R. Millett and Anne F. Trupp (Columbus: Mershon Center of the Ohio State University, 1981), pp. 42–63.

45. See Herbert C. Puscheck, "Selective Service Registration: Success or Failure?" *Armed Forces and Society* 10 (Fall, 1983): 5–25.

46. See Morris Janowitz, "Civic Consciousness and Military Performance," in *The Political Education of Soldiers*, ed. Morris Janowitz and Stephen D. Wesbrook (Beverly Hills, Calif.: Sage Publications, 1983), pp. 55–80; and Segal, "From Political to Industrial Citizenship".

CHAPTER 2. CHANGES IN UNITED STATES MILITARY MANPOWER POLICY

1. See John Whiteclay Chambers II, *To Raise an Army* (New York: Free Press, 1987).

2. John O'Sullivan and Allen M. Meckler, eds., *The Draft and Its Enemies* (Urbana: University of Illinois Press, 1974), pp. 4–5.

3. John Shy, *Toward Lexington* (Princeton, N.J.: Princeton University Press, 1965), p. 13.

4. James T. Flexner, *George Washington: The Forge of Experience, 1732–1775* (Boston, Mass.: Little, Brown, 1965), p. 138.

5. Ibid., p. 7.

6. *The Writings of George Washington*, ed. John C. Fitzpatrick, 39 vols. (Washington, D.C.: U.S. Government Printing Office, 1931–44), 26:374–91.

7. Walter Millis, *Arms and Men* (New York: Putnam, 1956), p. 46.

8. Lawrence Delbert Cress, *Citizens in Arms* (Chapel Hill: University of North Carolina Press, 1982), p. 89.

9. Richard H. Kohn, "The Creation of the American Military Establishment, 1783–1802," in *The Military in America*, ed. Peter Karsten (New York: Free Press, 1980), p. 76.

10. Millis, *Arms and Men*, p. 50.

11. Cress, *Citizens in Arms*, pp. 121–22.

12. Ibid. p. 126.

13. Chambers, *To Raise an Army*, pp. 29ff.

14. Millis, *Arms and Men*, p. 59.

15. Ibid. p. 69.

16. Ibid. p. 105.

17. Clement Eaton, *A History of the Southern Confederacy* (New York: Macmillan, 1954), p. 89.

18. Jack F. Leach, *Conscription in the United States* (Rutland, Vt.: Charles E. Tuttle, 1952), p. 160.

19. See William B. Hesseltine, *Lincoln and the War Governors* (New York: Knopf, 1948), pp. 273–307.

20. Chambers, *To Raise an Army*, p. 51.

21. See David R. Segal, "Leadership and Management: Organization Theory," in *Military Leadership*, ed. James H. Buck and Lawrence J. Korb (Beverly Hills, Calif.: Sage Publications, 1981) pp. 56–57.

22. Millis, *Arms and Men*, p. 179.

23. See Harry A. Marmion, "Historical Background of Selective Service in the United States," in *Selective Service and American Society*, ed. Roger W. Little (New York: Russell Sage Foundation, 1969), pp. 38–40; and Chambers, *To Raise an Army* pp. 103–51.

24. Millis, *Arms and Men*, p. 275.

25. J. Garry Clifford and Samuel R. Spencer, Jr., *The First Peacetime Draft* (Lawrence: University Press of Kansas, 1986).

26. Millis, *Arms and Men*, pp. 317–18.

27. James M. Gerhardt, *The Draft and Public Policy* (Columbus: Ohio State University Press, 1971), pp. 89–90.

28. See Herbert C. Puschek, "Selective Service Registration: Success or Failure?" *Armed Forces and Society* 10 (Fall, 1983): 5–25.

29. See Jeffrey M. Schevitz, *The Weaponsmakers* (Cambridge; Mass.: Schenkman, 1979), pp. 17–33.

30. David R. Segal, "Sociological and Economic Models of Military Manpower: An Attempt at Integration," in *The Challenge of Social Control: Citizenship and Institution-Building in Modern Society*, ed. Gerald D. Suttles and Mayer N. Zald (Norwood, N.J.: Ablex, 1985), pp. 161–80.

31. For analyses of the local boards and their dynamics see James W. Davis, Jr., and Kenneth M. Dolbeare, *Little Groups of Neighbors* (Chicago: Markham, 1968); and Gary L. Wamsley, "Decision-Making in Local Boards," in *Selective Service and American Society*, pp. 83–108.

32. See David R. Segal and John D. Blair, "Public Confidence in the U.S. Military" *Armed Forces and Society* 3 (Nov. 1976): 7.

33. See Davis and Dolbeare, *Little Groups of Neighbors*.

34. Marmion, "Historical Background of Selective Service," p. 47.

35. Neil D. Fligstein, "Who Served in the Military, 1940–73," *Armed Forces and Society* 6 (Winter 1980): 297–312.

36. Gilbert Badillo and G. David Curry, "The Social Incidence of Vietnam Casualties," *Armed Forces and Society* 2 (1976): 397–406.

37. Jerald G. Bachman, John D. Blair, and David R. Segal, *The All Volunteer Force* (Ann Arbor: University of Michigan Press, 1977), p. 12.

38. The conference proceedings are reported in *The Draft: A Handbook of Facts and Alternatives*, ed. Sol Tax (Chicago: University of Chicago Press, 1967).

39. Walter Y. Oi, "The Costs and Implications of an All-Volunteer Force," ibid., pp. 221–51; and comments by Harold Wool, ibid., especially pp. 322–25.

40. Morris Janowitz, "The Logic of National Service," ibid., pp. 73–90.

41. Milton Friedman, "Why Not a Voluntary Army?" ibid., pp. 200–207.

42. See Bruce K. Chapman, "Politics and Conscription: A Proposal to Replace the Draft," ibid., pp. 208–20.

43. See Segal, "Sociological and Economic Models of Military Manpower."

44. Gus C. Lee and Geoffrey Y. Parker, *Ending the Draft: The Story of the All Volunteer Force* (Alexandria, Va.: Human Resources Research Organization, 1977, report no. 77–1), prepared for the assistant secretary of defense (Manpower and Reserve Affairs), p. 29.

45. See Thomas S. Gates, Jr., et al., *The Report of the President's Commission on an All-volunteer Armed Force* (Washington, D.C.: U.S. Government Printing Office, 1970).

46. See Harry A. Marmion, *The Case against an All-Volunteer Army* (Chicago: Quadrangle Books, 1971).

47. Morris Janowitz, "Volunteer Armed Forces and Military Purpose," *Foreign Affairs* 50 (Apr. 1972): 427–43; idem, "Toward an All-Volunteer Military," *Public Interest* 27 (Spring 1972): 104–17; idem, *U.S. Forces and the Zero Draft*, Adelphi paper no. 94 (London: International Institute for Strategic Studies, 1973).

48. Morris Janowitz, "The All-Volunteer Military as a 'Sociopolitical' Problem," *Social Problems* 22 (Feb. 1975): 432–49.

49. Bachman, Blair, and Segal, *All-Volunteer Force.*

50. See Morris Janowitz and Charles C. Moskos, "Five Years of the All-Volunteer Force," *Armed Forces and Society* 5 (Winter 1979): 171–218.

51. United States, Office of the Secretary of Defense, *America's Volunteers* (Washington, D.C.: Office of the Assistant Secretary for Manpower, Reserve Affairs and Logistics, 1978); Richard V. L. Cooper, *Military Manpower and the All-Volunteer Force* (Santa Monica, Calif.: Rand Corporation, 1977).

52. See David R. Segal, "Military Organization and Personnel Accession," in *Conscripts and Volunteers*, ed. Robert K. Fullinwider (Totowa, N.J.: Rowman & Allanheld, 1983), pp 7–22.

53. E.g., Cooper, *Military Manpower.*

54. Melvin R. Laird, *People, Not Hardware* (Washington, D.C.: American Enterprise Institute Special Analysis, 1980).

55. See, e.g., Robert F. McNown, Bernard Udis, and Colin Ash, "Economic Analysis of the All-Volunteer Force," *Armed Forces and Society* 7 (Fall 1980): 113–32; and Charles Dale and Curtis Gilroy, "Determinants of Enlistments," ibid., 10 (Feb. 1984): 192–210.

56. United States, Office of the Assistant Secretary of Defense (Manpower, Reserve Affairs and Logistics), *Profile of American Youth: 1980 Nationwide Administration of the Armed Services Vocational Aptitude Battery* (Washington, D.C.: Office of the Secretary of Defense, Mar., 1982).

57. See William E. Dupuy, "Technology and Manpower: Army Perspective," in *The All-Volunteer Force after a Decade*, ed. William Bowman, Roger Little, and G. Thomas Sicilia (Washington, D.C.: Pergamon-Brassey's, 1986), pp. 122–35.

58. Military Manpower Task Force, *A Report to the President on the Status and Prospects of the All Volunteer Force* (Washington, D.C.: Office of the Secretary of Defense, October, 1982).

59. See Puschek, "Selective Service Registration."

60. See, e.g., James B. Jacobs and Dennis McNamara, "Selective Service without a Draft," *Armed Forces and Society* 10, no. 3 (Spring 1984): 361–79.

CHAPTER 3. CHANGES IN UNITED STATES SOCIAL AND MILITARY ORGANIZATION

1. See David R. Segal and Mady Wechsler Segal, "Change in Military Organization," *Annual Review of Sociology* 9 (1983): 151–70.

2. David Riesman, *The Lonely Crowd* (New Haven, Conn.: Yale University Press, 1950).

3. Maurice R. Stein, *The Eclipse of Community: An Interpretation of American Studies* (Princeton, N.J.: Princeton University Press, 1960); see also Arthur J. Vidich and Maurice R. Stein, "The Dissolved Identity in Military Life," in *Identity and Anxiety*, ed. Maurice R. Stein, Arthur J. Vidich, and David M. White (Glencoe, Ill.: Free Press, 1960), pp. 493–506.

4. Seymour Martin Lipset, *The First New Nation* (New York: Basic Books, 1963).

5. Max Weber, *The Theory of Social and Economic Organization*, trans. A. M. Henderson and Talcott Parsons (Glencoe, Ill.: Free Press, 1947).

6. See Frederick W. Taylor, *The Principles of Scientific Management* (New York: Harper & Row, 1911).

7. David R. Segal, "Leadership and Management: Organization Theory," in *Military Leadership*, ed. James H. Buck and Lawrence J. Korb (Beverly Hills, Calif.: Sage Publications, 1981), pp. 46ff.

8. See David R. Segal and Joseph J. Lengermann, "Professional and Institutional Considerations," in *Combat Effectiveness*, ed. Sam C. Sarkesian (Beverly Hills, Calif.: Sage Publications, 1980), p. 172.

9. See F. J. Roethlisberger and W. J. Dickson, *Management and the Worker* (Cambridge, Mass.: Harvard University Press, 1939).

10. E.g., Warren G. Bennis and Phillip E. Slater, *The Temporary Society* (New York: Harper & Row, 1968).

11. While the air war was dramatic and widely publicized, evaluations of the effects of strategic bombing with conventional explosives showed that this was not an effective means of waging war, a fact that had been forgotten by the air force and the Department of Defense by the time of the Vietnam War: see Morris Janowitz, "Consequences of Social Research on the U.S. Military," *Armed Forces and Society* 8 (1982): 522–23.

12. See Elian Huzar, *The Power and the Purse* (Westport, Conn.: Greenwood Press, 1971), pp. 161ff.

13. See Walter Millis, *Arms and Men* (New York: Putnam, 1956), p. 313.

14. Thomas S. Gates, Jr., et al., *The Report of the President's Commission on an All-Volunteer Armed Force* (Washington, D.C.: U.S. Government Printing Office, 1970).

15. See Eric Trist, "Work Improvement and Industrial Democracy," paper presented to the Conference of the Commission of European Communities on Work Organization, Technical Development, and Motivations of the Individual, Brussels, Belgium, 1974.

16. See David R. Segal, "Worker Representation in Military Organization," in *The Changing World of the American Military*, ed. Franklin D. Margiotta (Boulder, Colo.: Westview Press, 1978), pp. 223–46.

17. See George Ritzer, "Implications of and Barriers to Industrial Democracy in the United States and Sweden," in *Equity, Income, and Policy*, ed. Irving Louis Horowitz (New York: Praeger, 1977), pp. 49–60.

18. There is very little evidence that the experiments attempted in industrial settings have the desired effects: see David Bowers, "OD Techniques and Their Results in Twenty-three Organizations," *Journal of Applied Behavioral Science* 9 (1973): 21–43.

19. Segal and Lengermann, "Professional and Institutional Considerations," pp. 178ff.

20. Robert A. Gregory, "Organizational Development Efforts in the United States Air Force," paper presented at the eighty-fifth annual convention of the American Psychological Association, San Francisco, Calif., Sept., 1977.

21. Robert L. Forbes, Jr., "A *Cause Celebre*: Organizational Development in the United States Navy," paper presented at the eighty-fourth annual convention of the American Psychological Association, Washington, D.C., Sept., 1976.

22. David R. Segal, Barbara Ann Lynch, and John D. Blair, "The Changing American Soldier," *American Journal of Sociology* 85 (July, 1979): 105.

23. See Segal, "Leadership and Management."

24. Auguste Comte, *System of Positive Philosophy: or Treatise on Sociology* (London: Burt Franklin, 1875).

25. Emile Durkheim, *The Division of Labor in Society* (New York: Macmillan, 1933).

26. Georg Simmel, "Sociability," in *The Sociology of Georg Simmel*, ed. Kurt Wolff (New York: Macmillan, 1950), pp. 40–57.

27. Weber, *Theory of Social and Economic Organization*, p. 88.

28. K. Lewin, R. Lippitt, and R. K. White, "Patterns of Aggressive Behavior in Experimentally Created Social Climates," *Journal of Social Psychology* 10 (1939): 271–79.

29. E.g., Fred Fiedler, *A Theory of Leadership Effectiveness* (New York: McGraw-Hill, 1967); and U.S. Army War College, *Leadership for the 1970s* (Carlisle Barracks, Pa.: Army War College, 1971). For a recent example see Jerome Adams et al., "West Point: Critical Incidents of Leadership," *Armed Forces and Society* 10 (1984): 597–611.

30. J. E. McGrath and I. Altman, *Small Group Research* (New York: Holt, Rinehart & Winston, 1966), p. 50.

31. See Richard Hofstadter, *Social Darwinism in American Thought* (Boston, Mass.: Beacon Press, 1955).

32. See Robert L. Heilbroner, *The Worldly Philosophers* (New York: Simon & Schuster, 1953).

33. See, e.g., R. Blake and J. Mouton, *Corporate Excellence through Grid Organizational Development* (Houston, Tex.: Gulf Publishing, 1968); Peter F. Drucker, *The Practice of Management* (New York: Harper & Row, 1954); W. L. French and C. H. Bell, Jr., *Organizational Development* (Englewood Cliffs, N.J.: Prentice-Hall, 1973).

34. Morris Janowitz, *The Professional Soldier* (Glencoe, Ill.: Free Press, 1960).

35. Ardant de Picq, *Battle Studies*, trans. from the eighth French edition by John N. Greely and Robert C. Cotton, (New York: Macmillan, 1921).

36. S. L. A. Marshall, *Men against Fire* (New York: Morrow, 1947).

37. Samuel A. Stouffer et al., *The American Soldier, vol. 2: Combat and Its Aftermath* (Princeton, N.J.: Princeton University Press, 1949), p. 118.

38. Edward A. Shils and Morris Janowitz, "Cohesion and Disintegration in the Wehrmacht in World War II," *Public Opinion Quarterly* 12 (1948) 280–315.

39. Roger W. Little, "Buddy Relations and Combat Performance," in *The New Military*, ed. Morris Janowitz (New York: W. W. Norton, 1969), pp. 195–223.

40. John H. Faris, "An Alternative Perspective to Savage and Gabriel," *Armed Forces and Society* 3 (1977): 457–62.

41. D. J. Chesler, N. J. Van Steenberg, and E. Brueckel, "Effect on Morale of Infantry Team Replacement and Individual Replacement Systems," *Sociometry* 18 (1955): 73–81.

42. See David R. Segal, "Sociological and Economic Models of Military Manpower: An Attempt at Integration," in *The Challenge of Social Control: Citizenship and Institution-Building in Modern Society*, ed. Gerald D. Suttles and Mayer N. Zald (Norwood, N.J.: Ablex, 1985), pp. 161–80.

43. Personnel Research and Procedures Division, *Attitudes of Enlisted Men toward Unit Rotation (GYROSCOPE)*, OEU report 57-4 (Washington, D.C.: Adjutant General).

44. Compare Bruce E. Petree and Robert L. Schroeder, "Rx for Turbulence," *Army* 31 (Nov., 1981): 14–20, and Dandridge M. Malone, "A Context for Cohesion," U.S. Army Delta Force Concept Paper (Carlisle Barracks, Pa.: U.S. Army Delta Force, 1982).

45. Charles C. Moskos, *The American Enlisted Man* (New York: Russell Sage Foundation, 1970), pp. 144–45.

46. Paul L. Savage and Richard A. Gabriel, "Cohesion and Disintegration in the American Army," *Armed Forces and Society* 2 (1976): 340–76.

47. Moskos, *American Enlisted Man*; and Faris, "An Alternative Perspective."

48. John Helmer, *Bringing the War Home* (New York: Free Press, 1974).

49. See Robert L. Goldich, *The U.S. Army's New Manning System*, (Washington, D.C.: Congressional Research Service, 1983).

50. Janowitz, "Consequences of Social Research on the U.S. Military."

51. See, e.g., Savage and Gabriel, "Cohesion and Disintegration in the American Army."

52. Shils and Janowitz, "Cohesion and Disintegration in the Wehrmacht."

53. Edward A. Shils, "Primary Groups in the American Army," in *Continuities in Social Research: Studies in the Scope and Method of 'The American Soldier,'* ed. Robert K. Merton and Paul F. Lazarsfeld (New York: Free Press, 1950) pp. 16–39.

54. Moskos, *American Enlisted Man.*

55. Charles C. Moskos, "The Military," *Annual Review of Sociology* 2 (1976): 55–77.

56. See, e.g., Morris Janowitz, "The Logic of National Service," in *The Draft: A Handbook of Facts and Alternatives*, ed. Sol Tax (Chicago: University of Chicago Press, 1967), pp. 73–90.

57. See David R. Segal, "Worker Representation."

58. Robert L. Kaplan, with Patricia T. Harris, *The Measurement of High School Students' Attitudes toward Recruiting Incentives* (Fort Sheridan, Ill: U.S. Army Recruiting Command, 1983), p. 7.

59. Morris Janowitz, "The Citizen-Soldier and National Purpose," *Air University Review*, Nov.–Dec. 1979, pp. 31–39.

60. Morris Janowitz, "Observations on the Sociology of Citizenship," *Social Forces* 59 (Sept., 1980): 1–24.

61. Morris Janowitz, "Patriotism and the All-Volunteer Military," *Air University Review*, Jan.–Feb. 1982, pp. 31–39.

62. David R. Segal, "Military Service in the Nineteen-Seventies: Attitudes of Soldiers and Civilians," in *Manning the American Armed Forces*, ed. Allan R. Millett and Anne F. Trupp (Columbus: Mershon Center of the Ohio State University, 1981), pp. 42–63.

63. James S. Burk, with John H. Faris, *The Persistence and Importance of Patriotism in the All-Volunteer Force* (Fort Sheridan, Ill.: U.S. Army Recruiting Command, 1972), p. 13.

64. Stephen D. Wesbrook, "Historical Notes," in *The Political Education of Soldiers*, ed. Morris Janowitz and Stephen D. Wesbrook (Beverly Hills, Calif.: Sage Publications, 1983), pp. 251–84.

65. Ibid., and Wesbrook, "Sociopolitical Training in the Military," ibid., p. 15.

66. See, Moskos, *American Enlisted Man*, pp. 148–51.

67. Harmon Zeigler, *The Political Life of American Teachers* (Englewood Cliffs, N.J.: Prentice-Hall, 1967).

68. See, e.g., Gilbert T. Sewall, "The Diminished Past: Conditions and Ideals in the Social Studies," in *Against Mediocrity*, ed. Chester E. Finn, Jr., Diane Ravitch, and Robert T. Fancher (New York: Holmes & Meier, 1984), pp. 115–29.

69. Gertrude Himmelfarb, "Denigrating the Rule of Reason," *Harper's*, Apr., 1984, pp. 84–90.

70. Morris Janowitz, "Civic Consciousness and Military Performance," in *Political Education of Soldiers*, pp. 55–80; and David R. Segal, "From Political to Industrial Citizenship," ibid., pp. 285–306.

71. Morris Janowitz, *The Reconstruction of Patriotism* (Chicago: University of Chicago Press, 1983).

72. John H. Faris, "Economic and Noneconomic Factors of Personnel Recruitment and Retention in the AVF," *Armed Forces and Society* 10 (1984) 251–75.

73. Morris Janowitz, *Sociology and the Military Establishment*, rev. ed. (New York: Russell Sage Foundation, 1965), p. 17.

74. David R. Segal and Mady W. Segal, "Models of Civil-Military Relationships at the Elite Level," in *The Perceived Role of the Military*, ed. M. Van Gils (Rotterdam: Rotterdam University Press, 1971), pp. 279–92.

75. Morris Janowitz, "The Emergent Military," in *Public Opinion and the Military Establishment*, ed. Charles C. Moskos (Beverly Hills, Calif.: Sage Publications, 1971), pp. 255–70.

76. Moskos, *American Enlisted Man*, p. 170.

77. Charles C. Moskos, "The Emergent Military," *Pacific Sociological Review* 16 (1973): 255–79.

78. William L. Hauser, *America's Army in Crisis* (Baltimore, Md.: Johns Hopkins University Press, 1973).

79. Statement of Dr. Charles C. Moskos, Hearing before the Military Personnel Subcommittee on Armed Services on the Continuing Review of the All-Volunteer Force, 95th Cong., 2d sess., July 11, 1978.

80. Thomas S. Gates Jr., et al., *The Report of the President's Commission on an All-Volunteer Armed Force* (Washington, D.C.: U.S. Government Printing Office, 1970).

81. Assembly of Western European Union, *Conditions of Service in the Armed Forces*, document 650, Twentieth Ordinary Session, Nov., 1974.

82. Charles C. Moskos, "Studies on the American Soldier," paper presented at the annual meeting of the American Sociological Association, New York City, Aug. 1973.

83. Charles C. Moskos, "From Institution to Occupation," *Armed Forces and Society* 4 (1977): 41–50.

84. Janowitz, *Professional Soldier*, p. 117.

85. Leonard Shyles and Mark Ross, "Recruitment Rhetoric in Brochures Advertising the All-Volunteer Force," mimeo., (College Park: University of Maryland).

86. See Ezra S. Krendel and Bernard L. Samoff, eds., *Unionizing the Armed Forces* (Philadelphia: University of Pennsylvania Press, 1977); Alan Ned Sabrosky et al., eds., *Blue-Collar Soldiers? Unionization and the U.S. Military* (Philadelphia: Foreign Policy Research Institute, 1977); William J. Taylor, Roger J. Arango, and Robert S. Lockwood, eds., *Military Unions* (Beverly Hills, Calif.: Sage Publications, 1977).

87. Segal, "Military Service in the Nineteen-Seventies," pp. 44–45.

88. David R. Segal, "Measuring the Institutional/Occupational Change Thesis," *Armed Forces and Society* 12 (Spring 1986): 351–75.

89. See Michael J. Stahl, T. Roger Manley, and Charles W. McNichols, "Operationalizing the Moskos Institution-Occupation Model," *Journal of Applied Psychology* 63 (1978): 422–27; idem, "An Empirical Example of the Moskos Institution-Occupation Model," *Armed Forces and Society* 6 (1980): 257–69; and idem, "A Longitudinal Test of the Moskos Institution-Occupation Model," *Journal of Political and Military Sociology* 9 (1981): 43–7.

90. C. A. Cotton, "Institutional and Occupational Values in Canada's Army," *Armed Forces and Society* 8 (1981): 99–110.

91. David R. Segal, John D. Blair, Joseph J. Lengermann, and Richard C. Thompson, "Institutional and Occupational Values in the U.S. Military," in *Changing U.S. Military Manpower Realities*, ed. Franklin D. Margiotta, James Brown, and Michael J. Collins (Boulder, Colo.: Westview Press, 1983), pp. 107–27.

92. See Janowitz, *Reconstruction of Patriotism*.

93. See Morris Janowitz, "Toward a Redefinition of Military Strategy in International Relations," *World Politics* 26 (1974): 499–500, and "Beyond Deterrence: Alternative Conceptual Dimensions," in *The Limits of Military Intervention*, ed. Ellen P. Stern (Beverly Hills, Calif.: Sage Publications, 1977), pp. 384–85; also see Jonathan Alford, "Deterrence and Disuse: Some Thoughts on the Problem of Maintaining

Volunteer Forces," *Armed Forces and Society* 6 (Winter 1980): 247–56.

94. Gregory D. Foster, "The Effect of Deterrence on the Fighting Ethic," *Armed Forces and Society* 10 (Winter 1984): 276–92.

95. Charles W. Brown and Charles C. Moskos, "The American Volunteer Soldier: Will He Fight?" *Military Review* 56 (June 1976): 8–17.

96. David F. Burrelli and David R. Segal, "Definitions of Mission among Novice Marine Corps Officers," *Journal of Political and Military Sociology* 10 (Fall 1982): 299–306.

97. William C. Cockerham and Lawrence E. Cohen, "Volunteering for Foreign Combat Missions," *Pacific Sociological Review* 24 (July 1981): 325–54; David R. Segal et al., "Paratroopers as Peacekeepers," *Armed Forces and Society* 10, no. 4 (Aug. 1984): 487–506.

98. David Gottlieb, *Babes in Arms* (Beverly Hills, Calif.: Sage Publications, 1980).

99. David R. Segal and Young Hee Yoon, "Institutional and Occupational Models of the Army in the Career Force," *Journal of Political and Military Sociology* 12 (1984): 243–56.

100. See Edward N. Luttwak, *The Pentagon and the Art of War* (New York: Simon & Schuster, 1985), and Richard A. Gabriel, *Military Incompetence* (New York: Hill & Wang, 1985).

CHAPTER 4. THE WELFARE STATE
AND MILITARY SERVICE

1. Kathi V. Friedman, *Legitimation of Social Rights and the Western Welfare State* (Chapel Hill: University of North Carolina Press, 1981), p. 3.

2. Morris Janowitz, *Social Control of the Welfare State* (Chicago: University of Chicago Press, 1976), p. 3.

3. Kenneth E. Boulding, *The Economy of Love and Fear* (New York: Praeger, 1981), p. 28.

4. Ibid., p. 80.

5. See Mancur Olson, *The Rise and Decline of Nations* (New Haven, Conn.: Yale University Press, 1982).

6. W. Andrew Achenbaum, *Old Age in the New Land* (Baltimore, Md.: Johns Hopkins University Press, 1979), p. 84.

7. Theda Skocpol and John Ikenberry, "The Political Formation of the American Welfare State in Historical and Comparative Perspective," *Comparative Social Research* 6 (1983): 95.

8. Judith Treas, "The Historical Decline in Late-Life Labor Force Participation in the United States," in *Age, Health and Employment*, ed. James E. Birran and Judy Livington (Englewood Cliffs, N.J.: Prentice-Hall, 1985).

9. See, e.g., Robert F. Hale, "Congressional Perspectives on Defense Manpower Issues," *Armed Forces and Society* 11, no. 3 (Spring 1985): esp. 348–50.

10. Robert L. Goldich, *Military Retirement: Budgetary Implications of the 5th QRMC Proposals* (Washington, D.C.: Congressional Research Service Report no. 85-31 F, Jan. 31, 1985).

11. Mady W. Segal, "The Military and the Family as Greedy Institutions," *Armed Forces and Society* 13, no. 1 (Fall 1986): 9–38.

12. Bernard Beck, "The Military as a Welfare Institution," in *Public Opinion and the Military Establishment*, ed. Charles C. Moskos (Beverly Hills, Calif.: Sage Publications, 1971), p. 142.

13. Sue E. Berryman, "Images and Realities," in *Life in the Rank and File*, ed. David R. Segal and H. Wallace Sinaiko (New York: Pergamon, 1986), pp. 9–34.

14. Beck, "The Military as a Welfare Institution," p. 139.

15. This "interest-group liberalism" is discussed by Daniel Bell in *The Coming of Post-Industrial Society* (New York: Basic Books, 1973); see also Theodore J. Lowi, *The End of Liberalism: The Second Republic of the United States*, 2d ed. (New York: Norton, 1979).

16. See Walter A. Friedlander, *Introduction to Social Welfare* (Englewood Cliffs, N.J.: Prentice-Hall, 1968), chaps. 1 and 2.

17. Friedman, *Legitimation*, p. 15.

18. Morris Janowitz, *The Last Half-Century* (Chicago: University of Chicago Press, 1981), p. 138.

19. See Neil D. Fligstein, "The G.I. Bill: Its Effect on the Educational and Occupational Attainment of Veterans," working paper 76–9 (Madison: Center for Demography and Ecology, University of Wisconsin, 1976); and William M. Mason, *On the Socioeconomic Effects of Military Service* (Ph.D. diss., University of Chicago, 1970).

20. W. L. Hansen and B. A. Weisbrod, "Economics of the Military Draft," *Quarterly Journal of Economics* 31 (1967): 395–421; and Walter Y. Oi, "The Economics of the Draft," *American Economic Review* 57 (1967): 39–63.

21. Melanie Martindale and Dudley L. Poston, Jr., "Variations in Veteran/Nonveteran Earnings Patterns among World War II, Korea, and Vietnam War Cohorts," *Armed Forces and Society* 5 (1979): 219–43; Wayne J. Villemez and John D. Kasarda, "Veteran Status and Socioeconomic Attainment," *Armed Forces and Society* 2 (1976): 174–200; Dudley L. Poston, Jr., Mady W. Segal, and John S. Butler, "The Influence of Military Service on the Civilian Earnings Patterns of Female Veterans," in *Women in the United States Armed Forces*, ed. Nancy Loring Goldman (Chicago: Inter-University Seminar on Armed Forces and Society, 1984), pp. 152–71.

22. See Paul Starr, *The Discarded Army* (New York: Charterhouse, 1973), pp. 184–87.

23. See G. David Curry, *Sunshine Patriots* (South Bend, Ind.: Notre Dame University Press, 1984).

24. Janowitz, *The Last Half-Century*, p. 142; see also Kirsten A. Grønbjerg, *Mass Society and the Extension of Welfare, 1960–1970* (Chicago: University of Chicago Press, 1977).

25. Harold L. Wilensky, *The Welfare State and Equality* (Berkeley: University of California Press, 1975), p. 79.

26. Ibid., p. 80.

27. Albert Szymanski, *The Logic of Imperialism* (New York: Praeger, 1981), p. 520.

28. See, e.g., Seymour Melman, *Our Depleted Society* (New York: Holt, Rinehart, & Winston, 1965), and Bruce M. Russett, *What Price Vigilance?* (New Haven, Conn.: Yale University Press, 1970).

29. See, e.g., Seymour Melman, "Twelve Propositions on Productivity and War Economy," *Armed Forces and Society* 1 (Summer 1975): 490–97. An opposing theoretical perspective is presented by Harry G. Johnson in "Egregious Economics as Pacifist Propaganda," ibid., pp. 498–504.

30. This discussion draws heavily on James L. Clayton, *On the Brink: Defense, Deficits, and Welfare Spending* (New York: Ramapo Press, 1984).

31. See Kirsten A. Grønbjerg, "Welfare Entitlements in the No-Growth Society," in *The Challenge of Social Control: Citizenship and Institution-Building in Modern Society*, ed. Gerald D. Suttles and Mayer N. Zald (Norwood, N.J.: Ablex, 1985), pp. 98–118.

32. Charles C. Moskos, "From Institution to Occupation," *Armed Forces and Society* 4 (1977): 41–50.

33. Sue E. Berryman, *Who Serves? The Persistent Myth of the Underclass Army* (Boulder, Colo.: Westview Press, 1988), pp. 2–3.

34. Alex Mintz and Alexander Hicks, "Military Keynesianism in the United States: Disaggregating Military Expenditures and Their Determinants," *American Journal of Sociology* 90 (Sept. 1984) 411–17.

35. Morris Janowitz, *The Reconstruction of Patriotism* (Chicago: University of Chicago Press, 1983), pp. 7–8.

36. See "Opinion Roundup," in *Public Opinion*, June/July 1982, p. 27.

37. Debate on this amendment appears in the *Congressional Record* for July 28, 1982, pp. H 4756–72.

38. Jerald G. Bachman, "American High School Seniors View the Military," *Armed Forces and Society* 10, no. 1 (Fall 1983): 86–104.

39. David R. Segal and Jerald G. Bachman, "The Military as an Educational and Training Institution," *Youth and Society* 10 (Sept. 1978): 47–63.

40. David R. Segal, "Personnel," in *American Defense Annual, 1986–1987*, ed. Joseph Kruzel (Lexington, Mass.: D. C. Heath, 1986), pp. 142–48.

41. David R. Segal, "Military Service in the Nineteen-Seventies: Attitudes of Soldiers and Civilians," in *Manning the American Armed Forces*, ed. Allan R. Millett and Anne F. Trupp (Columbus: Mershon Center of the Ohio State University, 1981), p. 56.

CHAPTER 5. RACE, GENDER,
AND THE UNITED STATES MILITARY

1. Alvin J. Shexnider and John Sibley Butler, "Race and the All-Volunteer System," *Armed Forces and Society* 2 (Spring 1976): 421–32.

2. Charles C. Moskos, "The American Dilemma in Uniform: Race in the Armed Forces," *Annals of the American Academy of Political and Social Science* 406 (Mar. 1973): 94–106.

3. Benjamin Quarles, *The Negro in the American Revolution* (Chapel Hill: University of North Carolina Press, 1961), p. ix; and Martin Binkin and Mark J. Eitelberg, with Alvin J. Schexnider and Marvin M. Smith, *Blacks in the Military* (Washington, D.C.: Brookings Institution, 1982), p. 13.

4. Richard J. Stillman II, *Integration of the Negro into the U.S. Armed Forces* (New York: Praeger, 1968), pp. 8–9.

5. Dennis D. Nelson, *The Integration of the Negro into the United States Navy* (New York: Farrar, Straus & Young, 1951), p. 5.

6. Ulysses Lee, "The Draft and the Negro," *Current History* 55 (July 1968): 29–30.

7. See John Hope Franklin, *From Slavery to Freedom*, 5th ed., (New York: Knopf, 1980), p. 224.

8. Richard O. Hope, *Racial Strife in the U.S. Military* (New York: Praeger, 1979), p. 12.

9. Binkin et al., *Blacks in the Military*, p. 14.

10. Hope, *Racial Strife*.

11. Herbert R. Northrup, Steven M. DiAntonio, John A. Brinker, and Dale F. Daniel, *Black and Other Minority Participation in the All-Volunteer Navy and Marine Corps* (Philadelphia: Wharton School, 1979), p. 10.

12. Jack D. Foner, *Blacks and the Military in American History* (New York: Praeger, 1974), pp. 52–55.

13. Stephen E. Ambrose, *Duty, Honor, Country* (Baltimore, Md.: Johns Hopkins Press, 1966), p. 233.

14. Foner, *Blacks and the Military*, p. 77.

15. See Marvin Fletcher, *The Black Soldier and Officer in the United States Army, 1891–1917* (Columbia: University of Missouri Press, 1974), pp. 119–52.

16. Binkin et al., *Blacks in the Military*, p. 16.

17. Fletcher, *Black Soldier*, p. 154.

18. Foner, *Blacks and the Military*, pp. 113–16.

19. Northrup et al., *Black and other Minority Participation*, p. 11.

20. Stephen E. Ambrose, "Blacks in the Army in Two World Wars," in *The Military in American Society*, ed. Stephen E. Ambrose and James A. Barber, Jr. (New York: Free Press, 1962), pp. 178–79.

21. Franklin, *From Slavery to Freedom*, pp. 444–68.

22. See Lee Nichols, *Breakthrough on the Color Front* (New York: Random House, 1954), p. 33.

23. Moskos, "American Dilemma," p. 96.

24. Richard M. Dalfiume, *Desegregation of the U.S. Armed Forces* (Columbia: University of Missouri Press, 1969), p. 39.

25. Northrup et al., *Black and other Minority Participation*, p. 11.

26. Foner, *Blacks and the Military*, p. 152.

27. Binkin et al., *Blacks in the Military*, p. 21.

28. Samuel A. Stouffer et al., *The American Soldier*, vol. 1: *Adjustment during Army Life* (Princeton, N.J.: Princeton University Press, 1949), p. 586.

29. See Foner, *Blacks and the Military*, p. 177.

30. Hope, *Racial Strife*, p. 29.

31. Binkin et al., *Blacks in the Military*, p. 28.

32. Leo Bogart, ed., *Social Research and the Desegregation of the U.S. Army* (Chicago: Markham, 1969).

33. Moskos, "American Dilemma," p. 98.

34. See Alan L. Gropman, *The Air Force Integrates* (Washington, D.C.: Office of Air Force History, 1978).

35. President's Committee on Equal Opportunity in the Armed Forces, *Equality of Treatment and Opportunity for Negro Military Personnel Stationed within the United States* (Washington, D.C.: Government Printing Office, 1964).

36. Binkin et al., *Blacks in the Military*, p. 32.

37. Hope, *Racial Strife*, pp. 38–39; Binkin et al., *Blacks in the Military*, p. 36; Adam Yarmolinsky, *The Military Establishment* (New York: Harper & Row, 1971), p. 344; Gropman, *Air Force Integrates*, pp. 215–16; Northrup et al., *Black and Other Minority Participation*, pp. 18–19.

38. Dale K. Brown and Peter G. Nordlie, *Changes in Black and White Perceptions of the Army's Race Relations/Equal Opportunity Program, 1972–1974* (McLean, Va.: Human Sciences Research, Inc., 1975).

39. See David R. Segal, Jerald G. Bachman, and Faye E. Dowdell, "Military Service for Female and Black Youth," *Youth and Society* 10 (Dec. 1978): 127–34.

40. Sally Cook Lopreato and Dudley L. Poston, Jr., "Differences in Earnings and Earning Ability between Veterans and Nonveterans in the United States," *Social Science Quarterly* 57 (Mar. 1977): 750–66.

41. These processes are discussed by David R. Segal and Peter G. Nordlie in "Racial Inequality in Army Promotions," *Journal of Political and Military Sociology* 7 (Spring 1979): 135–42.

42. See Hope, *Racial Strife*, especially pp. 37–48.

43. Linda Grant De Pauw, "Women in Combat: The Revolutionary War Experience," *Armed Forces and Society* 7 (Winter 1981): 209.

44. Janice E. McKenney, "Women in Combat: Comment," *Armed Forces and Society* 8 (Summer 1982): 686–92.

45. Jeanne Holm, *Women in the Military* (Novato, Calif.: Presidio Press, 1982), p. 5.

46. See Nancy Loring Goldman, "Introduction," in *Female Soldiers: Combatants or Noncombatants?* ed. Goldman (Westport, Conn.: Greenwood Press, 1982), p. 7.

47. See John Laffin, *Women in Battle* (New York: Abelard-Schuman, 1967), pp. 116–24.

48. See Holm, *Women in the Military*, pp. 7–9.

49. Patricia J. Thomas, *Utilization of Enlisted Women in the Military* (San Diego, Calif.: Navy Personnel Research and Development Center, 1975), p. 4.

50. Holm, *Women in the Military*, p. 12.

51. Martin Binkin and Shirley J. Bach, *Women and the Military* (Washington, D.C.: Brookings Institution, 1977), p. 6.

52. Holm, *Women in the Military*, p. 31.

53. Ibid., p. 67.

54. Ibid., pp. 64–65.

55. Binkin and Bach, *Women and the Military*, p. 10.

56. See Holm, *Women in the Military*, pp. 148–65.

57. Mady Wechsler Segal and David R. Segal, "Social Change and the Participation of Women in the American Military," in *Research in Social Movements, Conflict and Change*, vol. 5, ed. Louis Kriesburg (Greenwich, Conn.: JAI Press, 1983), pp. 235–58.

58. Mady Wechsler Segal, "Women's Roles in the U.S. Armed Forces," in *Conscripts and Volunteers*, ed. Robert K. Fullinwider (Totowa, N.J.: Rowman & Allanheld, 1983), pp. 201–2.

59. See David H. Marlowe, "The Manning of the Force and the Structure of Battle: Part 2—Men and Women," in *Conscripts and Volunteers*, p. 194.

60. M. C. Devilbiss, "Gender Integration and Unit Deployment," *Armed Forces and Society* 11 (Summer 1985): 523–52.

61. Samuel A. Stouffer, *Social Research to Test Ideas* (New York: Free Press, 1962), pp. 291–92.

62. David R. Segal, Nora Scott Kinzer, and John C. Woelfel, "The Concept of Citizenship and Attitudes toward Women in Combat," *Sex Roles* 3, no. 5 (1977): 471.

CHAPTER 6. ARMS AND THE MAN
TOWARD THE YEAR 2000

1. See Carl von Clausewitz, *On War*, ed. and with an introduction by Anatol Rapoport (Baltimore, Md.: Penguin Books, 1968), pp. 19–20.

2. See Morris Janowitz, *Military Conflict* (Beverly Hills, Calif.: Sage Publications, 1975), pp. 70–88; and Jacques Van Doorn, "The Decline of the Mass Army in the West," *Armed Forces and Society* 1, no. 2 (Winter 1975): 147–57.

3. Stephen J. Cimbala, "Forever MAD: Essence and Attributes," *Armed Forces and Society* 12 (1985): 95–107.

4. David R. Segal et al., "Deterrence, Peacekeeping, and Combat Orientation in the U.S. Army," in *Challenges to Deterrence in the 1990s*, ed. Stephen J. Cimbala (New York: Praeger, 1987), pp. 41–53.

5. Morris Janowitz, *The Professional Soldier* (Glencoe, Ill.: Free Press, 1960), pp. 257–79.

6. Ibid., p. 418 (emphasis added).

7. Ibid., p. 420.

8. Ibid., p. 419.

9. Ibid., pp. 424–25.

10. Ibid., pp. 417–42.

11. Morris Janowitz, "Civic Consciousness and Military Performance," in *The Political Education of Soldiers*, ed. Morris Janowitz and Stephen D. Wesbrook (Beverly Hills, Calif.: Sage, 1983), pp. 55–80.

12. Lawrence J. Korb, "The FY 1981–1985 Defense Program," *AEI Foreign Policy and Defense Review* 2 (1980) 2–63.

13. See David R. Segal and Katharine Swift Gravino, "Peacekeeping as a Military Mission," in *The Hundred Percent Challenge*, ed Charles Duryea Smith (Washington, D.C.: Seven Locks Press, 1985), pp. 38–68.

14. Larry L. Fabian, *Soldiers without Enemies* (Washington, D.C.: Brookings Institution, 1971).

15. Charles C. Moskos, *Peace Soldiers: The Sociology of a Unified United Nations Military Force* (Chicago: University of Chicago Press, 1976).

16. Mala Tabory, *The Multinational Force and Observers in the Sinai* (Boulder, Colo.: Westview Press, 1986), p. 19.

17. Tom W. Smith, "American Attitudes toward the Soviet Union and Communism," *Public Opinion Quarterly* 47, no. 2 (Summer 1983): 277–92.

18. Hazel Gaudet Erskine, "The Polls: Atomic Weapons and Nuclear Energy," *Public Opinion Quarterly* 27, no. 2 (Summer 1964): 155–90.

19. Thomas W. Graham and Bernard M. Kramer, "Attitudes toward Nuclear Defense, 1945–1985," *Public Opinion Quarterly* 50, no. 1 (Spring 1986): 125–34.

20. James A. Davis and Paul B. Sheatsley, *Americans View the Military: A 1984 Update*, National Opinion Research Center Report, no. 132 (Chicago: University of Chicago, Dec. 1985).

21. See David R. Segal et al., "Paratroopers as Peacekeepers," *Armed Forces and Society* 10, no. 4 (Aug. 1984): 487–506.

22. Segal et al., "Deterrence, Peacekeeping, and Combat Orientation."

23. Barbara Foley Meeker and David R. Segal, "Soldiers' Perceptions of Conflict Intensity," *Journal of Political and Military Sociology* 15 (Spring 1987): 105–15.

24. David R. Segal, "Personnel," in *American Defense Annual, 1986–1987*, ed. Joseph Kruzel (Lexington, Mass.: D. C. Heath, 1986), pp. 139–52.

25. See Morris Janowitz, "Toward a Redefinition of Military Strategy in International Relations," *World Politics* 26 (1974): 499–500, and "Beyond Deterrence: Alternative Conceptual Dimensions," in *The Limits of Military Intervention*, ed. Ellen P. Stern (Beverly Hills, Calif.: Sage Publications, 1977), pp. 369–89.

26. Jonathan Alford, "Deterrence and Disuse: Some Thoughts on the Problem of Maintaining Volunteer Forces," *Armed Forces and Society* 6 (Winter 1980): 247–56.

27. Gregory D. Foster, "The Effect of Deterrence on the Fighting Ethic," *Armed Forces and Society* 10 (Winter 1984): 276–92.

28. David Gottlieb, *Babes in Arms* (Beverly Hills, Calif.: Sage Publications, 1980).

29. See Charles W. Brown and Charles C. Moskos, "The American Volunteer Soldier: Will He Fight?" *Military Review* 56 (June 1976): 8–17; William C. Cockerham and Lawrence E. Cohen, "Volunteering for Foreign Combat Missions," *Pacific Sociological Review* 24 (July 1981): 325–54; David F. Burrelli and David R. Segal,

"Definitions of Mission among Novice Marine Corps Officers," *Journal of Political and Military Sociology* 10 (Fall 1982): 299–306.

30. Janowitz, "Beyond Deterrence."

31. Jesse J. Harris and David R. Segal, "Observations from the Sinai: The Boredom Factor," *Armed Forces and Society* 11 (Winter 1985): 235–48.

32. Segal and Gravino, "Peacekeeping as a Military Mission," p. 66.

33. See David R. Segal, "American Paratroopers Would Rather Fight Than Switch," *Sociology and Social Research* 70, no. 2 (Jan. 1986): 172–73.

34. See David R. Segal and Katharine Swift Gravino, "The Empire Strikes Back: Military Professionalism in the South Atlantic War," in *The Regionalization of Warfare*, ed. James Brown and William P. Snyder (New Brunswick, N.J.: Transaction Books, 1985), pp. 17–36.

35. Lawrence Freedman, "The War of the Falkland Islands, 1982," *Foreign Affairs* 61 (Fall 1982): 207.

36. United States, Department of the Army, *Operations* (Field Manual 100-5) (Fort Monroe, Va.: U.S. Army Training and Doctrine Command, 1981).

37. See W. R. Richardson, "Winning on the Extended Battlefield," *Army* 31, no. 6 (1981): 35–42; and D. A. Starry, "Extending the Battlefield," *Military Review* 61, no. 3 (1981): 31–35.

38. David R. Segal, "Management, Leadership, and the Future Battlefield," in *Leadership on the Future Battlefield*, ed. James G. Hunt and John D. Blair (Washington, D.C.: Pergamon-Brassey's, 1985), p. 210.

39. James M. Gavin, *On to Berlin* (New York: Viking Press, 1978).

CHAPTER 7. MISSIONS AND
OPTIONS FOR THE 1990s

1. Irving Louis Horowitz, "Human Resources and Military Manpower Requirements," *Armed Forces and Society* 12 (Winter 1986): 173–92.

2. See David F. Burrelli, *National Guard Overseas Training Missions: An Issue for U.S. Military Manpower Policy* (Washington, D.C.: Congressional Research Service, Nov. 21, 1986).

3. For a discussion of the military dimensions of terrorism see Robert H. Kupperman et al., "Terrorism: The Challenge to the Military in the 1990s," in *Strategic Requirements for the Army to the Year 2000*, ed. Robert H. Kupperman and William J. Taylor (Lexington, Mass.: D. C. Heath, 1984), pp. 187–207.

4. See Louis René Beres, *Terrorism and Global Security: The Nuclear Threat* (Boulder, Colo.: Westview Press, 1979).

5. See James M. Garrett, "Theater Strategic Deterrence Reexamined," *Armed Forces and Society* 10 (Fall 1983): 26–58, for a discussion of the issues involved in theater nuclear weapons. The kind of resistance encountered among America's NATO allies is exemplified in Rob Kroes, "Cruise Missiles and the Western Party System," *Armed Forces and Society* 12 (Summer 1986): 581–90.

6. Howard Schuman, Jacob Ludwig, and Jon A. Krosnick, "The Perceived Threat of Nuclear War," *Public Opinion Quarterly* 50 (Winter 1986): 519–36.

7. David W. Dent and Wayne C. McWilliams, "What College Students Think about the International Role of the United States," *International Studies Notes* 12 (Fall 1986): 48–55.

8. See Stephen J. Cimbala, "Theater Nuclear and Conventional Force Improvements," *Armed Forces and Society* 11 (Spring 1984): 115–29.

9. E.g., Jeffrey Record, "Should America Pay for Europe's Security?" *Washington Quarterly* 5 (Summer 1982): 19–29.

10. United States, Congressional Budget Office, *The Army of the Nineties: How Much Will It Cost?* (Washington, D.C.: Congress of the United States, Dec. 1986).

11. Theodore McNelly, "The Renunciation of War in the Japanese Constitution," *Armed Forces and Society* 13 (Fall 1986): 81–106.

12. See Sir Wallace Rowling, "New Zealand and ANZUS," *Armed Forces and Society* 12 (Winter 1986): 169–72.

13. Dent and McWilliams, "What College Students Think."

14. See John R. Brinkerhoff and David W. Grissmer, "The Reserve Forces in an All-Volunteer Environment," in *The All-Volunteer Force after a Decade*, ed. William Bowman, Roger Little, and G. Thomas Sicilia (Washington, D.C.: Pergamon-Brassey's, 1986), pp. 206–29.

15. David R. Segal, "Personnel," chap. 7 in *American Defense Annual, 1986–1987*, ed. Joseph Kruzel (Lexington, Mass.: D. C. Heath, 1986), p. 148.

16. See David R. Segal, "Measuring the Institutional/Occupational Change Thesis," *Armed Forces and Society* 12 (Spring 1986): 351–75.

17. Robert H. Baldwin and Thomas V. Daula, "The Cost of High Quality Recruits," *Armed Forces and Society* 11 (Fall 1984): 96–114.

18. Brinkerhoff and Grissmer, "Reserve Forces," p. 213.

19. See David W. Grissmer and Sheila Nataraj Kirby, "Attrition and Retention in the Army Reserves and National Guard," in *Army Manpower Economics*, ed. Curtis L. Gilroy (Boulder, Colo.: Westview Press, 1986), pp. 169–97.

20. See, e.g., Roy A. Werner, "The Readiness of U.S. Reserve Components," in *Supplementary Military Forces*, ed. Louis A. Zurcher and Gwyn Harries-Jenkins (Beverly Hills, Calif.: Sage Publications, 1978), p. 87; also see John R. Brinkerhoff, "Future of the Army Reserves," in *Defense Manpower Planning*, ed. William J. Taylor, Jr., Eric T. Olson, and Richard A. Schrader (New York: Pergamon, 1981), p. 167.

21. Ellen Jones, *Red Army and Society* (Boston, Mass.: Allen & Unwin, 1985), esp. pp. 52–78.

22. See Reuven Gal, *A Portrait of the Israeli Soldier* (Wesport, Conn.: Greenwood Press, 1986).

23. William James, "The Moral Equivalent of War," *International Conciliation*, no. 27 (Feb. 1910).

24. For an insightful discussion of these initiatives see James B. Jacobs, "Compulsory and Voluntary National Service," in his *Socio-Legal Foundations of Civil-Military Relations* (New Brunswick, N.J.: Transaction Books, 1986), pp. 111–47.

25. Richard Danzig and Peter Szanton, *National Service: What Would It Mean?* (Lexington, Mass.: D. C. Heath, 1986).

Bibliography

Achenbaum, W. Andrew. *Old Age in the New Land*. Baltimore, Md.: Johns Hopkins University Press, 1979.

Adams, Jerome, Howard T. Prince II, Debra Instone, and Robert W. Rice. "West Point: Critical Incidents of Leadership." *Armed Forces and Society* 10 (1984): 597–611.

Alford, Jonathan. "Deterrence and Disuse: Some Thoughts on the Problem of Maintaining Volunteer Forces." *Armed Forces and Society* 6 (Winter 1980): 247–56.

Ambrose, Stephen E. "Blacks in the Army in Two World Wars." In *The Military in American Society*, edited by Stephen E. Ambrose and James A. Barber, Jr., pp. 178–79, New York: Free Press, 1962.

———. *Duty, Honor, Country*. Baltimore, Md.: Johns Hopkins Press, 1966.

Anderson, Martin, ed. *Registration and the Draft*. Stanford, Calif.: Hoover Institution Press, 1982.

Assembly of Western European Union. *Conditions of Service in the Armed Forces*. Document 650. Twentieth Ordinary Session, Nov., 1974.

Bachman, Jerald G. "American High School Seniors View the Military." *Armed Forces and Society* 10, no. 1 (Fall 1983): 86–104.

———, John D. Blair, and David R. Segal. *The All-Volunteer Force*. Ann Arbor: University of Michigan Press, 1977.

Badillo, Gilbert, and G. David Curry. "The Social Incidence of Vietnam Casualties." *Armed Forces and Society* 2 (1976): 397–406.

Baldwin, Robert H., and Thomas V. Daula. "The Cost of High Quality Recruits." *Armed Forces and Society* 11 (Fall 1984): 96–114.

Beck, Bernard. "The Military as a Welfare Institution." In *Public Opinion and the Military Establishment*, edited by Charles C. Moskos, pp. 137–48. Beverly Hills, Calif.: Sage Publications, 1971.

Bell, Daniel. *The Coming of Post-Industrial Society*. New York: Basic Books, 1973.

Bendix, Reinhard. *Nation-Building and Citizenship*. New York: Wiley, 1964.

Bennis, Warren G., and Phillip E. Slater. *The Temporary Society*. New York: Harper & Row, 1968.

Beres, Louis René. *Terrorism and Global Security: The Nuclear Threat*. Boulder, Colo.: Westview Press, 1979.

Berryman, Sue E. "Images and Realities." In *Life in the Rank and File*, edited by David R. Segal and H. Wallace Sinaiko, pp. 9–34. New York: Pergamon, 1986.

———. *Who Serves?: The Persistent Myth of the Underclass Army*. Boulder, Colo.: Westview Press, 1988.

Beyer, Glen H. *Housing and Society*. New York: Macmillan, 1965.

Binkin, Martin. *Military Technology and Defense Manpower*. Washington, D.C.: Brookings Institution, 1986.

———, and Shirley J. Bach. *Women and the Military*. Washington, D.C.: Brookings Institution, 1977.

Binkin, Martin, and Mark J. Eitelberg with Alvin J. Schexnider and Marvin M. Smith. *Blacks in the Military*. Washington, D.C.: Brookings Institution, 1982.

Blake, R., and J. Mouton. *Corporate Excellence through Grid Organizational Develop-ment*. Houston, Tex.: Gulf Publishing, 1968.

Bogart, Leo, ed. *Social Research and the Desegregation of the U.S. Army*. Chicago: Markham, 1969.

Boulding, Kenneth E. *The Economy of Love and Fear*. New York: Praeger, 1981.

Bowers, David. "OD Techniques and their Results in Twenty-three Organizations." *Journal of Applied Behavioral Science* 9 (1973): 21–43.

Brinkerhoff, John R. "Future of the Army Reserves." In *Defense Manpower Plan-ning*, edited by William J. Taylor, Jr., Eric T. Olson, and Richard A. Schrader. New York: Pergamon, 1981.

_____, and David W. Grissmer. "The Reserve Forces in an All-Volunteer Environ-ment." In *The All-Volunteer Force after a Decade*, edited by William Bowman, Roger Little, and G. Thomas Sicilia, pp. 206–29. Washington, D.C.: Pergamon-Brassey's, 1986.

Brown, Charles W., and Charles C. Moskos. "The American Volunteer Soldier: Will He Fight?" *Military Review* 56 (June 1976): 8–17.

Brown, Dale K., and Peter G. Nordlie. *Changes in Black and White Perceptions of the Army's Race Relations/Equal Opportunity Program 1972–1974*. McLean, Va.: Human Sciences Research, Inc., 1975.

Burk, James S., with John H. Faris. *The Persistence and Importance of Patriotism in the All-Volunteer Force*. Fort Sheridan, Ill.: U.S. Army Recruiting Command, 1972.

Burrelli, David F. *National Guard Overseas Training Missions: An Issue for U.S. Military Manpower Policy*. Washington, D.C.: Congressional Research Service, Nov. 21, 1986.

_____, and David R. Segal. "Definitions of Mission among Novice Marine Corps Officers." *Journal of Political and Military Sociology* 10 (Fall 1982): 299–306.

Chambers, John Whiteclay, II. *To Raise an Army*. New York: Free Press, 1987.

Chapman, Bruce K. "Politics and Conscription: A Proposal to Replace the Draft." In *The Draft: A Handbook of Facts and Alternatives*, edited by Sol Tax, pp. 208–20. Chicago: University of Chicago Press, 1967.

Chesler, D. J., N. J. Van Steenberg, and E. Brueckel. "Effect on Morale of Infantry Team Replacement and Individual Replacement Systems." *Sociometry* 18 (1955): 73–81.

Cimbala, Stephen J. "Forever MAD: Essence and Attributes." *Armed Forces and Society* 12 (1985): 95–107.

_____. "Theater Nuclear and Conventional Force Improvements." *Armed Forces and Society* 11 (Spring 1984): 115–29.

Clausewitz, Carl von. *On War*. Edited and with an introduction by Anatol Rapoport. Baltimore, Md.: Penguin Books, 1968.

Clayton, James L. *On the Brink: Defense, Deficits, and Welfare Spending*. New York: Ramapo Press, 1984.

Clifford, J. Garry, and Samuel R. Spencer, Jr. *The First Peacetime Draft*. Lawrence: University Press of Kansas, 1986.

Cockerham, William, C., and Lawrence E. Cohen. "Volunteering for Foreign Com-bat Missions." *Pacific Sociological Review* 24 (July 1981): 325–54.

Comte, Auguste. *System of Positive Philosophy: or Treatise on Sociology*. London: Burt Franklin, 1875.

Cooper, Richard V. L. *Military Manpower and the All-Volunteer Force*. Santa Monica, Calif.: Rand Corporation, 1977.

Cotton, C. A. "Institutional and Occupational Values in Canada's Army." *Armed Forces and Society* 8 (1981): 99–111.

Cress, Lawrence Delbert. *Citizens in Arms*. Chapel Hill: University of North Carolina Press, 1982.

Curry, G. David. *Sunshine Patriots*. South Bend, Ind.: Notre Dame University Press, 1984.

Dahl, Robert A. *Who Governs?* New Haven, Conn.: Yale University Press, 1961.

Dale, Charles, and Curtis Gilroy. "Determinants of Enlistments." *Armed Forces and Society* 10 (Feb. 1984): 192–210.

Dalfiume, Richard M. *Desegregation of the U.S. Armed Forces*. Columbia: University of Missouri Press, 1969.

Danzig, Richard, and Peter Szanton. *National Service: What Would It Mean?* Lexington, Mass.: D. C. Heath, 1986.

Davis, James A., and Paul B. Sheatsley. *Americans View the Military: A 1984 Update*. National Opinion Research Center Report no. 132. Chicago: University of Chicago (Dec. 1985).

Davis, James W., Jr., and Kenneth M. Dolbeare. *Little Groups of Neighbors*. Chicago: Markham, 1968.

Davis, Vincent. "Levée en Masse, C'est Fini." In *New Civil-Military Relations*, edited by John P. Lovell and Philip S. Kronenberg, pp. 89–108. New Brunswick, N.J.: Transaction Books, 1974.

Dent, David W., and Wayne C. McWilliams. "What College Students Think about the International Role of the United States." *International Studies Notes* 12 (Fall 1986): 48–55.

De Pauw, Linda Grant. "Women in Combat: The Revolutionary War Experience." *Armed Forces and Society* 7 (Winter 1981): 209–26.

de Picq, Ardant. *Battle Studies*. Translated from the eighth French edition by John N. Greely and Robert C. Cotton. New York: Macmillan, 1921.

Devilbiss, M. C. "Gender Integration and Unit Deployment." *Armed Forces and Society* 11 (Summer 1985): 523–52.

Drucker, Peter F. *The Practice of Management*. New York: Harper & Row, 1954.

Dupuy, William E. "Technology and Manpower: Army Perspective." *The All-Volunteer Force after a Decade*, edited by William Bowman, Roger Little, and G. Thomas Sicilia, pp. 122–35. Washington, D.C.: Pergamon-Brassey's, 1986.

Durkheim, Emile. *The Division of Labor in Society*. New York: Macmillan, 1933.

Eaton, Clement. *A History of the Southern Confederacy*. New York: Macmillan, 1954.

Erskine, Hazel Gaudet. "The Polls: Atomic Weapons and Nuclear Energy." *Public Opinion Quarterly* 27, no. 2 (Summer 1964): 155–90.

Fabian, Larry L. *Soldiers without Enemies*. Washington, D.C.: Brookings Institution, 1971.

Faris, John H. "An Alternative Perspective to Savage and Gabriel." *Armed Forces and Society* 3 (1977): 457–62.

———. "Economic and Noneconomic Factors of Personnel Recruitment and Retention in the AVF." *Armed Forces and Society* 10 (1984): 251–75.

Fiedler, Fred. *A Theory of Leadership Effectiveness*. New York: McGraw-Hill, 1967.

Fletcher, Marvin. *The Black Soldier and Officer in the United States Army, 1891–1917*. Columbia: University of Missouri Press, 1974.

Flexner, James T. *George Washington: The Forge of Experience, 1732–1775*. Boston, Mass.: Little, Brown, 1965.

Fligstein, Neil D. "The G.I. Bill: Its Effect on the Educational and Occupational Attainment of Veterans." Working paper 76–9. Madison: Center for Demography and Ecology, University of Wisconsin, 1976.

_____. "Who Served in the Military, 1940–73." *Armed Forces and Society* 6 (Winter 1980): 297–312.

Foner, Jack D. *Blacks and the Military in American History.* New York: Praeger, 1974.

Forbes, Robert L., Jr. "A *Cause Celebre*: Organizational Development in the United States Navy." Paper presented at the eighty-fourth annual convention of the American Psychological Association, Washington, D. C., Sept. 1976.

Foster, Gregory D. "The Effect of Deterrence on the Fighting Ethic." *Armed Forces and Society* 10 (Winter 1984): 276–92.

Franklin, John Hope. *From Slavery to Freedom.* 5th ed. New York: Knopf, 1980.

Freedman, Lawrence. "The War of the Falkland Islands, 1982." *Foreign Affairs* 61 (Fall 1982), pp. 196–210.

French, W. L., and C. H. Bell, Jr. *Organizational Development.* Englewood Cliffs, N.J.: Prentice-Hall, 1973.

Friedlander, Walter A. *Introduction to Social Welfare.* Englewood Cliffs, N.J.: Prentice-Hall, 1968.

Friedman, Kathi V. *Legitimation of Social Rights and the Western Welfare State.* Chapel Hill: University of North Carolina Press, 1981.

Friedman, Milton. "Why Not a Voluntary Army?" In *The Draft: A Handbook of Facts and Alternatives,* edited by Sol Tax, pp. 200–207. Chicago: University of Chicago Press, 1967.

Gabriel, Richard A. *Military Incompetence.* New York: Hill & Wang, 1985.

Gal, Reuven. *A Portrait of the Israeli Soldier.* Westport, Conn.: Greenwood Press, 1986.

Garrett, James M. "Theater Strategic Deterrence Reexamined." *Armed Forces and Society* 10 (Fall 1983): 26–58.

Gates, Thomas S., Jr., et al. *The Report of the President's Commission on an All-Volunteer Armed Force.* Washington, D.C.: U.S. Government Printing Office, 1970.

Gavin, James M. *On to Berlin.* New York: Viking Press, 1978.

Gerhardt, James M. *The Draft and Public Policy.* Columbus: Ohio State University Press, 1971.

Gold, Philip. *Evasions: The American Way of Military Service.* New York: Paragon, 1985.

Goldich, Robert L. *Military Retirement: Budgetary Implications of the 5th QRMC Proposals.* Washington, D.C.: Congressional Research Service Report no. 85–31 F, Jan. 31, 1985.

_____. *The U.S. Army's New Manning System.* Washington, D.C.: Congressional Research Service, 1983.

Goldman, Nancy Loring, ed. *Female Soldiers—Combatants or Noncombatants?* Westport, Conn.: Greenwood Press, 1982.

Goodpaster, Andrew J., Lloyd H. Elliot, and J. Alan Hovey, Jr. *Toward a Consensus on Military Service.* New York: Pergamon, 1982.

Gottlieb, David. *Babes in Arms.* Beverly Hills, Calif.: Sage Publications, 1980.

Graham, Thomas W., and Bernard M. Kramer. "Attitudes toward Nuclear Defense, 1945–1985." *Public Opinion Quarterly* 50, no. 1 (Spring 1986): 125–34.

Greisman, Harvey C., and Kurt Finsterbusch. "Modernization of Warfare." *Society* 12 (1975): 53–57.

Gregory, Robert A. "Organizational Development Efforts in the United States Air Force." Paper presented at the eighty-fifth annual convention of the American Psychological Association, San Francisco, Calif., Sept. 1977.

Grissmer, David W., and Sheila Nataraj Kirby. "Attrition and Retention in the Army Reserves and National Guard." In *Army Manpower Economics,* edited by Curtis L. Gilroy, pp. 169–97. Boulder, Colo.: Westview Press, 1986.

Grønbjerg, Kirsten A. *Mass Society and the Extension of Welfare, 1960–1970.* Chicago: University of Chicago Press, 1977.

_____. "Welfare Entitlements in the No-Growth Society." In *The Challenge of Social Control: Citizenship and Institution-Building in Modern Society,* edited by Gerald D. Suttles and Mayer N. Zald, pp. 98–118. Norwood: Ablex, 1958.

Gropman, Alan L. *The Air Force Integrates.* Washington, D.C.: Office of Air Force History, 1978.

Hale, Robert F. "Congressional Perspectives on Defense Manpower Issues." *Armed Forces and Society* 11, no. 3 (Spring 1985): 329–56.

Hansen, W. L., and B. A. Weisbrod. "Economics of the Military Draft." *Quarterly Journal of Economics* 31 (1967): 395–421.

Harries-Jenkins, Gwyn. "Armed Forces and the Welfare State." In *Civil-Military Relations,* edited by Morris Janowitz, pp. 231–57. Beverly Hills, Calif.: Sage, 1981.

Harris, Jesse J., and David R. Segal. "Observations from the Sinai: The Boredom Factor." *Armed Forces and Society* 11 (Winter 1985): 235–48.

Hauser, William L. *America's Army in Crisis.* Baltimore, Md.: Johns Hopkins University Press, 1973.

Heilbroner, Robert L. *The Worldly Philosophers.* New York: Simon & Schuster, 1953.

Helmer, John. *Bringing the War Home.* New York: Free Press, 1974.

Hesseltine, William B. *Lincoln and the War Governors.* New York: Knopf, 1948.

Himmelfarb, Gertrude. "Denigrating the Rule of Reason." *Harper's,* Apr., 1984, pp. 84–90.

Hofstadter, Richard. *Social Darwinism in American Thought.* Boston, Mass.: Beacon Press, 1955.

Holm, Jeanne. *Women in the Military.* Novato, Calif.: Presidio Press, 1982.

Hope, Richard O. *Racial Strife in the U.S. Military.* New York: Praeger, 1979.

Horowitz, Irving Louis. "Human Resources and Military Manpower Requirements." *Armed Forces and Society* 12 (Winter 1986): 173–92.

Huntington, Samuel P. *The Soldier and the State.* Cambridge, Mass.: Harvard University Press, 1957.

Huzar, Elian. *The Power and the Purse.* Westport, Conn.: Greenwood Press, 1971.

Jacobs, James B. *Socio-Legal Foundations of Civil-Military Relations.* New Brunswick, N.J.: Transaction Books, 1986.

Jacobs, James B., and Leslie Anne Hayes. "Aliens in the U.S. Armed Forces." *Armed Forces and Society* 7 (1981): 187–208.

Jacobs, James B., and Dennis McNamara. "Selective Service without a Draft." *Armed Forces and Society* 10, no. 3 (Spring 1984): 361–79.

James, William. "The Moral Equivalent of War." *International Conciliation,* no. 27 (Feb. 1910): 3–20.

Janowitz, Morris. "The All-Volunteer Military as a 'Sociopolitical' Problem." *Social Problems* 22 (Feb. 1975): 432–49.

_____. "Beyond Deterrence: Alternative Conceptual Dimensions." In *The Limits of Military Intervention,* edited by Ellen P. Stern, pp. 369–89. Beverly Hills, Calif.: Sage Publications, 1977.

_____. "The Citizen-Soldier and National Purpose." *Air University Review,* Nov.–Dec. 1979, pp. 31–39.

_____. "Civic Consciousness and Military Performance." In *The Political Education of Soldiers,* edited by Morris Janowitz and Stephen D. Wesbrook, pp. 55–80. Beverly Hills, Calif.: Sage Publications, 1983.

_____. "Consequences of Social Research on the U.S. Military." *Armed Forces and Society* 8 (1982): 522–23.

_____. "The Emergent Military." In *Public Opinion and the Military Establishment*, edited by Charles C. Moskos, pp. 255–70. Beverly Hills, Calif.: Sage Publications, 1971.

_____. *The Last Half-Century*. Chicago: University of Chicago Press, 1981.

_____. "The Logic of National Service." In *The Draft: A Handbook of Facts and Alternatives*, edited by Sol Tax, pp. 73–90. Chicago: University of Chicago Press, 1967.

_____. *Military Conflict*. Beverly Hills, Calif.: Sage Publications, 1975.

_____. "Observations on the Sociology of Citizenship." *Social Forces* 59 (Sept. 1980): 1–24.

_____. "Patriotism and the All-Volunteer Military," *Air University Review*, Jan.–Feb. 1982, pp. 31–39.

_____. *The Professional Soldier*. Glencoe, Ill.: Free Press, 1960.

_____. *The Reconstruction of Patriotism*. Chicago: University of Chicago Press, 1983.

_____. *Social Control of the Welfare State*. Chicago: University of Chicago Press, 1976.

_____. *Sociology and the Military Establishment*. rev. ed. New York: Russell Sage Foundation, 1965.

_____. "Toward an All-Volunteer Military." *Public Interest* 27 (Spring 1972): 104–17.

_____. "Toward a Redefinition of Military Strategy in International Relations." *World Politics* 26 (1974): 473–508.

_____. *U.S. Forces and the Zero Draft*. Adelphi paper no. 94. London: International Institute for Strategic Studies, 1973.

_____. "Volunteer Armed Forces and Military Purpose." *Foreign Affairs* 50 (Apr. 1972): 427–43.

_____, ed. *The New Military*. New York: W. W. Norton, 1969.

_____, and Charles C. Moskos. "Five Years of the All-Volunteer Force." *Armed Forces and Society* 5 (Winter 1979): 171–218.

Johnson, Harry G. "Egregious Economics as Pacifist Propaganda." *Armed Forces and Society* 1 (Summer 1975): 498–504.

Jones, Ellen. *Red Army and Society*. Boston, Mass.: Allen & Unwin, 1985.

Kaplan, Robert L., with Patricia T. Harris. *The Measurement of High School Students' Attitudes toward Recruiting Incentives*. Fort Sheridan, Ill.: U.S. Army Recruiting Command, 1983.

Kohn, Richard H. "The Creation of the American Military Establishment, 1783–1802." In *The Military in America*, edited by Peter Karsten, pp. 73–84. New York: Free Press, 1980.

Korb, Lawrence J. "The FY 1981–1985 Defense Program." *AEI Foreign Policy and Defense Review* 2 (1980): 2–63.

Krendel, Ezra S., and Bernard L. Samoff, eds. *Unionizing the Armed Forces*. Philadelphia: University of Pennsylvania Press, 1977.

Kroes, Rob. "Cruise Missiles and the Western Party System." *Armed Forces and Society* 12 (Summer 1986): 581–90.

Kupperman, Robert H., Yonah Alexander, Debra Van Opstal, and David Williamson, Jr. "Terrorism: The Challenge to the Military in the 1990s." In *Strategic Requirements for the Army to the Year 2000*, edited by Robert H. Kupperman and William J. Taylor, Jr., pp. 187–207. Lexington, Mass.: D. C. Heath, 1984.

Laffin, John. *Women in Battle*. New York: Abelard-Schuman, 1967.

Laird, Melvin R. *People, Not Hardware*. Washington, D.C.: American Enterprise Institute Special Analysis, 1980.

Lasswell, Harold D. "The Garrison State." *American Journal of Sociology* 46 (1941): 455–68.

_____. "The Garrison State Hypothesis Today." In *Changing Patterns of Military Politics*, edited by Samuel P. Huntington, pp. 51–70. New York: Free Press, 1962.

_____. "Sino-Japanese Crisis: The Garrison State versus the Civilian State." *China Quarterly* 11 (1937): 643–49.

Leach, Jack F. *Conscription in the United States*. Rutland, Vt.: Charles E. Tuttle, 1952.

Lee, Gus C., and Geoffrey Y. Parker. *Ending the Draft: The Story of the All Volunteer Force*. Report no. 77-1, prepared for the assistant secretary of defense, Manpower and Reserve Affairs. Alexandria, Va.: Human Resources Research Organization, 1977.

Lee, Ulysses. "The Draft and the Negro." *Current History* 55 (July 1968): 28–33, 47–48.

Lewin, K., R. Lippitt, and R. K. White. "Patterns of Aggressive Behavior in Experimentally Created Social Climates." *Journal of Social Psychology* 10 (1939): 271–79.

Lipset, Seymour Martin. *The First New Nation*. New York: Basic Books, 1963.

Little, Roger W. "Buddy Relations and Combat Performance." In *The New Military*, edited by Morris Janowitz, pp. 195–223. New York: W. W. Norton, 1969.

Lopreato, Sally Cook, and Dudley L. Poston, Jr. "Differences in Earnings and Earning Ability between Veterans and Nonveterans in the United States." *Social Science Quarterly* 57 (Mar. 1977): 750–66.

Lowi, Theodore J. *The End of Liberalism: The Second Republic of the United States*. 2d ed. New York: Norton, 1979.

Luttwak, Edward N. *The Pentagon and the Art of War*. New York: Simon & Schuster, 1985.

McGrath, J. E., and I. Altman. *Small Group Research*. New York: Holt, Rinehart & Winston, 1966.

McKenney, Janice E. "Women in Combat: Comment." *Armed Forces and Society* 8 (Summer 1982): 686–92.

McNelly, Theodore. "The Renunciation of War in the Japanese Constitution." *Armed Forces and Society* 13 (Fall 1986): 81–106.

McNown, Robert F., Bernard Udis, and Colin Ash. "Economic Analysis of the All-Volunteer Force." *Armed Forces and Society* 7 (Fall 1980): 113–32.

Malone, Dandridge M. "A Context for Cohesion." U.S. Army Delta Force Concept Paper. Carlisle Barracks, Pa.: U.S. Army Delta Force, 1982.

Marlowe, David H. "The Manning of the Force and the Structure of Battle: Part 1—The AVF and the Draft." In *Conscripts and Volunteers*, edited by Robert K. Fullinwider, pp. 46–57. Totowa, N.J.: Rowman & Allanheld, 1983.

_____. "The Manning of the Force and the Structure of Battle: Part 2—Men and Women." In *Conscripts and Volunteers*, pp. 189–99.

Marmion, Harry A. *The Case against an All-Volunteer Army*. Chicago: Quadrangle Books, 1971.

_____. "Historical Background of Selective Service in the United States." In *Selective Service and American Society*, edited by Roger W. Little, pp. 35–52. New York: Russell Sage Foundation, 1969.

Marshall, S. L. A. *Men against Fire*. New York: Morrow, 1947.

Marshall, T. H. *Citizenship and Social Class*. Cambridge, Eng.: Cambridge University Press, 1950.

Martindale, Melanie, and Dudley L. Poston, Jr. "Variations in Veteran/Nonveteran Earnings Patterns among World War II, Korea, and Vietnam War Cohorts." *Armed Forces and Society* 5 (1979): 219–43.

Mason, William M. *On the Socioeconomic Effects of Military Service*. Ph.D. diss., University of Chicago, 1970.

Meeker, Barbara Foley, and David R. Segal. "Soldiers' Perceptions of Conflict Intensity." *Journal of Political and Military Sociology* 15 (Spring 1987): 105–15.

Melman, Seymour. *Our Depleted Society.* New York: Holt, Rinehart, & Winston, 1965.

———. "Twelve Propositions on Productivity and War Economy." *Armed Forces and Society* 1 (Summer 1975): 490–97.

Military Manpower Task Force. *A Report to the President on the Status and Prospects of the All Volunteer Force.* Washington, D.C.: Office of the Secretary of Defense, Oct., 1982.

Millis, Walter. *Arms and Men.* New York: Putnam, 1956.

Mintz, Alex, and Alexander Hicks. "Military Keynesianism in the United States: Disaggregating Military Expenditures and Their Determinants." *American Journal of Sociology* 90 (Sept. 1984): 411–17.

Moskos, Charles C. "The American Dilemma in Uniform: Race in the Armed Forces." *Annals of the American Academy of Political and Social Science* 406 (Mar. 1973): 94–106.

———. *The American Enlisted Man.* New York: Russell Sage Foundation, 1970.

———. "The Emergent Military." *Pacific Sociological Review* 16 (1973): 255–79.

———. "From Institution to Occupation." *Armed Forces and Society* 4 (1977): 41–50.

———. "The Military." *Annual Review of Sociology* 2 (1976): 55–77.

———. *Peace Soldiers: The Sociology of a Unified United Nations Military Force.* Chicago: University of Chicago Press, 1976.

———. Statement before the Military Personnel Subcommittee on Armed Services on the Continuing Review of the All-Volunteer Force, 95th Cong., 2d sess., July 11, 1978.

———. "Studies on the American Soldier." Paper presented at the annual meeting of the American Sociological Association, New York, Aug. 1973.

———. "UN Peacekeepers." *Armed Forces and Society* 1 (1975): 388–401.

Nelson, Dennis D. *The Integration of the Negro into the United States Navy.* New York: Farrar, Straus & Young, 1951.

Nichols, Lee. *Breakthrough on the Color Front.* New York: Random House, 1954.

Northrup, Herbert R., Steven M. DiAntonio, John A. Brinker, and Dale F. Daniel. *Black and Other Minority Participation in the All-Volunteer Navy and Marine Corps.* Philadelphia: Wharton School, 1979.

Oi, Walter Y. "The Costs and Implications of an All-Volunteer Force." In *The Draft: A Handbook of Facts and Alternatives,* edited by Sol Tax, pp. 221–51. Chicago: University of Chicago Press, 1967.

———. "The Economics of the Draft." *American Economic Review* 57 (1967): 39–63.

Olson, Mancur. *The Rise and Decline of Nations.* New Haven, Conn.: Yale University Press, 1982.

O'Sullivan, John, and Allen M. Meckler, eds. *The Draft and Its Enemies.* Urbana: University of Illinois Press, 1974.

Pellegrino, Edmund D., et al. *The Successor Generation.* Washington, D.C.: Atlantic Council, 1981.

Petree, Bruce E., and Robert L. Schroeder. "Rx for Turbulence," *Army* 31 (Nov. 1981): 14–20.

Poston, Dudley L., Jr., Mady W. Segal, and John S. Butler. "The Influence of Military Service on the Civilian Earnings Patterns of Female Veterans." In *Women in the United States Armed Forces,* edited by Nancy L. Goldman, pp. 152–71. Chicago: Inter-University Seminar on Armed Forces and Society, 1984.

President's Committee on Equal Opportunity in the Armed Forces. *Equality of Treat-*

ment and Opportunity for Negro Military Personnel Stationed within the United States. Washington, D.C.: Government Printing Office, 1964.

Puscheck, Herbert C. "Selective Service Registration: Success or Failure?" *Armed Forces and Society* 10 (Fall 1983): 5–25.

Quarles, Benjamin. *The Negro in the American Revolution.* Chapel Hill: University of North Carolina Press, 1961.

Record, Jeffrey. "Should America Pay for Europe's Security?" *Washington Quarterly* 5 (Summer 1982): 19–29.

Richardson, W. R. "Winning on the Extended Battlefield." *Army* 31, no. 6 (1981): 35–42.

Riesman, David. *The Lonely Crowd.* New Haven, Conn.: Yale University Press, 1950.

Rimlinger, Gaston V. "Social Security, Incentives, and Controls in the U.S. and U.S.S.R." *Comparative Studies in Society and History* 4 (1961): 104–24.

Ritzer, George. "Implications of and Barriers to Industrial Democracy in the United States and Sweden." In *Equity, Income, and Policy,* edited by Irving Louis Horowitz, pp. 49–60. New York: Praeger, 1977.

Roethlisberger, F. J., and W. J. Dickson. *Management and the Worker.* Cambridge, Mass.: Harvard University Press, 1939.

Rowling, Sir Wallace. "New Zealand and ANZUS." *Armed Forces and Society* 12 (Winter 1986): 169–72.

Russett, Bruce M. *What Price Vigilance?* New Haven, Conn.: Yale University Press, 1970.

Sabrosky, Alan N. et al., eds. *Blue-Collar Soldiers? Unionization and the U.S. Military.* Philadelphia: Foreign Policy Research Institute, 1977.

Savage, Paul L., and Richard A. Gabriel. "Cohesion and Disintegration in the American Army." *Armed Forces and Society* 2 (1976): 340–76.

Schevitz, Jeffrey M. *The Weaponsmakers.* Cambridge, Mass.: Schenkman, 1979.

Schuman, Howard, Jacob Ludwig, and Jon A. Krosnick. "The Perceived Threat of Nuclear War." *Public Opinion Quarterly* 50 (Winter 1986): 519–36.

Scowcroft, Brent, ed. *Military Service in the United States.* Englewood Cliffs, N.J.: Prentice-Hall, 1982.

Segal, David R., "American Paratroopers Would Rather Fight Than Switch." *Sociology and Social Research* 70, no. 2 (Jan. 1986): 172–73.

———. "From Political to Industrial Citizenship." In *The Political Education of Soldiers,* edited by Morris Janowitz and Stephen D. Wesbrook, pp. 285–306. Beverly Hills, Calif.: Sage Publications, 1983.

———. "Leadership and Management: Organization Theory." In *Military Leadership,* edited by James H. Buck and Lawrence J. Korb, pp. 41–69. Beverly Hills, Calif.: Sage Publications, 1981.

———. "Management, Leadership, and the Future Battlefield." In *Leadership on the Future Battlefield,* edited by James G. Hunt and John D. Blair, pp. 201–13. Washington, D.C.: Pergamon-Brassey's, 1985.

———. "Measuring the Institutional/Occupational Change Thesis." *Armed Forces and Society* 12 (Spring 1986): 351–75.

———. "Military Organization and Personnel Accession." In *Conscripts and Volunteers,* edited by Robert K. Fullinwider, pp. 7–22. Totowa, N.J.: Rowman & Allanheld, 1983.

———. "Military Service in the Nineteen-Seventies: Attitudes of Soldiers and Civilians." In *Manning the American Armed Forces,* edited by Allan R. Millett and Anne F. Trupp, pp. 42–63. Columbus: Mershon Center of the Ohio State University, 1981.

_____. "Personnel." In *American Defense Annual, 1986–1987*, edited by Joseph Kruzel, pp. 139–52. Lexington, Mass.: D. C. Heath, 1986.

_____. "Sociological and Economic Models of Military Manpower: An Attempt at Integration." In *The Challenge of Social Control*, edited by Gerald D. Suttles and Mayer N. Zald, pp. 161–80. Norwood, N.J.: Ablex, 1985.

_____. "Worker Representation in Military Organization." In *The Changing World of the American Military*, edited by Franklin D. Margiotta, pp. 223–46. Boulder, Colo.: Westview Press, 1978.

_____, et al. "Trends in the Structure of Army Families." *Journal of Political and Military Sociology* 4 (Spring 1976): 135–38.

_____, and Jerald G. Bachman. "The Military as an Educational and Training Institution." *Youth and Society* 10 (Sept. 1978): 47–63.

_____, Jerald G. Bachman, and Faye E. Dowdell. "Military Service for Female and Black Youth." *Youth and Society* 10 (Dec. 1978): 127–34.

_____, and John D. Blair. "Public Confidence in the U.S. Military." *Armed Forces and Society* 3 (Nov. 1976): 3–11.

_____, John D. Blair, Joseph J. Lengermann, and Richard C. Thompson. "Institutional and Occupational Values in the U.S. Military." In *Changing U.S. Military Manpower Realities*, edited by Franklin D. Margiotta, James Brown, and Michael J. Collins, pp. 107–27. Boulder, Colo.: Westview Press, 1983.

_____, and Katharine Swift Gravino. "The Empire Strikes Back: Military Professionalism in the South Atlantic War." In *The Regionalization of Warfare*, edited by James Brown and William Snyder, pp. 17–36. New Brunswick, N.J.: Transaction Books, 1985.

_____, and Katharine Swift Gravino. "Peacekeeping as a Military Mission." In *The Hundred Percent Challenge*, edited by Charles Duryea Smith, pp. 36–68. Washington, D.C.: Seven Locks Press, 1985.

_____, Jesse Harris, Joseph Rothberg, and David H. Marlowe. "Paratroopers as Peacekeepers." *Armed Forces and Society* 10, no. 4 (Aug. 1984): 487–506.

_____, Nora Scott Kinzer, and John C. Woelfel. "The Concept of Citizenship and Attitudes toward Women in Combat." *Sex Roles* 3, no. 5 (1977): 469–77.

_____, and Joseph J. Lengermann. "Professional and Institutional Considerations." In *Combat Effectiveness*, edited by Sam C. Sarkesian, pp. 154–84. Beverly Hills, Calif.: Sage, 1980.

_____, Barbara Ann Lynch, and John D. Blair. "The Changing American Soldier." *American Journal of Sociology* 85 (July 1979): 95–108.

_____, and Peter G. Nordlie. "Racial Inequality in Army Promotions." *Journal of Political and Military Sociology* 7 (Spring 1979): 135–42.

_____, Joseph M. Rothberg, Jesse J. Harris, and David H. Marlowe. "Deterrence, Peacekeeping, and Combat Orientation in the U.S. Army." In *Challenges to Deterrence in the 1990s*, edited by Stephen J. Cimbala, pp. 41–53. New York: Praeger, 1987.

_____, and Mady Wechsler Segal. "Change in Military Organization." *Annual Review of Sociology* 9 (1983): 151–70.

_____, and Mady W. Segal. "Models of Civil-Military Relationships at the Elite Level." In *The Perceived Role of the Military*, edited by M. Van Gils, pp. 279–92. Rotterdam: Rotterdam University Press, 1971.

_____, and Young Hee Yoon. "Institutional and Occupational Models of the Army in the Career Force." *Journal of Political and Military Sociology* 12 (1984): 243–56.

Segal, Mady W. "The Military and the Family as Greedy Institutions." *Armed Forces and Society* 13, no. 1 (Fall 1986): 9–38.

_____. "Women's Roles in the U.S. Armed Forces." In *Conscripts and Volunteers*, edited by Robert K. Fullinwider, pp. 200–213. Totowa, N.J.: Rowman & Allanheld, 1983.

Segal, Mady W., and David R. Segal. "Social Change and the Participation of Women in the American Military." In *Research in Social Movements, Conflicts and Change*, vol. 5, edited by Louis Kriesberg, pp. 235–58, Greenwich, Conn.: JAI Press, 1983.

Sewall, Gilbert T. "The Diminished Past: Conditions and Ideals in the Social Studies." In *Against Mediocrity*, edited by Chester E. Finn, Jr., Diane Ravitch, and Robert T. Fancher, pp. 115–29. New York: Holmes & Meier, 1984.

Shexnider, Alvin J., and John Sibley Butler. "Race and the All-Volunteer System." *Armed Forces and Society* 2 (Spring 1976): 421–32.

Shils, Edward A. "Primary Groups in the American Army." In *Continuities in Social Research: Studies in the Scope and Method of 'The American Soldier,'* edited by Robert K. Merton and Paul F. Lazarsfeld, pp. 16–39. New York: Free Press, 1950.

_____, and Morris Janowitz. "Cohesion and Disintegration in the Wehrmacht in World War II." *Public Opinion Quarterly* 12 (1948): 280–315.

Shy, John. *Toward Lexington*. Princeton, NJ.: Princeton University Press, 1965.

Shyles, Leonard, and Mark Ross. "Recruitment Rhetoric in Brochures Advertising the All-Volunteer Force." Mimeographed. College Park: University of Maryland.

Simmel, Georg. "Sociability." In *The Sociology of Georg Simmel*, edited by Kurt Wolff, pp. 40–57. New York: Macmillan, 1950.

Skocpol, Theda, and John Ikenberry. "The Political Formation of the American Welfare State in Historical and Comparative Perspective." *Comparative Social Research* 6 (1983): 87–148.

Sleeman, J. F. *The Welfare State*. London: Allen & Unwin, 1973.

Smith, Tom W. "American Attitudes toward the Soviet Union and Communism." *Public Opinion Quarterly* 47, no. 2 (Summer 1983): 277–92.

Stahl, Michael J., Charles W. McNichols, and T. Roger Manley. "An Empirical Example of the Moskos Institution-Occupation Model." *Armed Forces and Society* 6 (1980): 257–69.

Stahl, Michael J., Charles W. McNichols, and T. Roger Manley. "A Longitudinal Test of the Moskos Institution-Occupation Model. *Journal of Political and Military Sociology* 9 (1981): 43–47.

Stahl, Michael J., T. Roger Manley, and Charles W. McNichols. "Operationalizing the Moskos Institution-Occupation Model." *Journal of Applied Psychology* 63 (1978): 422–27.

Starr, Paul. *The Discarded Army*. New York: Charterhouse, 1973.

Starry, D. A. "Extending the Battlefield." *Military Review* 61, no. 3 (1981): 31–35.

Stein, Maurice R. *The Eclipse of Community: An Interpretation of American Studies*. Princeton, N.J.: Princeton University Press, 1960.

Stillman, Richard J. II. *Integration of the Negro into the U.S. Armed Forces*. New York: Praeger, 1968.

Stouffer, Samuel A. *Social Research to Test Ideas*. New York: Free Press, 1962.

_____, Arthur A. Lumsdaine, Marion Harper Lumsdaine, Robin M. Williams, M. Brewster Smith, Irving L. Janis, Shirley A. Star, and Leonard S. Cottrell. *The American Soldier*, vol. 1: *Adjustment during Army Life* and vol. 2: *Combat and Its Aftermath*. Princeton, N.J.: Princeton University Press, 1949.

Szymanski, Albert. *The Logic of Imperialism*. New York: Praeger, 1981.

Tabory, Mala. *The Multinational Force and Observers in the Sinai*. Boulder, Colo.: Westview Press, 1986.

Tax, Sol, ed. *The Draft: A Handbook of Facts and Alternatives*. Chicago: University of Chicago Press, 1967.

Taylor, Frederick W. *The Principles of Scientific Management*. New York: Harper & Row, 1911.

Taylor, William J., Roger J. Arango, and Robert S. Lockwood, eds. *Military Unions*. Beverly Hills, Calif.: Sage Publications, 1977.

Thomas, Patricia J. *Utilization of Enlisted Women in the Military*. San Diego, Calif.: Navy Personnel Research and Development Center, 1975.

Treas, Judith. "The Historical Decline in Late-Life Labor Force Participation in the United States." In *Age, Health and Employment*, edited by James E. Birran and Judy Livington, pp. 158–75. Englewood Cliffs, N.J.: Prentice-Hall, 1985.

Trist, Eric. "Work Improvement and Industrial Democracy." Paper presented to the Conference of the Commission of European Communities on Work Organization, Technical Development, and Motivations of the Individual, Brussels, Belgium, 1974.

United States Army War College. *Leadership for the 1970s*. Carlisle Barracks, Pa.: Army War College, 1971.

United States. Adjutant General's Office. Personnel Research and Procedures Division. *Attitudes of Enlisted Men Toward Unit Rotation (GYROSCOPE)*. OEU Report 57-4. Washington, D.C.: Adjutant General.

United States. Congressional Budget Office. *The Army of the Nineties: How Much Will It Cost?* Washington, D.C.: Congress of the United States, Dec., 1986.

United States. Department of the Army. *Operations*. Field Manual 100-5. Fort Monroe, Va.: U.S. Army Training and Doctrine Command, 1981.

United States. Office of the Secretary of Defense. *America's Volunteers*. Washington, D.C.: Office of the Assistant Secretary for Manpower, Reserve Affairs and Logistics, 1978.

United States. Office of the Assistant Secretary of Defense (Manpower, Reserve Affairs and Logistics). *Profile of American Youth: 1980 Nationwide Administration of the Armed Services Vocational Aptitude Battery*. Washington, D.C.: Office of the Secretary of Defense, Mar. 1982.

Van Doorn, Jacques. "The Decline of the Mass Army in the West." *Armed Forces and Society* 1, no. 2 (Winter, 1975): 147–57.

———. *The Soldier and Social Change*. Beverly Hills, Calif.: Sage Publications, 1975.

Vidich, Arthur J., and Maurice R. Stein. "The Dissolved Identity in Military Life." In *Identity and Anxiety*, edited by Maurice R. Stein, Arthur J. Vidich, and David M. White, pp. 493–506. Glencoe, Ill.: Free Press, 1960.

Villemez, Wayne J., and John D. Kasarda. "Veteran Status and Socioeconomic Attainment." *Armed Forces and Society* 2 (1976): 174–200.

Wamsley, Gary L. "Decision-Making in Local Boards." In *Selective Service and American Society*, edited by Roger W. Little, pp. 83–108. New York: Russell Sage Foundation, 1969.

Washington, George. *The Writings of George Washington*. Edited by John C. Fitzpatrick. 39 vols. Washington, D.C.: U.S. Government Printing Office, 1931–44.

Weber, Max. *The Theory of Social and Economic Organization*. Translated by A. M. Henderson and Talcott Parsons. Glencoe, Ill.: Free Press, 1947.

Werner, Roy A. "The Readiness of U.S. Reserve Components." In *Supplementary Military Forces*, edited by Louis A. Zurcher and Gwyn Harries-Jenkins, pp. 69–90. Beverly Hills, Calif.: Sage Publications, 1978.

Wesbrook, Stephen D. "Historical Notes." In *The Political Education of Soldiers*, edited by Morris Janowitz and Stephen D. Wesbrook, pp. 251–84. Beverly Hills, Calif.: Sage, 1983.

_____. "Sociopolitical Training in the Military." In *The Political Education of Soldiers*, edited by Morris Janowitz and Stephen D. Wesbrook, pp. 15–54. Beverly Hills, Calif.: Sage, 1983.

Wilensky, Harold L. *The Welfare State and Equality*. Berkeley: University of California Press, 1975.

Wool, Harold. *The Military Specialist*. Baltimore, Md.: Johns Hopkins University Press, 1968.

Wrong, Dennis H. *Population and Society*. New York: Random House, 1977.

Yarmolinsky, Adam. *The Military Establishment*. New York: Harper & Row, 1971.

Zeigler, Harmon. *The Political Life of American Teachers*. Englewood Cliffs, N.J.: Prentice-Hall, 1967.

Index